JOURNAL FOR THE STUDY OF THE OLD TESTAMENT
SUPPLEMENT SERIES
402

Editors
Claudia V. Camp, Texas Christian University
and
Andrew Mein, Westcott House, Cambridge

Founding Editors
David J.A. Clines, Philip R. Davies and David M. Gunn

Editorial Board
Richard J. Coggins, Alan Cooper, J. Cheryl Exum, John Goldingay
Robert P. Gordon, Norman K. Gottwald, John Jarick,
Andrew D.H. Mayes, Carol Meyers, Patrick D. Miller

GENDER, CULTURE, THEORY
14

Editor
J. Cheryl Exum

To Jessie

Rewriting Moses

The Narrative Eclipse of the Text

Brian Britt

T&T CLARK INTERNATIONAL
A Continuum imprint
LONDON • NEW YORK

Copyright © 2004 T&T Clark International
A Continuum imprint

Published by T&T Clark International
The Tower Building, 11 York Road, London SE1 7NX
15 East 26th Street, Suite 1703, New York, NY 10010

www.tandtclark.com

British Library Cataloguing-in-Publication Data
A catalogue record for this book is available from the British Library

Typeset and edited for Continuum by Forthcoming Publications Ltd
www.forthcomingpublications.com

Printed on acid-free paper in Great Britain by MPG Books Ltd

ISBN 0-5670-8181-8 (HB)
ISBN 0-5670-8087-0 (PB)

CONTENTS

ACKNOWLEDGMENTS

I decided to write this book when my interest in biblical conceptions of writing and revelation led repeatedly to the figure of Moses. While I knew the project would be challenging, I could not know how much I would depend on others in shaping it and bringing it to completion. I especially wish to thank my colleagues in the Virginia Tech Interdisciplinary Reading Group: Jane Aiken, David Burr, John Christman, Joe Eska, Amy Nelson, Darleen Pryds, Ann-Marie Knoblauch, and Bailey Van Hook, who read many drafts of these chapters closely and provided insightful comments at all stages. Jane Aiken was extraordinarily helpful to me in the study of images and art.

I also wish to thank the following people for their responses to particular parts and the overall conception of the project: Ananda Abeysekara, Andrew Becker, Leslie Brisman, Stephen Britt, Arnold Davidson, Michael Fishbane, Terry Fretheim, Elizabeth Struthers Malbon, Jack C. Marler, James Nohrnberg, Terry Papillon, Paulo Polanah, Lynn Poland, Richard Rosengarten, Fabrice Teulon, Damian Treffs, Steve Weitzman, and Anthony Yu.

My students at Virginia Tech, especially those who participated in my courses on Moses and Monotheism and Religion and Literature, enabled me to see Freud, Hurston, and other texts and issues in new ways. They have also challenged me to make my analysis clear and relevant.

J. Cheryl Exum, my editor at Sheffield/Continuum, offered important suggestions, encouragement, and advice at several stages of this project. Duncan Burns and Rebecca Mulhearn carried the book through production with care and good humor. Lian Jian provided invaluable assistance in preparing the bibliography. Brandy Renee McCann and Paulette Jayabalan also provided research assistance.

I am grateful to the National Endowment for the Humanities, which funded a summer seminar at Yale University where I developed work on Chapter 6; the Virginia Foundation for Humanities, which provided support for work on Chapter 3; and Virginia Tech, which provided a Humanities stipend and research leave for this project. The staff of the Index of Christian Art in Princeton provided valuable assistance in my search for images of Moses. Several portions of this work were presented at national meetings of the Society of Biblical Literature, the American Academy of Religion, and at Religion 2000 in Boston. Earlier versions of Chapters 4 and 6 appeared in the journals *Religion and the Arts* (Volume 7, Issue 3 [2003], pp. 227-73) and *Biblical Interpretation* (Volume 8, Issue 4 [2000], pp. 358-74), respectively; I thank the editors and publishers of both journals for permission to publish these chapters here. All these groups and individuals share my gratitude but not my responsibility for any of the book's shortcomings.

I thank, finally, all the members of my family for their encouragement, good humor, and support, but my deepest, almost inexpressible gratitude goes to Jessica Meltsner, to whom I dedicate this book.

ABBREVIATIONS

AB	Anchor Bible
BDB	Francis Brown, S.R. Driver and Charles A. Briggs, *A Hebrew and English Lexicon of the Old Testament* (Oxford: Clarendon Press, 1907)
BibInt	*Biblical Interpretation: A Journal of Contemporary Approaches*
BN	*Biblische Notizen*
CBQ	*Catholic Biblical Quarterly*
GKC	*Gesenius' Hebrew Grammar* (ed. E. Kautzsch, revised and trans. A.E. Cowley; Oxford: Clarendon Press, 1910)
HTR	*Harvard Theological Review*
ICC	International Critical Commentary
Int	*Interpretation*
JBL	*Journal of Biblical Literature*
JSOTSup	*Journal for the Study of the Old Testament*, Supplement Series
LCL	Loeb Classical Library
LXX	Septuagint
NRSV	New Revised Standard Version
PMLA	Publications of the Modern Language Association of America
VT	*Vetus Testamentum*
VTSup	*Vetus Testamentum*, Supplements
ZAW	*Zeitschrift für die alttestamentliche Wissenschaft*
ZTK	*Zeitschrift für Theologie und Kirche*

INTRODUCTION

Philo of Alexandria begins his *Life of Moses* with a polemic: 'Greek men of letters have refused to treat him as worthy of memory, possibly through envy, and also because in many cases the ordinances of the legislators of the different states are opposed to his'.[1] Though he lived prosperously, Philo understood the precarious status of Jewish life under Roman rule. After anti-Jewish riots in Alexandria, he traveled to Rome in 39 CE to petition Emperor Caligula for the restoration of legal rights to Jews. Like Josephus after him, Philo defended Judaism and Moses against attacks from the Alexandrian grammarian Apion. For Philo and Josephus, Moses represented the pinnacle of Jewish tradition, and their Hellenistic biographies extol him in its defense. Most biographies of Moses, from late antiquity to the present, resemble the portraits of Philo and Josephus more closely than the Bible, placing the life story of the great man at the center of tradition.

Moses is a figure exalted but contained by scripture. His biblical portrait suggests a struggle between hero worship and a decision to subordinate his prestige to the tasks of resolving cultural crises and inaugurating written traditions. Both these elements—polemic and writing—follow Moses into his post-biblical rewritings, even those that depart radically from the details of the Bible. There is a great difference, even a tension, between the reputation of Moses and the biblical account of him.[2] Indeed, traditions have a way of neutralizing and forgetting what they enshrine in scripture.[3] But as Freud observes in his study of Moses, something of a tradition remains even in its forgetting.[4] This book analyzes biblical and post-biblical representations of Moses in order to explore ancient and contemporary ideas of scriptural tradition.

---

1.   Philo, *On the Life of Moses*, in *Philo*. VI. *On the Life of Moses* (ed. G.P. Goold; trans. F.H. Colson; Cambridge, MA: Harvard University Press, 1994), p. 277. For a thorough discussion of Philo's Moses in historical and cultural context, see Maren R. Niehoff, *Philo and Jewish Identity and Culture* (Tübingen: J.C.B. Mohr [Paul Siebeck], 2001), esp. pp. 5-9 and 69-70.

2.   Likewise, the reputation of the Bible as sacred scripture is often not matched by knowledge of what it says. See, for example, the results of a recent Gallup survey on Bible knowledge among Americans in David Gibson, 'We Revere the Bible… We Don't Read It', *Washington Post* (9 December 2000), B9.

3.   A similar phenomenon applies to the creation of memorials. See James E. Young, *Writing and Rewriting the Holocaust* (Bloomington: Indiana University Press, 1988), pp. 172-80, and *The Texture of Memory* (New Haven: Yale University Press, 1993).

4.   Sigmund Freud, *Moses and Monotheism* (trans. Katherine Jones; New York: Vantage Books, 1967), pp. 86-87.

    Popular images of Moses range from Charleton Heston's film portrayal in *The
Ten Commandments* to Michelangelo's statue of the biblical lawgiver clutching the
tablets of the law. Behind these familiar portraits, however, lie several biblical episodes that portray Moses in a complex and uncanny light. How do these episodes
and other versions of the Moses story depict him as an author and central figure of
biblical tradition? I argue that post-biblical models of biography have eclipsed the
biblical portrait of Moses, casting him as a hero, engaging him in ideological polemics, and minimizing the biblical elements of mystery and textuality. Yet biblical
traces always remain in later biographies of Moses, sometimes, paradoxically, in
the texts that depart most dramatically from biblical precedent. In many different
ways, rewritings of Moses reflect and refract the biblical portrait's interests in
written tradition and polemical controversy.
    Each chapter of this book analyzes cultural texts—from the Bible and contem-
porary culture[5]—in order to identify how the story of Moses relates to ideas of
scripture, revelation, and biblical tradition. Again and again, Moses is mobilized to
address fierce controversies of the day, bearing traces and complexities of biblical
tradition in diverse, subtle, and even hidden ways. The many uses of Moses belong
to a dynamic tradition of the sort defined by Alasdair MacIntyre as 'an historically
extended, socially embodied argument, and an argument precisely in part about the
goods which constitute that tradition'.[6] This story illuminates how rewritings of
Moses in hagiography, fiction, film, art, and scholarship reflect a biblical tradition
engaged in perennial questions about myth, sacred texts, and the nature of tradition
itself.
    Because of its unique cultural and religious position, the Bible continues to be an
object of unmatched commentary and contention. Despite modern and postmodern
theories of secularization, the Bible retains what could be called an 'aura'. According to Walter Benjamin, the quality of aura means three things: first, the auratic
object has the capacity to return the viewer's gaze; second, the closer one looks at
it, the more distant it seems; and third, aura denotes 'the associations which, at home
in the *mémoire involontaire*, tend to cluster around the object of a perception'.[7] All
three qualities describe the cultural function of biblical tradition described in this
book. First, the unique status of the Bible endows it with the capacity to respond
directly and meaningfully to the devout reader's gaze, which is one reason why the
religious biographies of Augustine, Luther, Buber, and so many others attribute
personal transformation to the Bible. Like a mirror or a skillful teacher, the Bible
reflects interests, intentions, and insecurities back onto the reader. On a larger cultural scale, the person-like quality of the Bible makes it possible to speak of people

---

    5.   By 'contemporary' I mean from the late-eighteenth century to the present, a period when
Enlightenment thought influenced biblical scholarship and literature as well as philosophy. Most
texts in this study, however, come from the twentieth century. The main exception to this pattern is
the analysis of Medieval and Renaissance Christian art in the book's 'Interlude' (Chapter 4).
    6.   Alasdair MacIntyre, *After Virtue: A Study in Moral Theory* (Notre Dame, IN: University
of Notre Dame Press, 1984), p. 222.
    7.   Walter Benjamin, *Charles Baudelaire* (trans. Harry Zohn; London: Verso, 1989),
pp. 145-48.

as books ('I can read you like a book') and books as people ('That book answered all my questions').

The Bible's aura also makes it perpetually distant: one can never fully grasp or comprehend it—its horizon constantly recedes from the reader. Famously difficult, complex, and even confusing, the Bible has generated endless streams of commentary. Drawing on the tradition of Romantic aesthetics, Benjamin argued that literary works from poetry to the Bible itself do not simply communicate meaning or mere content. Their value lies, at least in part, in their capacity to gesture messianically toward higher modes of language and life. In this elusive metaphysical maneuver, Benjamin also borrowed from allegorical and mystical modes of biblical interpretation, according to which the Bible's possible meanings seem infinite.[8]

Finally, and centrally to this study, the Bible's aura means that it carries all kinds of associations, some conscious and others unconscious or semi-conscious, a quality Benjamin describes in terms of Proust's *mémoire involontaire*. Biblical traditions convey a tremendous number of layered meanings; many, as scholars like Michael Fishbane have shown, already appear in the interpretive traditions of the biblical text itself; many require careful textual and cultural analysis to uncover. Other associations and meanings come from post-biblical traditions that may or may not be fully conscious to the reader. Here we find ourselves close to Freud's notion of the unconscious and his understanding of religious tradition in *Moses and Monotheism*. The question is how we can speak of an unconscious tradition.

This question was recently posed in a critical way by Yosef Yerushalmi in *Freud's Moses: Judaism Terminable and Interminable*, and has since been taken up by Jan Assmann, Jacques Derrida, and others. For Yerushalmi, Freud's suggestion that Moses' Egyptian identity and patricidal death at the hands of the Hebrews were repressed and later resurfaced in Judaism and Christianity is insufficiently explained by Freud in terms of a quasi-biological or 'Lamarckian' mechanism of transmission. Yerushalmi also challenges Freud's anti-religious and scientific biases here, even at the level of Freud's self-understanding as a Jew.[9] A debate about Freud's eccentric treatment of Moses has thus become a debate on the nature of religious tradition and modernity itself. Is it possible to speak of repressed knowledge on a cultural and historical scale? What accounts for the uncanny return of traditional concerns and *topoi* in texts that ignore or even reject the traditions they embody?

This study contributes to these debates by drawing attention to the biblical text as well as its legacy. With a specific focus on Moses, I engage the question of the Bible's cultural 'aura'. Freud's speculations on Moses are not my focus, but the larger issue of tradition, including forms of tradition that are nearly hidden, unacknowledged, or inadvertent, does concern me. Without embracing his psychoanalytic and cultural theories, I find Freudian questions compelling and some of his

---

8.   As with many of his writings, Benjamin's essays on translation and language provide critical clarification of the cultural status of the Bible on a rhetorical rather than traditionally philosophical level.

9.   Yosef Yerushalmi, *Freud's Moses: Judaism Terminable and Interminable* (New Haven: Yale University Press, 1991), pp. 30-35, 81-85.

categories, such as repression, useful in a metaphorical sense. This project seeks to
go beyond Yerushalmi's debate between Freud, which in some ways is simply a
debate on the possibility of a secular form of Judaism.[10] Like Derrida and Assmann,
I follow Freud's general insight that traditions consist not only of deliberate, fully-
conscious and institutionally protected practices, but also of what Jacques Derrida
calls 'traces' that continue in the face of incidental or even willful distance from the
Bible. For Derrida, the structures and institutions of writing themselves help account for the manner in which tradition operates.[11] For Assmann, Moses performs
important cultural work for monotheistic culture. By means of an approach he calls
'mnemohistory' (the history of memory), Assmann identifies the 'Mosaic distinction' as a pattern that runs through centuries of tradition and counter-tradition.[12]

This book takes the problem of Moses and tradition as articulated by Freud,
Derrida, Assmann, and others, back to the text. By 'text' I mean the language,
structures, and meanings of the biblical text and such post-biblical texts as novels,
paintings, and films. Beneath these close readings of texts lies the conviction that
the texts themselves really matter to cultural and theoretical debates. With Benjamin, who wrote that the 'Bible must evolve the fundamental linguistic facts', I am
convinced that no understanding of the Bible's cultural significance is complete
without biblical studies.[13] On close inspection, the Bible often proves to be more
subtle and uncanny than traditions that claim to have surpassed it. But biblical studies, especially under the unacknowledged influence of theological and scientific
paradigms (see Chapter 3), often do not take full account of the sense in which the
object of their study constitutes the very ground on which they stand. For biblical
culture, the study of the Bible is always a reflexive venture, a problem that only an
awareness of the cultural and textual complexities can begin to unravel. Only the
study of texts themselves, using all the tools of the hermeneutical trade (including
ideological categories of race, gender, what Ricoeur, citing Freud, Marx, and
Nietzsche, calls 'hermeneutics of suspicion'), can provide the rich detail and context demanded by the cultural debates about Moses and tradition. Thus the combination of cultural and biblical texts and methods in this study.[14]

   10.   See Richard J. Bernstein, *Freud and the Legacy of Moses* (Cambridge: Cambridge University Press, 1998), pp. 108-16.
   11.   The concern preoccupies his early work, *Of Grammatology* (trans. Gayatri Spivak; Baltimore: Johns Hopkins University Press, 1976), as well as more recent studies such as *Archive Fever:
A Freudian Impression* (trans. Eric Prenowitz; Chicago: University of Chicago Press, 1996), which
specifically addresses the Freud–Yerushalmi debate.
   12.   Jan Assmann, *Moses the Egyptian: The Memory of Egypt in Western Monotheism* (Cambridge, MA: Harvard University Press, 1997), pp. 8-15.
   13.   Even though Benjamin's most substantial writings concern modernity, his work is, in his
words, 'saturated with theology as a blotter is with ink' (Walter Benjamin, *Gesammelte Schriften*
[ed. Rolf Tiedemann and H. Schweppenhäuser; 7 vols.; Frankfurt: Suhrkamp, 1991], V, p. 588).
   14.   My method is Benjaminian in this sense: much to the dismay of critics in his day and ever
since, Benjamin insisted on juxtaposing religious terms and traditions with the most anti-religious
cultural forms of modern life.

1. *The Biblical Moses*

The earliest known version of Moses' life appears in the biblical books of Exodus through Deuteronomy. Together with Genesis, Leviticus and Numbers, these books constitute the five books of Moses, known also as the Torah of Moses, or the Pentateuch. For Jewish and Christian traditions, the association of these books with Moses can mean that Moses is their author *and* that Moses is their subject. How are these two beliefs related? Modern biblical scholarship challenged the first belief, and today Mosaic authorship of the Pentateuch no longer has support outside traditionalist communities of faith. But the second belief, that the Torah of Moses is *about* Moses, still motivates many accounts of the Pentateuch. The lasting popularity of this view requires explanation, since the Pentateuch devotes no more than fourteen of its 167 chapters primarily to the story of Moses' life, and even these chapters bear faint resemblance to conventional ideas of biography or hagiography. The claim that the Pentateuch is *about* Moses insists that Moses is important *to* the Pentateuch, but it disregards the text. What accounts for this confusion, and what are its consequences?

Except for the brief narrative of Moses' birth, rescue, upbringing and flight to Midian in Exodus 2–3, the biblical account of Moses' life follows the public career of a divinely commissioned servant of YHWH. Though he performs many 'signs and wonders', promulgates and administers divine law, and leads the people from Egypt to Kadesh, Sinai, and the Plains of Moab, Moses rarely seems to act on his own initiative. Readers learn less from the Bible about the personality and life story of Moses than they do about Joseph, David, or perhaps even Esther. Much of what the Bible does say is ambiguous. Even the story of Moses' name hints at Hebrew and Egyptian identity. The brief story of Moses' birth appears in the context of oppression and infanticide against all Hebrews; the Bible is silent about Moses' childhood and youth, and he next appears as an adult in the scene where he kills the Egyptian overseer and flees to Midian. The encounter with YHWH in Exodus 3–4 never explains why Moses is selected to be the Hebrews' leader. Subsequent episodes on the plagues, passover, and Red Sea crossing present Moses less as a protagonist than as an agent of divine will. Except for the incident at Massah-Meribah (Exod. 17; Num. 20), the Korah rebellion (Num. 16), and the golden calf episode (Exod. 32–34), Moses rarely seems to act spontaneously.

The long specifications of priestly law in Exodus, Leviticus, and Numbers interrupt the narrative of Moses with the divinely given speech of Moses. His articulation of priestly law and covenant in Deuteronomy displace Moses the character with Moses the messenger. The traditional blurring of Moses as writer and Moses as writings finds its strongest support in these extended pronouncements. Except for the 'farewell speech' of Moses, almost nothing happens in Deuteronomy, except for the death of Moses. Moses and text are interconnected in the Pentateuch, and Deuteronomy makes these connections visible and central.

Like the tragedies of Aeschylus or the history plays of Shakespeare, the Pentateuch approaches Moses as if he is already a mythic figure of the past (see, e.g.,

Num. 12; Deut. 34).[15] But unlike these literary portraits, Moses does not occupy center stage in the Bible. The biblical narrator makes no attempt to establish the prominence of Moses, but rather seems concerned not to allow Moses a central role in the Pentateuch. Divine displeasure with Moses appears in several places (Exod. 4; Num. 20; Deut. 3; 31), and his actions sometimes invite human opprobrium as well (Exod. 2; Num. 12). The story of Moses in the Pentateuch suggests a variety of perspectives, perhaps reflecting internal rivalries in ancient Israel, but it also suggests that Moses is a known figure, a theme on whom the Pentateuch performs variations and makes allusions. My analysis of biblical episodes (Exod. 1–2; 4.10-17; 34.29-35; Deut. 31–34) is selective, and I make no attempt to resolve the many historical-textual debates on Pentateuch narrative. I take the complexity of Moses in the Pentateuch as axiomatic, and my studies of biblical episodes seek to explore the implications of this complexity for the relationship between biblical ideas of biography and revelation.

The biblical portrait of Moses reflects the complexity of the Pentateuch. Doublets, fragments, legends, interpolations, and narrative gaps complicate the attempt to imagine Moses with great precision or detail.[16] The circumstances of his youth, education, personality, physical appearance and abilities, and family are all missing or uncertain in the biblical accounts. His leadership role is too complex and ambiguous to sum up in terms of prophet, judge, priest, or servant. (Philo did just that, however, by dividing his biography of Moses into sections according to the offices as prophet, priest, philosopher, lawgiver, and king.) The ambiguous episodes of his birth, commission, Sinai revelation, and death call attention to biblical ideas of writing and sacred text, especially as they relate the writing of Moses (in Exodus and Deuteronomy). By making the identity and actions of Moses ambiguous, the Bible underlines the connection between Moses and the text.[17]

The complexities of the biblical Moses have rarely been the subject of interpretive reflection. From the time of Philo and Josephus, the story of Moses has more typically been the seamless story of a legendary hero of multiple talents. Even since the nineteenth century, when textual-historical scholarship divided the Pentateuch into distinct traditions, popular images of Moses have retained the familiar form of heroic biography. Yet even the most univocal and coherent narratives of Moses bear the traces of biblical complexity, often in ways that reflect contemporary rather than ancient categories and preoccupations. My studies of scholarship, commentary, works of art, fiction, and film show the power of biographical traditions and the equally powerful but often suppressed legacy of biblical complexity, a complexity tied to the fact that Moses is, in the words of Jacques Derrida, a 'writing

    15.   See Ronald Hendel, 'The Exodus in Biblical Memory', *JBL* 120 (2001), pp. 601-22, which applies Jan Assmann's notion of 'mnemohistory' to develop this point.
    16.   Erich Auerbach, *Mimesis* (trans. Willard R. Trask; Princeton, NJ: Princeton University Press, 1954), pp. 11-15. See James W. Watts, 'The Legal Characterization of Moses in the Rhetoric of the Pentateuch', *JBL* 117 (1998), pp. 415-26.
    17.   Biblical notions of sacred text are the focus of my first book, *Walter Benjamin and the Bible* (New York: Continuum, 1996).

being' and a 'being written'.[18] This central ambivalence, along with many other tensions within the biblical Moses, is often expressed by the splitting or doubling of Moses, especially in film and fiction.

2. *Moses in Post-Biblical Tradition*

Two major streams of post-biblical tradition are Hellenistic and rabbinic. The Hellenistic tradition includes Philo, Josephus, Paul, and Christian versions of the Moses story. The rabbinic tradition includes, broadly speaking, midrash, Talmud, and centuries of responsa. This study claims no comprehensive survey of either tradition. The bibliography alone of either tradition would surpass the scope of this book. It would also be misguided to apply the cliché of Athens and Jerusalem by distinguishing rabbinic from Hellenistic sources. As any student of Josephus or midrash knows, the texts resist any such distinction. Nevertheless, I do argue that the contemporary cultural phenomena analyzed here, particularly scholarship, fiction, films, and visual art, have a stronger connection to Hellenistic tradition than they do to rabbinic Judaism. If there is one simple way to mark a distinction between rabbinic and Hellenistic traditions about Moses, it is that rabbinic tradition is *more likely* to occur within a context guided by reading and interpretation of the biblical text, commentary on words, sentences, and questions of narrative and halakhic meaning. Hellenistic tradition, from Philo to later post-biblical traditions, is *more likely* to operate according to concepts, patterns, and questions external to the biblical text.

To take one illustration, the story of the child Moses taking Pharaoh's crown appears in both Josephus and *Exodus Rabbah*, but only in the latter does it serve to explain another text, namely the speech impediment of Exod. 4.10-17.[19] (The midrash may also be an allusion to the burnt mouth of another prophet: Isaiah [see Isa. 6.6-7].) The origins and transmission of this story are unclear, but its appearance in the Hellenistic text of Josephus and the rabbinic midrash underscores the impossibility of making a clear dichotomy between the two traditions. As my analysis of episodes and traditions (especially the veil of Moses) will show, the lines of tradition and transmission are unpredictable. Narrative elements from one biblical text can be displaced onto the interpretation of another; the gender and moral character of a character may change completely while a detail of characterization (e.g. the role of veils in prophetic figures discussed in Chapter 4) remains intact.

The Moses of midrash appears in many roles and settings, but his identity is overwhelmingly based on his role as a giver, writer, and teacher of Torah. More than any episode of his life, including his birth, upbringing, leadership of the people, and death, the uniqueness of Moses comes from the Torah. In fact, midrash often associates the major episodes of Moses' life with his role as writer and giver of the Torah; the extensive traditions on the death of Moses, discussed in Chapter 8, are a

---

18. Derrida, *Of Grammatology*, p. 18.
19. The two versions are given together in Kugel, *The Bible as It Was* (Cambridge, MA: Harvard University Press, 1997), pp. 297-98.

case in point. One of my contentions is that the emphasis on the text and writing of Torah in the midrash is also present in the biblical tradition. The focus of this study, then, will be the conjunctions and disjunctions between selected contemporary and biblical images of Moses. Far from the continuities between Torah and midrash, governed by normative practices of commentary on the Hebrew text, the trajectories from the Bible to contemporary culture through Hellenistic tradition are complex and various.

Contemporary versions of Moses' life echo the structural and thematic tensions of the Pentateuch. The tendency to express contrary themes within a traditional context is basic to many contemporary Moses texts. For historians, the sketchy and legendary elements of the narrative cast doubt on the historicity of Moses. Many of the novels and scholarly accounts express ambivalence on the question of Moses' ethnicity, while the feature films divide the traditional role of Moses among male and female characters. Another area of ambivalence in some accounts is the moral character of Moses himself. As Freud's *Moses and Monotheism* and Assmann's *Moses the Egyptian* show, the complexities of biblical tradition often mirror the complexities of Moses.

Ambiguous and 'fraught with background', the biblical Moses perpetually invites and deflects attention; his person and his place in tradition are intertwined.[20] But in post-biblical traditions, Moses is often the center of polemical biographies (e.g. Philo, Josephus, and more recently, Freud) that cast him unequivocally as prophet, lawgiver, or liberator. At the same time, there are significant counter-traditions (e.g. Moses the magician in Hurston's *Moses, Man of the Mountain*) that cut against this grain and preserve the ambiguity and mystery of Moses. I suggest that these counter-traditions function to retrieve some of the features of the biblical Moses that are obscured by modern retellings.

In *The Eclipse of Biblical Narrative*,[21] Hans Frei argues that modern historical research on the Bible displaced scholarly attention to biblical narrative. Research on the Bible was driven either by concerns for historicity or the development of systematic theology, neither of which paid close attention to biblical stories. For Frei there is an apparent trade-off between interest in narrative and biblical scholarship: while novels flourished in England, historical research on the Bible grew up in Germany. The cultural divide between fact and fiction, he writes, 'becomes impenetrable; one is either on one side of it or the other, and the decision between them is the crucial issue'.[22] What Frei's analysis overlooks, however, is the flourishing of cultural forms like the biblical novel, which cross the boundaries between historical science and fictional art.

This book argues that Frei's thesis is only half right, for while some disregarded biblical narrative, others rewrote it through what I call the narrative eclipse of the Bible. Many scholars and artists *did* attend to biblical narrative by imposing non-biblical forms such as Hellenistic biography on the Bible. This study analyzes the

20. Auerbach, *Mimesis*, p. 12.
21. Hans Frei, *The Eclipse of Biblical Narrative* (New Haven: Yale University Press, 1974), p. 142.
22. Frei, *The Eclipse of Biblical Narrative*, p. 150.

narrative eclipse of the Bible in rewritings of Moses. Modern biographies of Moses share much in common, and like their forebears, Philo, Josephus, and Gregory of Nyssa, they have roots in polemical controversies that focus on Moses in order to valorize particular virtues or group identities. At the same time, I argue that rewritings of Moses reflect tensions internal to the biblical text—especially the tension between Moses and Torah, great person and written tradition. It is a paradox that some of the most 'biblical' features of biographies and novels about Moses are at odds with their own narrative purposes.

My methods are literary and cultural analysis, informed by the theoretical insights of Benjamin, Freud, Derrida, Assmann, Mieke Bal, and others. I explicate selected texts in context, but I do not propose grand historical narratives or theological exegeses. Instead, my analysis shows a variety of contexts in which biographical models of interpretation have eclipsed the central biblical concern for ideas of revelation. I also identify how biblical ambiguities are preserved and transformed in contemporary portraits of Moses. Although these portraits eclipse the biblical text, they still reflect the complexity of the Bible. Through explication and description of 'texts' about Moses, the book builds an argument about writing, biography, and ideas of revelation. My analyses draw on the methods of literary studies, gender studies, and cultural studies, but they are all guided by the question of how Moses and writing are related. This book does not represent an exhaustive survey of primary or secondary literature. I have selected texts that represent a range of discourses, constituencies, and traditions, but they are concentrated in Jewish and Christian cultures, especially in Europe and North America.

The texts chosen for this study bear on my interest in Moses' role in writing and revelation, but they are also influential and representative of larger cultural and literary patterns. The 'contemporary' chapters on novels, film, and scholarship deal with the post-Enlightenment period; the chapter on the veil of Moses relates a passage of Exodus to medieval Christian art. Biblical passages are the focus of the remaining chapters, with some history of interpretation. The book thus begins with popular images of Moses from novels, films, and scholarship, and progresses from these images to earlier, less familiar ones. With this structure I attempt to follow the hermeneutical position of the contemporary reader gradually toward the 'horizon' of the biblical text itself.

Readers of this book should thus expect to be 'defamiliarized' by biblical texts and surprised by how even the most distant and rewritten versions of the Moses story bear traces of the Bible's core concerns. My approach is theory-laden, at times even guided by such theoretical concerns as writing, textuality, ideology, and identity. These lines of inquiry are not as unlikely as they may seem. I agree with Yvonne Sherwood that the Bible turns out to embody and illustrate the principles of some postmodern theory.[23] But the book offers new evidence as well as new readings, using time-tested methods of close reading, research, and analysis.

23. Yvonne Sherwood, *A Biblical Text and its Afterlives* (Cambridge: Cambridge University Press, 2000), pp. 196-201.

The gap between traditional and new approaches in religious and biblical studies is unnecessary in my view; contemporary scholars should read innovative journals like *Semeia* as well as the venerable *Zeitschrift für die alttestamentliche Wissenschaft*. Traditional historical and philological methods continue to produce fresh insights by themselves, and they become even more fruitful in combination with such contemporary approaches as hermeneutics, structuralism, post-structuralism, and ideological criticism. Ancient text and contemporary context go together, and this book is an attempt to practice and justify such a holistic methodological view.

The book divides into two sections: Contemporary Images of Moses and Uncanny Biblical Texts. They are connected by a chapter that analyzes the biblical episode of Moses' veil and its interpretations, especially in Christian art. My analysis thus moves backward in time, from contemporary culture to the ancient text, in order to retrieve elements of the biblical portrait that are present but transformed in post-biblical culture. At the same time, each chapter attempts to bring biblical and post-biblical texts and contexts together.

The study begins with the chapters on the popular culture of fiction and film. Over twenty fictional accounts of Moses appeared in English and German between 1920 and 1998. This chapter identifies and explains the form and popularity of these retellings. With three main exceptions, these novels follow standard religious, romantic, and humanistic formulas. The exceptions are Lincoln Steffens' *Moses in Red* (1926), Zora Neale Hurston's *Moses, Man of the Mountain* (1939) and Thomas Mann's *The Tables of the Law* (1943), which subvert the great-man formula by their emphasis on violence and magic, and thereby retrieve the biblical link between Moses and writing.

Film rewrites the Bible in unique and powerful ways. While the biblical Moses appears in an ambiguous and distant light, the movie Moses is necessarily vivid and physically present. In addition to the two versions of *The Ten Commandments* by Cecil B. DeMille (1923 and 1956), I analyze two other significant films about Moses: *Moon of Israel* (1924), and the recent animated feature, *Prince of Egypt* (1998). Chapter 3 argues that films about Moses, forced by the medium to physical depiction, create 'double Moses' characters—male and female, Egyptian and Hebrew—in order to accommodate contradictory elements of biblical tradition and contemporary culture.

The third chapter, on scholarly portraits of Moses, exposes some of the most well-hidden narrative reshapings of the Moses story. Shaped by Western Classical and Romantic models of biography, modern studies of Moses often cast the biblical narrative in the form of heroic legends, stressing his individual accomplishments as a lawgiver and liberator. I examine five influential modern scholars: Julius Wellhausen, Hugo Gressmann, Martin Noth, Gerhard von Rad, and Martin Buber. In their pursuit of the historical Moses, these scholars would often overlook the contours of the biblical text. As the glue holding the fragments of the Pentateuch together, Moses comes to embody legend itself.

What contemporary portraits of Moses most often overlook is the category of writing in the biblical narrative. The remaining chapters address this dimension of the biblical portrait through literary and cultural analysis. One of the most neglected and confusing biblical texts about Moses is Exod. 34.29-35, where it is said that Moses put a veil (מסוה) over his face after speaking with God. I analyze the passage in its context and correlate it with images of the veil or mask from art history. Artistic images of Moses' veil are rare, and they never cover his face completely. A more common image is the related female (and anti-Jewish) figure of Synagogue with a veil or blindfold. Traditional views of the veil have been typically moralistic, judging it to be a punishment for Israelite disobedience, or, in Christian tradition (following 2 Cor. 3), a sign of the law rather than the gospel. The veil generates a kind of anxiety, I suggest, that relates also to an anxiety before the text. My readings of texts and images propose the veil as an element of Moses' prophetic work and thus a metaphor for scripture as a dynamic of concealment and revelation, silence and speech.

Chapter 5, 'Moses' Heavy Mouth', is a study of how the objection that Moses is unable to speak well in Exod. 4.10-17 suggests the importance of another form of communication: writing. The role of speech and writing in Deuteronomy 31–32 is the focus of Chapter 6, which proposes a biblical idea of the sacred text as a memorial. The poetic texts of Moses' final speech, the Song and the Blessing of Deuteronomy 32–33, represent a kind of orally transmitted scripture. The Blessing, on the other hand, recalls the blessing of Jacob in Genesis 48–49 and anticipates the division of territories in Joshua. Both the Song and the Blessing interrupt the narrative of Moses' farewell and death poetically to link past, present, and future.

My final chapter draws together the links between Moses and writing through a comparison of his birth and death stories. What do the ambiguities of Moses' birth and death contribute to biblical ideas of scripture? This chapter surveys biblical and post-biblical legends of Moses' birth and death in light of this question. The combination of legendary material with biblical tradition in Exodus 1–2 suggests a hero tradition that has been truncated and incorporated into a narrative for other purposes. The reason for Moses' death is not entirely clear: Is it his own guilt (Deut. 32.51) or the guilt of the people (Deut. 3.26)? Is he strong and healthy or weak and enfeebled? Freud's hypothesis that Moses was murdered by the Israelites may be untrue literally but insightful nevertheless. I understand the mysterious circumstances of Moses' birth and death to contribute directly to the idea of texts in the Bible. In post-biblical stories of Moses, the balance between the life of Moses and the writing of Moses changes, but even here, in a legend about the struggle over the body of Moses, the repressed dimension of texts returns.

Part I

Contemporary Images of Moses

Chapter 1

SUBVERTING THE GREAT MAN:
VIOLENCE AND MAGIC IN MOSES FICTION

Compelling as it was non-biblical, the story of Moses as a heroic protagonist animated modern novels and biblical scholarship alike (see Chapter 3). But while text-critical research remained obscure to general readers, fiction writers filled bookshelves and imaginations with portraits of Moses. Energized by spectacular archaeological discoveries and questions about the Bible's historical accuracy, dozens of novels and plays about Moses appeared during the nineteenth and twentieth centuries. The discoveries most relevant to Moses were the Egyptian excavations at Amarna and the Valley of the Kings. Though none of this evidence pointed directly at Moses, it produced vivid images of Egyptian life, raised questions about the relationship between Egypt and Israel, and reactivated the longstanding European fascination with ancient Egypt.

Most modern novels about Moses depict him as a hero who blends the best of Enlightenment and Romantic ideals: Howard Fast calls him a rationalist 'within the crippling limitations of his own time',[1] and W.G. Hardy describes his experience on Sinai as a 'timeless rapture' during which he 'felt himself so at one with the Power that there was now no dividing line between himself and it'.[2] The novels vary in focus from the early life of Moses in Egypt to retellings of Pentateuch narratives; from Moses as a lawgiver to Moses as an emancipator; from pious to humanist perspectives; and from ancient romance to contemporary social statement. This chapter surveys modern literary portraits of Moses and then examines three works that differ strikingly from the others (see Table 1, below). I argue that most modern novels about Moses inherit a standard biographical model rooted in ancient polemics (Philo and Josephus) and adapt it to Romantic and humanistic values and the purposes of mass culture. Three of the novels, by Lincoln Steffens, Zora Neale Hurston, and Thomas Mann, avoid this pattern through an emphasis on violence, magic, and contemporary politics. By their resistance to dominant patterns of biographical fiction, these exceptional cases affirm, in different ways, the biblical Moses.

---

1. Howard Fast, *Moses, Prince of Egypt* (New York: Crown, 1958), p. 272.
2. W.G. Hardy, *All the Trumpets Sounded* (New York: Popular Library, 1957), p. 222.

Table 1. *Selected Modern Moses Fiction/Literature*[3]

1.	1859:	J.H. Ingraham, *Pillar of Fire*
2.	1861:	François René de Chateaubriand, *Moïse, tragédie en cinq actes*
3.	1869:	Frances Ellen Watkins Harper, *Moses*
4.	1873:	A.L.O.E. (anon.), *Rescued from Egypt*
5.	1889:	Georg Ebers, *Joshua: A Story of Biblical Times*
6.	1903:	August Strindberg, *Through Deserts to Ancestral Lands (Moses)*
7.	1905:	Ivan Franko, *Moses* (Ukranian; narrative in verse)
8.	1916:	Isaac Rosenberg, *Moses* (play in verse)
9.	1919:	H. Rider Haggard, *Moon of Israel*
10.	1925:	Robert Graves, *My Head! My Head!*
11.	1926:	Lincoln Steffens, *Moses in Red*
12.	1927:	Jansen, Werner, *Die Kinder Israel*
13.	1928:	Louis Untermeyer, *Moses, A Novel* and *Burning Bush* (poetry)
14.	1932:	Arnold Schoenberg, *Moses und Auron* (opera)
15.	1931:	Lissauer, Ernst, *Der Weg des Gewaltigen* (drama)
16.	1937–39:	Sigmund Freud, *Moses and Monotheism*
17.	1939:	Zora Neale Hurston, *Moses, Man of the Mountain*
18.	1939:	Rev. Arthur E. Southon, *On Eagles' Wings*
19.	1942:	W.G. Hardy, *All the Trumpets Sounded*
20.	1943:	Thomas Mann, *Tables of the Law* (*Das Gesetz*)
21.	1949:	Dorothy Clarke Wilson, *Prince of Egypt*
22.	1951:	Scholem Asch, *Moses*
23.	1952:	Joan Grant, *So Moses Was Born*
24.	1953:	Leibert, Julius, *The Lawgiver*
25.	1956:	Leon Kolb, *Moses, the Near Easterner*
26.	1958:	Howard Fast, *Moses, Prince of Egypt*
27.	1965:	Janos Kodolanyi, *Az Ego Csipkebokor* (Hungarian)
28.	1968:	Manuel van Loggem, *Mozes* (Dutch)
29.	1973:	Samuel Sandmel, *Alone Atop the Mountain*
30.	1975:	Thomas Keneally, *Moses the Lawgiver*
31.	1976:	Anthony Burgess, *Moses* (verse; based on screenplay)
32.	1991:	Alouph Hareven, *Panim el Panim* (Hebrew)
33.	1995:	Judith Tarr, *Pillar of Fire*
34.	1998:	Lynne Reid Banks, *Moses in Egypt:* *A Novel Inspired by 'The Prince of Egypt'*

From J.H. Ingraham's 1859 *Pillar of Fire* to Judith Tarr's 1995 novel of the same name, novels about Moses appeared against the backdrop of modern biblical scholarship, wars of nationalism, the Holocaust, DeMille's two film versions of *The Ten Commandments* (1923 and 1956), and the civil rights movement. They address matters as various as Christian–Jewish relations (Ingraham, Asch, Leibert), race (Jansen, Untermeyer, Hurston, Fast), ideology (Steffens, Untermeyer, Wilson/ DeMille, Fast[4]), and modernity (Untermeyer, Mann, Kolb). Lincoln Steffens

---

3.   This list represents as many European and American literary works about Moses as I could find. The present study surveys the full-length novels and concentrates on the three by Steffens, Hurston, and Mann.

4.   Fast, a popular author who belonged to the Communist Party until 1957, published *Moses, Prince of Egypt* in 1958.

portrayed Moses in a socialist context in his 1926 *Moses in Red*. Zora Neale Hurston depicted Moses as an African American in *Moses, Man of the Mountain* (1939). A survey of Moses fiction would thus share much in common with Theodore Ziolkowski's *Fictional Transfigurations of Jesus*.[5] But more often than not, the novels deal indirectly with social issues. Instead, most of the novels paint heroic portraits of Moses in the tradition of the *Bildungsroman* and fit easily within one of the following four very broad worldviews: Christian, Jewish, Romance/ Orientalist, and Humanist/Secularist (see Table 2, below).

Table 2. *Full-Length Moses Novels Grouped by Predominant World View*[6]

Christian:	1.	Ingraham (1859)
	2.	Southon (1939)
Romance/Orientalist:	3.	Jansen (1927)
	4.	Wilson (1949)
	5.	Grant (1952)
	6.	Tarr (1995)
	7.	Banks (1998)
Jewish:	8.	Asch (1951)
	9.	Leibert (1953)
Humanist/Secularist:	10	Hardy (1942)
	11.	Kolb (1956)
	12.	Fast (1958)
Sui Generis:	14.	Steffens (1926)
	15.	Untermeyer (1928)[7]
	16.	Hurston (1939)
	17.	Mann (1943)

5.   Theodore Ziolkowski, *Fictional Transfigurations of Jesus* (Princeton, NJ: Princeton University Press, 1972).

6.   These broad distinctions are meant only to group the full-length novels into a small number of clear groups. Many of the novels could be described as a hybrid of two or more of these world-views, but in cases where none of these distinctions applies, the novels are listed as *Sui Generis*. While the Jewish and Christian worldviews are fairly self-explanatory, a word about the other two categories is in order. Romance/Orientalist novels are those that tell the story of Moses as taking place in a distant time and place in which reality is fundamentally *different* (usually more exotic, more noble, more vivid, and more mysterious) from modern Western culture. These novels, set predominantly in Egypt, participate in a Romantic tradition of Orientalism most famously described by Edward Said in *Orientalism*. Like other romance fiction, these novels accentuate the success of the hero in an exotic environment. Novels in the 'Humanist/Secularist' category, on the other hand, portray Moses as a great man who upholds modern principles of the Enlightenment, such as liberty and equality. These novels also display a strong de-mythologizing tendency, preferring naturalistic explanations of events to miracles and magic. Kolb is the best example of this phenomenon.

7.   Untermeyer's ambitious novel, divided like the Pentateuch into five books, can best be described as a deliberate and exuberant mixture of Romance, Humanist, and Jewish worldviews, coming together in what Mikhail Bakhtin (*The Dialogic Imagination* [ed. Michael Holquist; trans. Caryl Emerson and Michael Holquist; Austin: University of Texas Press, 1981], p. 311) calls a 'heteroglot' novel.

Most of the novels also represent the narrative eclipse of the Bible (as my inversion of Hans Frei's title goes), gathering up familiar ingredients of plot, history, and culture and recombining them in a newly subjective, individualized Moses. The Moses of modern fiction is the great man seen up close and depicted as everyman. Most of the novels tell a coming-of-age story in which an Egyptian prince becomes a Hebrew hero, but ambiguous scenes from the Bible are nearly always left out, such as the 'bridegroom of blood' episode (Exod. 4.24-26), or Moses' wearing of a veil (Exod. 34.29-35). Heroic images of Moses as an Egyptian commander, a great philosopher, an Egyptian prince, or a priest of the cult of Aton fill in gaps and resolve ambiguities in the biblical tradition. Like children's Bibles, popular novels about Moses create the impression of a faithful but more accessible retelling of the biblical story. All the questions about Moses' motives and agency, along with the story's contemporary meaning, dissolve in the face of the standard plot. By highlighting humanist and Romantic ideals in the charismatic figure of Moses, these novels repress the complexity of biblical and post-biblical traditions.

The novels allude to important cultural issues (such as the authority of the Bible, ideology, race, and modernity) without exploring them. They recombine and reflect elements from popular culture—Orientalism, great-man mythology, Egyptian artifacts, and romance fiction. Like the 'dream kitsch' and cultural debris at the center of Walter Benjamin's late work, these elements of popular fiction call for critical analysis.[8] A complete social history of Moses fiction (which this is not) would examine the fluidity of these elements as they appear in fiction as well as in films like DeMille's 1956 *The Ten Commandments*. For many viewers subject to the powerful imagery of mass culture, Charleton Heston *is* Moses. The Christian overtones of the film, taken in part from Southon's *On Eagle's Wings*, are woven effortlessly together with the Orientalist romance of Wilson's *Prince of Egypt*, a work that has more in common with popular 'bodice-ripper' fiction than the Bible. At the same time, the film makes almost no reference either to the complexities and polemics surrounding Moses traditions or to the social issues of the 1950s.

Sigfried Kracauer wrote in 1930 that the rise of biography as a bourgeois 'art form' was due in part to the 'crisis of the novel', triggered by a breakdown in traditional structures of meaning.[9] Biography provides readers with a sense of assurance that its story is history and that history is comprised of a succession of heroes: 'The moral of the biography is that, in the chaos of current artistic practices, it is the only seemingly necessary prose form'.[10] If the novel is the premier literary form of a world abandoned by God, as Georg Lukacs contends, then biblical novels embody a literary paradox: novels that affirm religious traditions are undercut by their secular genre. Novels typically challenge religious tradition, but they might unwittingly affirm it by making Moses the central hero. Contemporary biographical

8.   See Walter Benjamin, 'Traumkitsch', in *idem*, *Gesammelte Schriften*, II, pp. 620-22; and Susan Buck-Morss, *The Dialectics of Seeing* (Cambridge: MIT Press, 1989), p. 272.

9.   Sigfried Kracauer, 'The Biography as an Art Form of the New Bourgeoisie', in *idem*, *The Mass Ornament* (trans. Thomas Y. Levin; Cambridge, MA: Harvard University Press, 1995), pp. 101-105 (102).

10.   Kracauer, 'Biography', p. 103.

novels about Moses cannot be understood as self-contained literary artifacts, because few of these novels would withstand the aesthetic scrutiny of the New Criticism. Moses can better be seen as a means to various ideological ends in the modern novels. The polemical use of Moses has roots in ancient biographical polemics of the Bible, Philo, and Josephus.

The Moses novels are a hybrid of genres: biography, history, myth, and novel. Each of these forms has a distinct history and set of meanings in the modern period, but there has been no study of novels as a group. Since the story of Moses is familiar to most modern readers, the sheer number and sameness of the novels must lie in social and historical realities rather than literary invention. My contention is that modern Moses novels typically appropriate the legitimacy of religious tradition and literary genres (biography, history, myth, and novel) to repress and naturalize a range of cultural conflicts.[11]

Modern fiction continues the literary tradition of 'naturalism' or 'realism' (what the structuralists call *vraisemblablisation*), which Georg Lukacs, M.H. Abrams, Alan Watt and others identify with secularization.[12] This kind of realism obtains legitimacy in modern literature, but in the Moses novels it would seem to collide with the authority of religious tradition. Not only was realism defined as non-religious or anti-religious, but modern scholarly doubt about the historicity of the Bible made it even less amenable to realistic fiction. The novels about Moses thus represent a specific kind of crisis: the contradiction between modern realism and religious tradition. As such, the novels of Moses illustrate the capacity of myths to express contradictions, as Levi-Strauss argues in *Structural Anthropology*.[13] Modern crises of meaning, religious tradition, identity, race, class, and gender, all appear in the Moses novels, but they usually lie beneath the surface. Anxious to address crises but loathe to confront them, most of the novels follow familiar patterns to form a literature of repression.

11. This approach resembles other socially oriented modes of criticism, such as Fredric Jameson's well-known idea of the 'political unconscious', in which works of culture are symbolic acts that, through analysis, reveal ideological content: *The Political Unconscious* (Ithaca, NY: Cornell University Press, 1981), pp. 32-79. My approach is less theoretically ambitious, however; the connections I make between social realities and the novels are relatively local and textually based. See my essay on Hurston and Untermeyer, 'Contesting History and Identity in Modern Fiction About Moses', in Eric Ziolkowski (ed.), *Literature, Religion, and East-West Comparison: Essays in Honor of Anthony C. Yu* (Newark, DL: University of Delaware Press, forthcoming). On the question of fiction and history, see also R.G. Collingwood, *The Idea of History* (Oxford: Clarendon Press, 1946), pp. 242-26. The present study was already complete before the appearance of Melanie Wright's *Moses in America: The Cultural Uses of Biblical Narrative* (Oxford: Oxford University Press, 2003), which includes detailed social history and cultural analyses of the Steffens and Hurston novels, as well as DeMille's 1956 *The Ten Commandments*.

12. Georg Lukacs writes: 'The novel is the epic of a world that has been abandoned by God', in *idem*, *The Theory of the Novel* (trans. Anna Bostock; Cambridge: MIT Press, 1971), p. 88. See also Ian Watt, *The Rise of the Novel* (London: Penguin Books, 1966), pp. 82-85; and M.H. Abrams, *Natural Supernaturalism* (New York: W.W. Norton, 1973).

13. Claude Levi-Strauss, *Structural Anthropology* (New York: Basic Books, 1963).

Most of the Moses novels are relatively modest in literary terms. They lack origi-
nality, depth, and historical plausibility. Some resemble each other uncannily.[14]
Nevertheless, they constitute a striking and overlooked *corpus* of popular culture.
Several authors of Moses novels (Thomas Mann, Sholem Asch, Howard Fast,
Thomas Keneally, Anthony Burgess, and Judith Tarr) are well-known and highly
prolific. Is the Moses novel a set piece or sub-genre for authors of historical fiction?
Why are there so many Moses books? One reason given by the authors is the deep
pleasure they ascribe to writing about Moses. Lincoln Steffens observes: 'It would
be a fine arts practice if every writer, scientist and statesman—if everybody would
read, after every enlightening experience or discovery of theirs, the beautiful old
stories of the Bible and then write or tell them again in the fresh glow of their new
light'.[15] Arthur Southon echoes these sentiments: 'Nothing I have ever imagined
and written has given me a tenth of the joy I have found in writing this imaginative
reconstruction of one of the most familiar series of incidents in the Bible'.[16] The
biblical Moses has been an edifying object of interpretation for centuries, and
contemporary fiction is only one of its many forms.

If the majority of the novels represent the literature of repression, a small minority could be called the literature of confrontation. These novels, especially Hurston's
Moses Man of the Mountain (1939), resist the image of Moses as a modern idealist hero. Three other notable cases are Steffens' *Moses in Red* (1926), Mann's 1943
Tables of the Law, and Freud's *Moses and Monotheism* (1939), a work which Freud
described as *ein historischer Roman* and is thus itself a kind of Moses fiction.[17]

Instead of presenting Moses as a great liberator and lawgiver, the novels of confrontation highlight three elements that challenge that image directly: magic, violence, and contemporary politics. The novels of confrontation are no more faithful
to the biblical narrative than the novels of repression. In fact, there are several
novels by Leibert, Southon, and Asch, that follow the Bible *very* closely. These
pious and traditionalist novels tend to follow the biblical account through paraphrase and even quotation. Southon and Asch, for example, quote the rarely mentioned biblical episode of Moses' heavy mouth; the episode also appears in the
1878 work *Rescued From Egypt*, a didactic novel about Jewish–Christian relations
interspersed with sermons on the life of Moses.[18] But what sets Hurston, Steffens,
and Mann apart from the other novels is a self-consciousness about representation
and a subversion of prevalent ideals. The novels of confrontation perform the
critical task of subverting the great-man myth.

14.   Joan Grant's *So Moses Was Born* (repr., New York: Arno Press, 1980 [1952]), for instance,
strongly resembles Dorothy Clarke Wilson's *Prince of Egypt* (repr., New York: Pocket Books,
1951 [1949]).

15.   Lincoln Steffens, *Moses in Red* (Philadelphia: Dorrance & Co., 1926), p. 44.

16.   Arthur E. Southon, *On Eagles' Wings* (New York: McGraw–Hill, 1939), p. viii.

17.   Freud, cited in Yosef Yerushalmi, *Freud's Moses*, p. 16. Since Freud's book is the object
of so many valuable studies, especially Yerushalmi's, my focus here is on the novels by Hurston,
Steffens, and Mann.

18.   Southon, *On Eagles' Wings*, p. 165; Sholem Asch, *Moses* (trans. Maurice Samuel; New
York: Putnam, 1951), p. 111, and Anonymous, *Rescued from Egypt* (London: Thomas Nelson,
1873), p. 290.

Hurston's novel, for instance, presents Moses in contradictory terms as a liberator and hoodoo man, a public leader and a solitary mystic. This mixture creates the literary effect of what the Russian formalists call 'estrangement', or even the 'alienation effect', a term borrowed from Brecht's theory of epic theater to describe the capacity to distance and historicize events in literature.[19] This quality appears also in Steffens' *Moses in Red*, which includes lengthy excurses on twentieth-century politics and the necessity of violence in revolutions. Mann's *Tables of the Law* also presents Moses in a shockingly violent light. A second quality present in Hurston but missing from most of the novels is an attention to the magical and hermetic dimensions of Moses traditions. By confronting the contemporary hero myth of Moses, Hurston, Steffens and Mann initiate a critical rewriting of the biblical Moses, a figure usually obscured by the legacy of Philo and Josephus.

1. Ancient Polemical Roots of the Modern Moses Novels

Representations of Moses have always been polemical. In the Bible, stories exalting Moses coexist with stories criticizing him. In Numbers 11–12, for example, Moses prevails over Aaron and Miriam after they challenge him. Most scholars account for the controversial status of Moses by analyzing the text into distinct documentary sources: E and D depict Moses favorably, while J tends to honor Aaron at the expense of Moses.[20] A second, theological reason scholars give for ambivalence toward Moses in the Bible is the need to minimize the risk of deifying Moses or upstaging divine authority.[21]

The polemical tradition took a different turn in the Greek and Roman literature about Moses. In his 1972 book, *Moses in Greco-Roman Paganism*, John Gager surveys traditions about Moses dating from early in the third century BCE.[22] While most of these sources identify Moses as an important lawgiver, they are also predominantly anti-Jewish. In pre-Christian times, one motive for attacks on Moses was the threat of a monotheistic religious community, especially in Rome. These writers describe Moses as an Egyptian or Hebrew leader of a rebellion. In one form of the story, Moses is a leprous Egyptian priest whose followers are also lepers.[23]

19. Bertolt Brecht, *Brecht on Theater* (trans. John Willet; London: Methuen, 1974), p. 96.

20. See, e.g., Richard Elliott Friedman, *Who Wrote the Bible?* (New York: Harper & Row, 1989); and John H. Hayes and J. Maxwell Miller (eds.), *Israelite and Judean History* (Philadelphia: Trinity Press International, 1977).

21. The biblical story of Moses weaves the legend of an individual together with the story of a people. As Jonathan Cohen shows, the birth legend has strong roots in the Babylonian legend of Sargon. Yet after the first chapters of Exodus, this story is not mentioned again in the Hebrew Bible. Nevertheless, the birth legend and the heroic Moses resurface in gospel stories of Christ's birth and in later polemics, sometimes overshadowing the story of Israel's enslavement and deliverance. Jonathan Cohen, *The Origins and Evolution of the Moses Nativity Story* (Leiden: E.J. Brill, 1993), pp. 6-8, 59.

22. John G. Gager, *Moses in Greco-Roman Paganism* (Nashville: Abingdon Press, 1972).

23. The story is attested in Lysimachus and Apion, Nicharchus *et al.* See Gager, *Moses in Greco-Roman Paganism*, pp. 40, 129. See also Gohei Hata, 'The Story of Moses Interpreted Within

Moses is also depicted as a magician, in one case losing a magic contest with the Egyptians.[24]

The two main Jewish biographers of Moses in late antiquity are Philo of Alexandria and Josephus (first century CE). Both biographies were highly influential and also apologetic. As noted in the Introduction, Philo begins his neo-Platonic biography as follows: 'Greek men of letters have refused to treat him as worthy of memory, possibly through envy'.[25] Philo's account is thus apologetic from the beginning, emphasizing throughout the excellence of Moses as an individual. This Moses personifies all the best of Philo's culture: he is educated in mathematics, poetry, and philosophy; his body, mind, and soul are harmonized like a musical instrument.[26] To underline his purpose, Philo divides the second half of his biography into the distinct roles of Moses as king, philosopher, lawgiver, priest, and prophet.[27] Moses stands out most distinctly as 'the best of all lawgivers in all countries, better in fact than any that have ever arisen among either Greeks or the barbarians'; the laws of Moses are likewise excellent: 'firm, unshaken, immovable, stamped, as it were, with the seals of nature herself'.[28]

In his *Jewish Antiquities* and the apologetic *Contra Apionem*, Josephus echoes many elements of Philo's biography: Moses is history's greatest and most ancient lawgiver, a powerful and unselfish liberator, and a wise ruler. His laws are universal, harmonious, and merciful.[29] Moses is a good-looking hero who overcomes tremendous odds in the name of the people and the God of Israel.[30] In *Contra Apionem*, a point-by-point refutation of anti-Jewish writings, Josephus also denies the specific charge that Moses was an Egyptian priest expelled for leprosy.[31] The stories of Moses' birth and Egyptian youth are considerably more elaborate and textured in Josephus than in Philo. The legend of Moses' military campaign against Ethiopia, for instance, which appears in Artapanus, does not appear in Philo at all.[32] In general, then, the Moses of Josephus is at once more detailed and more apologetic than Philo's idealizing portrait.

Writing in Greek, Philo and Josephus polemically depict Moses as the greatest lawgiver in order to defend Moses not as an individual but as a representative of Jewish people and traditions. Their use of Hellenistic forms (biography, cf. Plato's *Phaedo*) and terms (e.g. philosophy) departs from the biblical emphasis on the

the Context of Anti-Semitism', in Louis H. Feldman and Gohei Hata (eds.), *Josephus, Judaism, and Christianity* (Detroit: Wayne State University Press, 1987), pp. 180-97.

24. Gager, *Mose in Greco-Roman Paganism*, p. 21.

25. Philo, *On the Life of Moses*, p. 277.

26. Philo, *On the Life of Moses*, pp. 287, 291.

27. Philo, *On the Life of Moses*, p. 455.

28. Philo, *On the Life of Moses*, p. 457.

29. Josephus (*Josephus*. I. *Against Apion* [trans. H.St.J. Thackeray; LCL; Cambridge, MA: Harvard University Press, 1966], pp. 359-65, 379).

30. Gager, *Moses in Greco-Roman Paganism*, p. 50. Physical beauty is also typical of the main characters in *Diasporanovelle*; see Meinhold von Arndt, 'Die Gattung der Josephsgeschichte und des Estherbuches: Diasporanovelle II', *ZAW* 88 (1976), pp. 72-93.

31. Josephus, *Against Apion*, p. 277.

32. Josephus, *Against Apion*, pp. 269-75.

people and God of Israel. As Patricia Cox shows in *Biography in Late Antiquity*, Hellenistic biography was *inherently* polemical.[33] Philo and Josephus would prove to be highly influential; many of the novels depict Moses in similarly heroic (and polemical) terms.

Christian traditions about Moses between the ancient and modern periods are too many and diverse to enumerate here, but the polemical nature of Moses established in biblical and Hellenistic traditions persisted. Since he prefigures Christ *and* personifies Judaism, Moses poses a delicate challenge. Christians often see Moses through the eyes of the New Testament. The brilliant, complex associations between Moses and Jesus in the Gospel of Matthew (as heroes, redeemers, and intercessors) effectively eclipse Moses with the image of Christ.[34] Paul uses allegory to accomplish similar ends, contrasting the veiled Moses to Christ, who removes the veil (2 Cor. 3). Most Christian references to the veil of Moses refer to 2 Corinthians rather than Exodus 34.[35]

Christian traditions also build on the polemical and Hellenistic legacy of Philo and Josephus.[36] For instance, Gregory of Nyssa's fourth-century *Life of Moses*, while Christian, borrows heavily from Philo in its favorable depiction of Moses as a figure of ideal Christian spirituality.[37] The allegorical and homiletic uses of Moses may be found in Christian sermons, art, and morality plays, but sustained biographies of Moses are rare in this period, and in an increasingly anti-Jewish Christian Europe, portraits of Moses can be ambivalent or negative.[38]

2. *Idealism and the Egyptian Moses*

While the ancient apologists elaborated and isolated Moses from his biblical context, they still viewed him from a distance. Modern writers viewed Moses for the first time at close range and from within. Fully human and recognizable, Moses was a great individual confronting the maxim 'Know thyself' in terms of idealist ethics and character. This Moses was more solitary than any that had appeared before.

Two general trends account for the number of popular works written about Moses. The first is the blend of Jewish and Christian traditions with the values of Enlightenment and Romantic thought in the nineteenth and twentieth centuries: Moses was a great lawgiver and heroic liberator. The Romantics' enthusiasm for Moses was informed by the Orientalist philosophy and philology of the nineteenth

33. Patricia Cox, *Biography in Late Antiquity* (Berkeley: University of California Press, 1983), p. 135.

34. See Dale Allison, Jr, *The New Moses* (Minneapolis: Fortress Press, 1993).

35. Chapter 4 of this book analyzes traditional interpretations of the veil of Moses.

36. See Arnaldo Momigliano, *The Development of Greek Biography* (Cambridge, MA: Harvard University Press, 1971), esp. pp. 78-87.

37. Gregory of Nyssa, *The Life of Moses* (trans. Abraham Malherbe and Everett Ferguson; New York: Paulist Press, 1978).

38. See V.A. Kolve, *The Play Called Corpus Christi* (Stanford: Stanford University Press, 1966), pp. 74-78; and Ruth Mellinkoff, *The Horned Moses in Medieval Art and Thought* (Berkeley: University of California Press, 1970).

century. The second trend was the twentieth-century explosion of popular interest
in ancient Egypt.

Modern portraits of Moses have thus concentrated on his Egyptian background.
It was Schiller who promoted the modern view that Moses was Egyptian in culture
if not in birth, in a set of lectures from 1790.[39] Borrowing heavily from a little-
known masonic treatise on the Egyptian identity of Moses, Schiller depicted Moses
as an Egyptian founder of Israelite religion.[40] At the same time, Schiller's Moses is
also a central figure in developing Enlightenment thought.[41] According to Schiller,
the religion and teaching of Moses drew heavily from Egyptian mystery cults. Like
the Moses of many later novels, Schiller's Moses is a princely figure who undergoes a dramatic personal transformation, culminating in the decision to save his
people: 'Great and glorious rises before his spirit the idea, "I will redeem this
people"'.[42] Merging Egypt, Israel, and his own Romantic idealism, Schiller's story
of the self-sacrifice and transformation of Moses presents a cultural shift from the
worldly greatness of Egypt to the sublimity of Hebrew religion.[43]

Schiller's view of Moses as an Enlightenment figure rooted in Egypt gained
momentum in the twentieth century with the rising popular interest in ancient Egypt.
One hypothesis that linked Egypt and Israel was the view that Mosaic religion bore
a strong resemblance to the religious reform of Amenhotep IV (fourteenth century),
a quasi-monotheistic religion. This suggestion drew attention when the Hymn to
Aton, a quasi-monotheistic text with parallels in Psalm 104, was first published in
English in 1908.[44] Another phase of popular interest in ancient Egypt coincided
with the exhibition of artifacts from the tomb of King Tutankahmun in the 1920s.

The Egyptian background of Moses and his law would come to have different
implications for different authors: a justification of Israelite greatness for some, and
a repudiation of the pious view of Moses' (and the Bible's) originality for others.[45]

---

39. See Friedrich Schiller, *Die Sendung Moses* (ed. Karl-Heinz Hahn; Schillers Werke:
Nationalausgabe, 17; Weimar: Hermann Böhlaus, 1970), pp. 377-413. Schiller's observations were
based largely on a treatise by masonic philosopher Karl Reinhold. See Assmann, *Moses the Egyptian*, p. 125.

40. Schiller, *Die Sendung Moses*, p. 377. See Assmann, *Moses the Egyptian*, pp. 125-39.

41. Schiller, *Die Sendung Moses*, p. 377.

42. Schiller, *Die Sendung Moses*, p. 389 (my translation).

43. Goethe depicts Moses as deciding to become the people's redeemer after pondering his
people's fate and fatherland: 'Nach manchem Zweifel und Zögern entschliesst er sich, zurückzuke-
hren und des Volkes Retter ze werden', *Israel in der Wüste*, in Thomas Mann, *Das Gesetz* (ed. Käte
Hamburger; Frankfurt: Ullstein, 1964), p. 182. Later, Heine's Moses would also reflect the values
of individual freedom, liberty, human rights; according to Bluma Goldstein, this humanism reflected Heine's ambivalence toward Christianity and Judaism. Goldstein, *Reinscribing Moses*
(Cambridge, MA: Harvard University Press, 1992), pp. 26-27.

44. See J.H. Breasted, *The Dawn of Conscience* (New York: Charles Scribner's Sons, 1933).

45. The mere juxtaposition of Egyptian and Hebrew cultures overlooks vast differences of
power and scale. Cf. Nietzsche on the ironies of the Roman encounter with Judaism as the background to Christendom, especially in the creation of *ressentiment* and 'bad conscience', in *idem, On
the Genealogy of Morals* (trans. Walter Kaufmann; New York: Vintage Books, 1967), pp. 32-36,
52-55.

Freud's *Moses and Monotheism* has been interpreted in both ways.[46] But in every case, the connection between Egypt and Israel made a link between the status of a great empire (Egypt) and the status of a great tradition (Israel).

The Orientalist fascination with the exotic Near East influenced many of the modern Moses novels. Rudyard Kipling, for instance, wrote a letter to support the publication of H. Rider Haggard's 1919 *Moon of Israel*.[47] Haggard's novel is also dedicated to the French Egyptologist Gaston Maspero, who commended the book for its fidelity to the 'inner spirit of the old Egyptians'.[48] Maspero's work on Egyptian mythology is also cited by Louis Untermeyer as a source for his 1928 *Moses*.[49] The role of Maspero and others in the formation of Moses fiction may be considerable, since Untermeyer's novel likely provided a model for others.

For the most part, then, modern novels about Moses poured the old wine of Romantic Orientalism and Enlightenment morality into the new skin of popular Egyptology. The images of the ancient Orient that run through books like Untermeyer's 1928 *Moses* and Wilson's 1949 *Prince of Egypt* predate the flourishing of popular interest in Egyptian archaeology that followed the discovery of Tutankhamun's tomb in 1922. In other words, the Moses novels demythologize and re-mythologize Moses according to modern doctrines of self, society, and history. Two related fascinations of the twentieth-century novels—Judaism and popular revolution—likewise have their roots and dominant narrative topoi in nineteenth-century thought.

3. *Identity and Recognition*

Most of the popular Moses novels turn on a central moment of recognition and decision: Moses realizes he is a Hebrew and that he must lead his people out of slavery. Even when this decision coincides with the burning bush episode, it remains an act of personal free will in the face of Moses' identity and destiny. It is always a difficult struggle, one that involves the sacrifice of Egyptian prestige and the risk of humiliation as a Hebrew.

This episode is so important that many of the novels omit or shift the birth narrative to this coming-of-age recognition. Moses' heroic freedom echoes the resolve described by the Romantic Moses of Schiller and Goethe and forms a variation on the maxim 'Know thyself'. At the same time, the decision is usually ethnically or racially grounded: Werner Jansen, as an obvious instance, described his novel as a '*Rasseroman*' that would demonstrate the power of blood.[50]

---

46.   Yerushalmi, for instance, retrieves Jewish elements within Freud's book, but he also challenges what he sees as Freud's misunderstanding of Jewish tradition (*Freud's Moses*, pp. 81-100). Bernstein, on the other hand, reads Freud's Moses as a fully Jewish (if somewhat secularized) figure (*Freud and the Legacy of Moses*, pp. 90-116).

47.   Morton Cohen, *Rider Haggard: His Life and Works* (London: Hutchinson, 1960), p. 50.

48.   Haggard, *Moon of Israel* (New York: Longmans, Green & Co., 1919), pp. v-vi; see Edward Said's mention of Maspero in *Orientalism* (New York: Vintage Books, 1978), p. 170.

49.   Louis Untermeyer, *Moses* (New York: Harcourt, Brace & Co., 1928), p. 389.

50.   Cited by Hamburger in Mann, *Das Gesetz*, p. 203; the novel was reprinted in 1941 with a pro-Nazi inscription.

The self-recognition scene takes many forms. In Ingraham's *Pillar of Fire*, Moses discovers his true identity by reading the secret Book of Thoth deep inside a pyramid. Thoth is the ibis-headed god of writing, counterpart to Hermes and central to Hermetic tradition.[51] In *On Eagle's Wings*, Miriam brings Moses to his dying mother, whose last request is that Moses should promise to deliver his people.[52] The death of Moses' mother also leads to discovery in Fast's *Moses, Prince of Egypt*: while Moses grieves over the ritual killing of his mother, a priest tells him the true story of his origins.[53] The discovery generates a typical inner conflict:

> 'So I am the son of slaves, of the dirty, dying wretches who live in the Land of Goshen', went through him, hour after hour, day after day, cutting apart his grief, filling him with anger and frustration and hatred of himself—and building resentment against his dead mother. Yet there was something in him, a core of solidity that allowed him to fight this resentment, to cling to the image of his mother as his mother—and not to turn against her the corroding humiliation that was eating out his heart.[54]

Another catalyst for Moses' self-recognition is his killing of the Egyptian overseer. After Untermeyer's Moses kills the overseer, the Egyptian Queen Thermutis tells Moses that his real father is the Hebrew Amram, the result of an illicit affair.[55] 'One of my boys will be a great leader yet', she tells him.[56] In Wilson's *Prince of Egypt*, Moses discovers his true identity when his resemblance to a Hebrew is noted.[57] A similar episode appears in Hurston's *Moses, Man of the Mountain*. In all cases, the self-recognition as a Hebrew coincides with Moses' destiny as a liberator.

In the tradition of *Bildungsroman*, the popular novels depict Moses more intimately than ancient sources. Though none of the novels presents Moses as a first-person narrator, their scope usually extends to the thoughts and feelings of the main character. Dorothy Clarke Wilson's young Prince Moses has especially vehement moments:

> The passivity in which he had been existing was gone. He felt warmly, virilely alive. He was acutely aware of every small detail in the garden about him: the crunch of his sandals on the red gravel walk, the fragrance of roses and bittersweet… But the mood of well-being was not to last. He exchanged it a few days later for a tumultuous unrest which beset his emotions like a fever, plunging them into alternate extremes of warmth and frigidity.[58]

---

51.   Brian P. Copenhaver (ed.), *Hermetica* (Cambridge: Cambridge University Press, 1992), pp. xiii-xvi. The legendary Book of Thoth appears also in Hurston's *Moses, Man of the Mountain* (Urbana: University of Illinois Press, 1984), pp. 73-75. The scene of self-discovery inside a pyramid also appears (without mention of Thoth) in the recent Dreamworks film, *Prince of Egypt* (Produced by Jeffrey Katzenberg, 1998).
    52.   Southon, *On Eagles' Wings*, pp. 68-74.
    53.   Fast, *Moses, Prince of Egypt*, pp. 80-83.
    54.   Fast, *Moses, Prince of Egypt*, p. 83.
    55.   Untermeyer, *Moses*, pp. 84-87.
    56.   Untermeyer, *Moses*, p. 86.
    57.   Wilson, *Prince of Egypt*, p. 258.
    58.   Wilson, *Prince of Egypt*, p. 73.

Intimate as Wilson's portrait is, it remains highly conventional, shaped more by the standards of romance and melodrama than original or biblically derived characterization.

Like the Moses of Philo and Josephus, the Moses of the novels is extraordinary: his intelligence, military skill, charisma, and good looks set him apart from all his contemporaries. These qualities unfold slowly in his youth, but after Moses claims his destiny, they flourish. Moses prevails as a superior exemplar of liberator and lawgiver according to the range of ideals represented by the novelists: Fast—liberal; Kolb—bureaucrat; Steffens—revolutionary; Tarr—former king; Leibert—rabbi; Untermeyer—passionate humanist.

4. *Stock Endings and Ideology*

The conclusion to each novel reflects its purpose and worldview. The guiding vision of Ingraham's epistolary novel *Pillar of Fire* is clear from the dedication:

> To the Men of Israel… This Book is Inscribed by the Author; With the Prayer, that You, of this Generation, Who are Dispersed in All the Earth, May Behold and Follow the Light of the Cross, As Your Fathers Followed the Pillar of Fire, and Enter at Last the Real Canaan, Under the True Joshua, Jesus, the Son of Abraham, Who Also Was the Son of God.[59]

In this way, the final scene of the golden calf and its aftermath allegorizes Israel as the Jewish People of the Old Testament and presents Joshua as a prefiguration of Jesus:

> Moses informs me that the Lord, in punishment of this sin of Israel, will cause them to wander many years in the wilderness ere He bring them to the land promised to their fathers, and will subject them to be harassed by enemies on all sides, some of whom have already attacked them, but were discomfited by the courage of a Hebrew youth, called Joshua, who promises to become a mighty warrior and leader in Israel, and whom Moses loves as an own son.[60]

The victory at the Red Sea is a popular final scene in the novels: in Wilson's *Prince of Egypt*, the values of self-sacrifice and universal freedom take precedence. The Cushite prince Nehsi manages to lead the Egyptians into the trap of the Red Sea, but he dies in the process. His daughter Tharbis, the wife and true love of Moses, joins him in reflection and celebration at the end of the story: '"Come", said Moses. Taking her hand, he led Tharbis along the shore of the Sea of Reeds to a high headland of sand and rock jutting out into the water. Together they climbed up the rocky include and stood side by side, the tortured confusion of the sea behind them, the new morning sun warm on their faces.'[61] Tharbis, an African captured by the Egyptians, shares the freedom of the Israelites. (Tharbis is used similarly in Hardy,

---

59. J.H. Ingraham, *The Pillar of Fire or Israel in Bondage* (Philadelphia: G.G. Evans, 1860), p. 3.
60. Ingraham, *The Pillar of Fire*, p. 594.
61. Wilson, *Prince of Egypt*, p. 436.

though with a misogynistic edge: after Moses spares her from stoning, Tharbis, bruised and naked, throws herself on Moses: 'He realized with a sick disgust that she was a woman who, if you beat her, loved you—at least, for the moment'.[62])

Another Red Sea ending appears in Judith's Tarr's *Pillar of Fire*, where Moses and Akhenaton, the quasi-monotheistic Pharaoh, are the same person. As the Egyptian king discovers the Hebrews (Hapiru in the novel), he gradually comes to embrace their religion and people: '"The Aten has revealed himself to me", he said, "in words of fire... I must go", the king said. "Into the desert. I must follow the god. By night he is a pillar of fire." '[63] The Egyptian king stages his own death and then emerges as the prophet Moshe. The central conflict between Egyptian and Hebrew thus unfolds dramatically within the central character. The final scene is the crossing of the Red Sea in which the body of the new Pharaoh, Ramses I, washes up on the shore. After the burial of the Egyptian Pharaoh, Miriam and the others begin to celebrate their freedom with the Song of the Sea (see Exod. 15). Tarr's novel represents the most dramatic connection between the Amarna phase of Egyptian history and Hebrew monotheism. Moses/Akhenaton represents the progress from slavery to freedom not in socio-economic terms, but rather as a kind of spiritual journey of transformation and enlightenment.

In Julius Leibert's 1953 account, the story of Moses ends with a modern retelling of rabbinic traditions about the death of Moses: when the angel of death appears at his doorstep, Moses sends him away, saying 'I have one more thing left to do'.[64] Then, after he blesses the people and leads them in recitation of the Shema (Deut. 6.4), God approaches him and denies his request to enter the promised land: 'Only small men die with their work done. Great men—never!'[65] When he asks why his burial place must remain unknown, God replies, 'It will free you and the Torah from the shackles of race and land!'[66] Then, according to the traditional rabbinic reading of the phrase that says Moses died '*al pi YHWH*—by the mouth of God', God ends Moses' life with a kiss. Leibert, a rabbi and a lawyer, combines a commitment to Jewish tradition with a humanistic vision of the law in this conclusion.[67]

Hardy's death of Moses conclusion reflects the importance of the law of Moses as well as the image of Moses as a compassionate and Romantic hero: the divine 'Face' reassures Moses that his lawgiving work is complete, and Moses has a vision of his birthplace: 'and the voice of Jochebed called to him. "Aunt Jochebed", he said. And then remembering: "Mother". And the night had come.'[68] In Arthur Southon's version of the Red Sea scene, Moses leaves the scene and the Hebrews direct their worship to God 'instead of exalting the human means employed'.[69]

62. Hardy, *All the Trumpets Sounded*, p. 233.
63, Judith Tarr, *Pillar of Fire* (New York: Forge, 1995), p. 172.
64. Julius Leibert, *The Lawgiver* (New York: Exposition Press, 1953), p. 354.
65. Leibert, *The Lawgiver*, p. 355.
66. Leibert, *The Lawgiver*, p. 356.
67. Jewish sources also inform the death of Moses scene in Sholem Asch, *Moses*, pp. 504-505.
68. Hardy, *All the Trumpets Sounded*, pp. 238-39.
69. Southon, *On Eagles' Wings*, p. 296.

By contrast to these standard scenes of the Red Sea, the golden calf, and Moses' death, which affirm familiar religious and humanist images of Moses as liberator, lawgiver, and hero, Hurston's final scene in *Moses, Man of the Mountain* begins as a standard death scene but shifts surprisingly to a scene where Moses returns to life as an African wise man. This difference illustrates Hurston's general challenge to the prevailing modern image of Moses (see below).

5. *Violence, Magic, and Critique*

Overall, the novels combine popular images of Egypt, the Bible, and modern culture in many variations on the basic coming-of-age plot. An appropriate hermeneutical stance toward the novels, then, is to see them as documents of social history, indicators of popular ideology and consciousness. Insofar as they conform to a common narrative template, the novels practice literary repression, whereas Hurston's exceptional use of magic and contemporary African-American dialect represents not a Romantic reiteration of traditional images, but a literature of confrontation. In different ways, Hurston, Steffens and Mann appear to challenge the commonly held stereotype of Moses as an idealist hero. As such, the elements of divine violence and magic stand against the tide of the great-man/idealist portraits of Moses. While Hurston's novel may resemble the biblical account even less than many others, it nevertheless represents an important critical step in recognizing the limitations of prevailing images. Very few novels are faithful to the specific details of puzzling biblical episodes, but Hurston, Steffens and Mann offer something else: a critical distance and a critical view of prevailing humanistic and Romantic portraits.

a. *Socialism, Fascism, and Violence: Steffens and Mann*
The two novels that confront ideological conflict most directly are Lincoln Steffens' *Moses in Red* (1926) and Thomas Mann's *The Tables of the Law* (1943). Steffens presents the Moses story through the autobiographical and historical lens of a leftist radical and muckraker; his narrative alternates between retelling the biblical story and relating it directly to modern Russia and revolutionary politics. Steffens repeatedly highlights the necessity of violence to the book of Exodus and in revolutions generally. He suggests that the death of Moses is not tragic but merciful, since revolutions take a generation to take root and their leaders are not suited to the realities of conquest and settlement.[70] With bluntness and no shred of irony, Moses and the God of Israel endorse dictatorship, violence, and political calculation as part of their revolutionary program.[71] The radical doctrine and tone of *Moses in Red* parallel Walter Benjamin's 1921 essay, 'Critique of Violence', in which divine justice and violence are also invoked in the context of political revolution: 'If mythical violence is lawmaking, divine violence is law-destroying; if the former

70. Steffens, *Moses in Red*, pp. 132-44.
71. Steffens, *Moses in Red*, pp. 113, 134.

sets boundaries, the latter boundlessly destroys them'.[72] For Benjamin, divine violence and revolutionary violence (especially in the form of syndicalism) share the capacity for positive social transformation. Far from endorsing violence for its own sake, Benjamin and Steffens challenge the repression of violence by idealist (rationalist and Romantic) social theory.[73]

Mann's *The Tables of the Law* depicts Moses as a grand Romantic hero whose passion and creativity form a people, invent written language, and deliver the law. Written in a condensed, high-blown style, and running to fewer than sixty pages in German, the novel at first appears to be a meditation on Moses as a great artist figure: while he is inventing the written alphabet (a tradition that dates to early Jewish tradition[74]), his head becomes so overheated that it sprouts horns. His mission to liberate the Hebrews is motivated primarily by the desire 'to stamp upon them the holy invisible God... They should put on a fold-shape distinct from all others, belonging to God, destined for the holy and spiritual life, distinguished from all others by reverence, awe, and abstention—in other words by fear before the ideas of purity, precept, and discipline.'[75]

But Mann's Moses is given to outbursts of anger, and there is also a streak of cruelty in him: 'he knew better than the innocent, that to kill is very fine [*köstlich*]'.[76] His genius for lawgiving has a tyrannical edge: 'His birth was irregular, hence it was he passionately loved order, the absolute, the shalt and shalt not'. After the episode of the golden calf, the novel concludes with the execution of those responsible and a set of extremely harsh warnings against covenant violations.[77]

Mann wrote the novel in the United States for a propagandistic anthology called *The Ten Commandments: Hitler's War Against the Moral Code*, which appeared in English in 1943.[78] The novel would thus seem to represent another installment in his attack on Hitler and fascism. In a letter to his son Klaus, who was serving in the US military at the time, Mann wrote: 'In any case, the realistic-grotesque story, whose subject, of course, is nothing less than the formation of civilized morality (the Golden Calf is a tragicomic relapse), greatly amuses me, and I have knocked off a hundred pages so rapidly that I felt I no longer have to be envious of your speed'.[79] Mann wrote in another letter that the story 'has a strong moral and timely

72. Walter Benjamin, 'Critique of Violence', in *idem*, *Reflections* (ed. Peter Demetz; trans. Edmund Jephcott; New York: Schocken Books, 1986), p. 297.

73. Violence—the Hebrews' murder of Moses—is also central in Freud's *Moses and Monotheism*. Like Steffens, Freud sees violence as generative of social and religious development.

74. According to Clement of Alexandria, this legend comes from the ancient Jewish historian Eupolemos (c. 150 BCE); see Gager, *Moses in Greco-Roman Paganism*, p. 77 n. 155. The tradition of Moses as the inventor of writing also appears in Leibert, *The Lawgiver*, pp. 302-303.

75. Thomas Mann, *The Tables of the Law* (trans. H.T. Lowe-Porter; New York: Knopf, 1943), p. 11.

76. Mann, *Tables of the Law*, p. 1.

77. Mann, *Tables of the Law*, p. 63.

78. See Frederick A. Lubich, ' "Fascinating Fascism": Thomas Manns "Das Gesetz" und seine Selbst-de-Montage als Moses–Hitler', *German Studies Review* 14 (1991, pp. 553-73 (554).

79. Letter to Klaus Mann, 9 March 1943, in Thomas Mann, *Letters of Thomas Mann* (trans. Richard and Clara Winston; New York: Knopf, 1971), p. 416.

touch and culminates in a curse of Hitler'.[80] The novella's final scene, which Mann read in wartime radio addresses to the German people,[81] is a speech of Moses that invokes moral tradition and terrible punishment for those who disobey it: 'In the stone of the mountains I engraved the ABC of human conduct, but no less shall it be graven in your flesh and blood, O Israel, so that everyone who breaks one of the ten commandments shall shrink within himself and before God, and it shall be cold about his heart because he overstepped God's bound'.[82] Moses' curse further targets the evil creator of the golden calf:

> 'Blood will flow in streams because of his black stupidity, so that the red pales form the cheek of mankind... And I will lift up my foot saith the Lord, and tread him into the mire—to the bottom of the earth will I tread the blasphemer, an hundred and twelve fathoms deep... And whosoever names his name shall spit towards the four quarters of the earth, and wipe his mouth and say "God save us all!" that the earth may be again the earth—a vale of troubles, but not a sink of iniquity. Say Amen to that!' And all the people said Amen.[83]

Though it may curse Hitler, this speech also depicts Moses, a man who has just ordered bloody executions, as the agent of a vengeful God. Its violent imagery of blood (a word Mann uses dozens of times here) evokes the war as well as the rhetoric of Nazism. The grandeur of the law is obscured by the Israelite, and hence Jewish, failure to obey it. Driven by a fanatical desire to forge a people full of fear and discipline and given to outbursts of rage in which he shakes his fists and a vein on his head swells, Mann's Moses is a dark parody of Hitler himself.

Hitler's own contribution to the gallery of Moses portraits appears in a 1924 dialogue between Hitler and the playwright Dietrich Eckart, *Der Bolschewismus von Moses bis Lenin*, in which Moses is sharply condemned as a proto-Bolshevik and representative of the Jewish people. In this incredibly erudite dialogue containing 149 scholarly footnotes to statements attributed to Hitler, Eckart jokes that Moses made the Egyptians happy with the exodus from Egypt; he and Hitler conclude with ominous reflections on the elimination of the Jews.[84] Whether Mann and the other contributors to the anthology were familiar with the bizarre dialogue between Eckart and Hitler, they certainly considered Hitler to be the enemy of Moses and biblical tradition.

The purpose of *The Ten Commandments: Ten Short Novels of Hitler's War Against the Moral Code* was to mobilize a public that understood the appeal of film

---

80. Letter to Fredric Warburg, 22 February 1945, in *Letters of Thomas Mann*, p. 463.

81. Käte Hamburger, 'Thomas Manns Mose-Erzählung "Das Gesetz" auf dem Hintergrund der Überlieferung und der religionswissenschaftlichen Forschung', in Mann, *Das Gesetz*, pp. 58-112 (94).

82. Mann, *Tables of the Law*, p. 62.

83. Mann, *Tables of the Law*, p. 63.

84. Dietrich Eckart and Adolf Hitler, *Der Bolschewismus von Moses bis Lenin* (Munich: Hoheniechen Verlag, 1924), pp. 49-50. Hitler's diatribe against Moses is highly unusual for the modern period. Even sectarian Christian writers like Ingraham and Southon depict Moses in a favorable light, though they sometimes characterize the Hebrews negatively.

and identified morality with biblical law.[85] In fact, the original plan of its organizer, Austrian expatriate Armin Robinson, was to produce a film called *Hitler and the Ten Commandments*.[86] In his Preface to the anthology, Hermann Rauschning (a one-time supporter of Hitler),[87] depicts a conversation among Hitler and his advisors on film as a political tool. The discussion then shifts to religion and morality; Hitler inveighs against Christianity as a Jewish sect and proponent of slave morality. Hitler concludes by saying that their struggle is against the Ten Commandments themselves.[88] Robinson's (and Mann's) project thus reflects the worldview and perhaps the impact of Cecil B. DeMille's 1923 film, *The Ten Commandments*, which combines the biblical Exodus with a modern morality tale. The film's prologue describes a moral crisis in the wake of World War I and modern decadence. To a world that laughs at the Ten Commandments, the film announces that 'They are not laws—they are the LAW'.[89]

But as politically appealing as it was, the didacticism of this project, which would present Hitler's objective as the destruction of biblical and hence moral law, did not match Mann's artistic sensibilities. Instead, he would attempt something more ambitious and risky: a satirical depiction of Moses as Hitler. By so doing, Mann created associations and puzzles that destabilize the heroic image of Moses. Was Moses degraded by this comparison to Hitler, or was Hitler ennobled? Was it a satire of biblical tradition or a heroic defense of it? What did it suggest about the role of heroes in German thought, especially the more sinister interpretations the Nazis gave Nietzsche? What did the parody suggest about Mann's views of religion, especially Judaism? Mann's notes for the novel reveal a careful program of study but little else; they assiduously track his reading and research on biblical tradition; beside the Bible, he carefully studied works by writers in the German idealist tradition: Johann Goethe, Max Weber, and Elias Auerbach.[90]

85. 'It is my hope that this book—Thomas Mann's story of the man who gave the world the Ten Commandments, and the other nine stories dealing with the men who have sought to destroy those Commandments—will help open the eyes of those who still do not recognize what Nazism really is', Armin Robinson, 'Editor's Foreword', in *The Ten Commandments* (New York: Simon & Schuster, 1944), p. v.

86. Klaus Makoschey, *Quellenkritische Untersuchungen zum Spätwerk Thomas Manns* (Thomas-Mann-Studien, 17; Frankfurt: Vittorio Klostermann, 1998), p. 21.

87. Hamburger, 'Thomas Manns Mose-Erzählung "Das Gesetz"', p. 93.

88. Hermann Rauschning, 'A Conversation With Hitler', in *The Ten Commandments*, pp. ix-xiii.

89. Cecil B. DeMille, *The Ten Commandments* (Famous Players-Lasky Corp., 1923). 'For James G. Williams, Mann's Moses is part of a 'great man' tradition: 'The effect of Mann's "great man" point of departure is to highlight the *achievement* of the law and to relegate to a marginal position in the story the *revelation* of the God of victims who stands with his people and delivers them. No doubt the commandments, the statutes, blessings, and curses of the covenant are an implied comment on the barbarism of fascist totalitarianism, and as such they represent Mann's view of the sort of regime that fosters violence and sacrificial thinking. However, Mann comes perilously close to throwing out...the benighted' (*The Bible, Violence and the Sacred* [San Francisco: HarperCollins, 1991], pp. 101-102).

90. Makoschey, 'Quellenkritische Untersuchungen zum Spätwerk Thamas Manns', pp. 59-81.

But the 'tragicomic' quality Mann described in the letter to his son is evident throughout the novella, especially with the giving of the law. Laws of ritual purity, for example, reflect Moses' (Hitlerlike) fanaticism with hygiene; Mann satirizes them with this edict on defecation: 'Next time let me see everybody with a trowel, or the avenging angel will be after you'.[91] Like the art student Hitler (as well as Michelangelo[92]), Moses leads the people with the absolute control of a sculptor: 'He chiselled, blasted, planed, and smoothed at the rebellious block with sturdy patience, with repeated forbearance, often forgiving, sometimes blasting with scorn and lashing out ruthlessly'.[93] Moses repeatedly denigrates the Israelites as a 'rabble' (*Pöbelvolk*), a term Hitler also used against the Jews.[94]

Mann's narrative puts his readers in an uncomfortable position. If Moses' insults are justified, then the Israelites (and the Jews) deserve the violence unleashed against them. If his anger is unjustified, then Moses is a tyrant. If the novella is taken only as a parody, then biblical tradition, German idealism, and the moral high ground against fascism all vanish. Noting these conundrums, Frederick Lubich argues that Mann's pairing of Moses and Hitler has unexpected consequences.[95] Lubich sees *Das Gesetz* as a *Doppeltext* that presents Moses and Hitler as a Janus-faced embodiment of race-based leadership, the quest for land, and harsh laws concentrating on purity and deference to authority. Perhaps overstating his case, Lubich speculates that Mann's novel reveals latent fascination and sympathy toward Hitler; nevertheless, the argument is revealing. Mann's own anti-Jewishness can be seen in a story about incest between a Jewish brother and sister, 'The Blood of the Walsungen' (1905). According to Sander Gilman, the story reflects a stereotype of Jews as corrupt.[96] In any case, the Hitler–Moses irony may not bear on Mann's personal ambivalence toward anti-Jewishness and totalitarianism. It seems more likely that Mann was unaware of the ironic links between his own worldview and fascism. But his novella certainly destabilizes the contemporary portrait of Moses from within the German idealist tradition.

Through surprising juxtapositions of modern politics and the Bible, as well as shocking arguments in favor of violence, Steffens and Mann defamiliarize the story of Moses. Far from a humanistic celebration of individual character, these novels offer disturbing but compelling images of violent social transformation. The shock value of such images challenges the reader to reconsider humanist and rationalist versions of the myth, and perhaps to observe their clash with biblical narrative. The images of violence thus have a critical function that can redirect readers to the

See my description of Elias Auerbach's *Moses* (trans. Robert Barclay and Israel O. Lehman; Detroit: Wayne State University Press, 1975), in Chapter 3, below.

91. Mann, *Tables of the Law*, p. 37.

92. Makoschey, 'Quellenkritische Untersuchungen zum Spätwerk Thamas Manns', pp. 99-114.

93. Mann, *Tables of the Law*, p. 43.

94. Mann, *Das Gesetz*, pp. 25, 35, 47, and 52. See Lubich, ' "Fascinating Fascism" ', p. 562. Hitler describes the Jews as *Pöbelvolk* in Eckart and Hitler, *Bolschewismus*, p. 7.

95. Lubich, ' "Fascinating Fascism" '.

96. Sander Gilman, *Difference and Pathology* (Ithaca, NY: Cornell University Press, 1985), pp. 158-59.

biblical text. In much the same way, Benjamin's 'Critique of Violence' argues against prevailing views of biblical law as humanistic. With the example of Korah's rebellion in Numbers 16, Benjamin maintains that divine law interrupts the order of things and may be enforced before it is given.[97] Like revelation and unlike human and mythical law, divine law needs no justification in human language or reasoning. Benjamin, like Steffens and Mann as well, seems to suggest that prevailing versions of humanism often minimize the presence of violence and divine fiat in the biblical tradition. Paradoxically, then, Steffens and Mann gain insight into biblical tradition by their focus on contemporary political violence; and by putting Moses at a distance, they actually bring him more clearly into focus.[98]

b. *Moses and Magic: Hurston*

Zora Neale Hurston's *Moses, Man of the Mountain* also depicts violence in ways that exceed and challenge the idealist norm. Despite the fact that he renounces his military career and violence in general, Moses presides over battles against enemies and directs the slaughter of many Israelites after the golden calf incident.[99] In a shocking reversal of tradition, Moses even kills Aaron when he continues to threaten Moses' nation-building goals.[100]

Like Steffens, then, Hurston shows and even invents violent dimensions in the Moses story, not to celebrate violence but to recognize it and, more importantly, to show the whitewashing of violence out of biblical retellings. The denial of violence, however unpleasant it may be, is arguably more toxic to advocates of social change than its recognition.[101] Like Janie's shooting of Tea Cake in *Their Eyes Were Watching God*, the killing of Aaron erupts into the story to defeat the hope for a happy ending. Yet both killings are necessary sacrifices that demonstrate the courage and strength of the protagonist.

Hurston's novel contains many of the same elements found in the majority of popular Moses fiction: Moses is handsome, inclined to solitary reflection, a heroic liberator and lawgiver whose character develops over time. But Hurston subverts the idealist qualities of Moses by means of two distinct narrative elements: magic and African-American political realism. Unlike the idealist Moses, Hurston claims that the greatness of her Moses does 'not flow from the Ten Commandments. It is his rod of power, the terror he showed before all Israel and to Pharaoh, and THAT MIGHTY HAND.'[102] For Hurston, a keen observer of popular culture, this state-

---

97. Walter Benjamin, 'On Language as Such and on the Language of Man', in *idem*, *Reflections*, pp. 277-300.

98. The distinctively modern idea that contemporary culture holds hidden religious content also appears in Matthew Arnold, Kracauer, and Benjamin.

99. Hurston, *Moses, Man of the Mountain*, pp. 109, 256, 292-93.

100. Hurston, *Moses, Man of the Mountain*, p. 336.

101. There is now an extensive literature on violence and religion, building on the work of René Girard, Walter Burkert, and Georges Bataille. Without summarizing all the debates in this area, this work can be credited with the insight that violence, symbolized especially in sacrifice rituals, lies at the core of religious tradition.

102. Hurston, *Moses, Man of the Mountain*, p. xxii.

ment unmistakably challenges the central point of Cecil B. DeMille's 1923 *The Ten Commandments*, that the Ten Commandments 'are not laws—they are the LAW'. DeMille presents the biblical law as the central and lasting value of the Moses story, while Hurston, who hoped to see her novel made into a film, denies DeMille's point from the very beginning.

From her first sentence, an awareness of representation is clear: 'Moses was an old man with a beard. He was the great law-giver. He had some trouble with Pharaoh about some plagues and led the Children of Israel out of Egypt and on to the Promised Land... But there are other concepts of Moses abroad in the world.'[103] Hurston suggests that what makes Moses special is his direct link to God, a fact that makes him the 'fountain of mystic powers'.[104] African, Haitian, and African-American traditions worship Moses not because he is a lawmaker but because of his 'rod of power' and 'that mighty hand'. Hurston's Moses is an Egyptian who speaks in African-American dialect, a magician who articulates Enlightenment principles, a peacemaker prone to bouts of violence, a charismatic leader who prefers solitary contemplation. By combining these contradictory tendencies in one figure, Hurston destabilizes stereotypes of Moses as a legendary hero, lawgiver, and liberator.

The image of Moses as magician has a long history, tied closely to his Egyptian upbringing. In *Moses the Egyptian*, Jan Assmann traces the connections between the Egyptian and magical dimensions of Moses, from ancient traditions to the Egyptian revival during the Renaissance, through the Enlightenment and Romantic periods, and down to the present. One contemporary text from this tradition is *The Sixth and Seventh Books of Moses*, a hermetic book of incantations, seals, and symbols mentioned by Hurston in her Introduction: 'There are millions of copies of a certain book, *The Sixth and Seventh Books of Moses*, being read and consulted in secret because the readers believe in Moses'.[105]

Another set of traditions associating Moses with magic arises in Africa and the African diaspora. *Moses, Man of the Mountain* is the best example of this tradition.[106] Other novelists introduce elements of African and African-American identity into the story, but often in stereotyped ways, such as the Ethiopian witch doctor, Doogana, whose magic is 'degraded by the pervading degradation of slavery', and

103.   Hurston, *Moses, Man of the Mountain*, p. xxi.
104.   Hurston, *Moses, Man of the Mountain*, p. xxii.
105.   Hurston, *Moses, Man of the Mountain*, p. xxii. An English copy of *The Sixth and Seventh Books of Moses* from around the turn of the century lists no author, date, or city of publication.
106.   The African-American literary background includes the following two works: Frances Ellen Watkins Harper, *Moses a Story of the Nile* (1869), in *Complete Poems of Frances E.W. Harper* (ed. Maryemma Graham; New York: Oxford University Press, 1988), pp. 34-66, and Charles W. Chesnutt, *The Conjure Woman* (repr., Ann Arbor: University of Michigan Press, 1969 [1899]), pp. 132-61, which contains stories of pre-Civil War conjuring told by old 'Uncle Julius' to a northern white businessman. The tale called 'Sis' Becky's Pickaninny' deals with the trade of a race horse for a slave woman who loses her baby in the trade; the baby's name is Mose, and through a series of magical transformations and 'conjurations', the baby is restored to its mother. When Mose grows up able to sing like a mockingbird, he works to set his mother and himself free.

the Kushite princess who seduces and tries to kill Moses in Fast's *Moses, Prince of Egypt*.[107]

The portrait of Moses as a magician means different things at different times. For Renaissance scholars such as Giordano Bruno, the view that 'Moses was a great Magus' only affirms the Renaissance humanism of his day, since magic represented the expression of human abilities.[108] A similar point could be made about Schiller's Moses, whose acquaintance with Egyptian mysteries establishes his credentials as a pre-eminent liberator and lawgiver. Romantic and Orientalist accounts of magic are common and reinforce prevailing ideas of the Hebrews and Egypt as an exotic other that is nevertheless tied to Western idealism. But calling Moses a magician also represents a counter-tradition in direct violation of religious and natural laws prohibiting magic (Exod. 22.18; Lev. 19.31; Deut. 18.9-14; 1 Sam. 28.3-19). I suggest that Hurston's Moses represents the counter-tradition that challenges prevailing views of Moses as an idealist hero.

Hurston's *Moses* is modern and surprising: the novel portrays Moses as a great hoodoo man in a complex and often satirically sketched African-American context. As John Lowe demonstrates, the novel's humor draws on African-American traditions of 'signification', folklore, and humor.[109] The focus is less on God and the moral order of the Ten Commandments than it is on the complexities of Moses and the dilemmas of leading a people out of slavery into nationhood. Hurston displays the Israelites as a people divided by issues of class, gender, and power dynamics. At the heart of these struggles, Moses himself is divided not so much between his Egyptian and Israelite identities as by a conflict between a desire for solitude and a duty to lead. As such, the novel represents a kind of Bakhtinian play on biblical tradition, decentering (or 'signifying on') God and reframing Moses as a powerful magician. Hurston thus performs what one critic calls a 'disruptive commentary' on traditional retellings of the Moses story.[110]

Hurston's use of magic must also be understood in the context of her anthropological studies with Franz Boas, which began in the 1920s. Her collection of folklore, *Mules and Men* (1935), along with her study of Haitian religion and culture, *Tell My Horse* (1939), earned Hurston a reputation as an important ethnographer. This research also gave her material for her novel on Moses. In *Tell My Horse*, she writes:

> This worship of Moses recalls the hard-to-explain fact that wherever the Negro is found, there are traditional tales of Moses and his supernatural powers that are not in the Bible, nor can they be found in any written life of Moses... All over the Southern United States, the British West Indies and Haiti there are reverent tales of Moses and his magic... It is more probable that there is a tradition of Moses as the great father of magic scattered over Africa and Asia. Perhaps some of his feats

107.   Fast, *Moses, Prince of Egypt*, pp. 209, 230-41, 277.
108.   Frances Yates, *Giordano Bruno and the Hermetic Tradition* (Chicago: University of Chicago Press, 1964), p. 353.
109.   John Lowe, *Jump at the Sun* (Urbana: University of Illinois Press, 1994).
110.   John Dorst, cited in Lowe, *Jump at the Sun*, p. 231.

recorded in the Pentateuch are the folk beliefs of such a character grouped about a
man for it is well established that if a memory is great enough, other memories
will cluster about it, and those in turn will bring their suites of memories to gather
about this focal point, because perhaps, they are all scattered parts of the one thing
like Plato's concept of the perfect thing.[111]

By carrying traditions of Moses and magic from her research to her fiction, Hurston
artfully blurs distinctions between fieldwork and storytelling, social science and
literary art, retelling and 'signifying'. By so doing, Hurston also resists prevailing
anthropological views of magic. For Durkheim, magic was distinguished from
religion by social context: unlike religion, magic takes place outside an organized
church or community.[112] Malinowski disagreed with Durkheim's view that religion
is essentially social.[113] He saw magic as more practical, simple, and circumscribed
than religion:

the practical art of magic has its limited, circumscribed technique: spell, rite, and
the condition of the performer form always its trite trinity. Religion, with its
complex aspects and purposes, has no such simple technique, and its unity can be
seen neither in the form of its acts nor even in the uniformity of its subject matter,
but rather in the function which it fulfills and in the value of its belief and ritual.[114]

A magician as well as the founder of a religion, Hurston's Moses challenges the
distinction made by Durkheim and Malinowski between magic and religion. This
view may reflect the influence of Boas, who is credited with counteracting racism
and making cultural relativism the norm in modern anthropology. In his letters to
Hurston, he urged her to write detailed, formal descriptions of the cultural practices
of magic she was studying.[115]

But even though Boas significantly influenced Hurston's work, Hurston's novel
exceeds the methodological boundaries of anthropology. Not only does the magic
of Moses challenge social scientific views that derogate magic, but it also stands
out against a cultural background that saw Moses as anything *but* a magician.
Hurston's *Moses* challenges the popular stereotype of Moses as an Enlighten-
ment/Romantic lawgiver.

Hurston's presentation of Moses as an African-American 'hoodoo man', like
much of her folklore research, faced the danger of reinforcing racial stereotypes.
But the novel avoids the stereotypes of African Americans as noble savages or
illogical 'Sambos' by calling attention to how images develop:

111.   Hurston, *Tell My Horse*, in *idem, Zora Neale Hurston: Folklore, Memoirs, and Other
Writings* (New York: Library of America, 1995), p. 378.
112.   Emile Durkheim, *The Elementary Forms of Religious Life* (trans. Karen E. Fields; New
York: Free Press, 1995), pp. 40-41.
113.   Bronislaw Malinowski, *Magic, Science and Religion* (Garden City, NY: Doubleday,
1954), p. 59.
114.   Malinowski, *Magic, Science and Religion*, p. 88.
115.   Letter from Boas to Hurston, 3 May 1937, cited in Lynda Marion Hill, *Social Rituals and
the Verbal Art of Zora Neale Hurston* (Washington, DC: Howard University Press, 1996), p. 139.

> Miriam told her story again and again to more believing ears. It grew with being
> handled until it was a history of the Hebrew in the palace, no less. Men claimed to
> have seen signs at the birth of the child, and Miriam came to believe every detail
> of it as she added them and retold them time and time again. Others conceived and
> added details at their pleasure and the legends grew like grass.[116]

Hurston presents Moses in such a detailed and complex light that it becomes impossible to reduce him to any set of essentialist categories.

For instance, the scene in which Moses becomes aware of his Hebrew identity, a basic part of all the Moses novels, begins with an act of racism. When he returns home from a successful military campaign, his Ethiopian-born treaty wife, who has learned that he is a Hebrew, recoils from him: 'You Hebrew! putting your hands on *me*!'[117] She continues, 'Get out of my room. The very idea of me being married to a Hebrew makes me sick at the stomach. Don't you dare to come near me. That gang of rapists and slaves.'[118] Moses kills the overseer immediately after this episode, after which he experiences a complete change of heart and renounces violence: 'he found a new sympathy for the oppressed of all mankind. He lost his taste for war… Henceforth he was a man of thought.'[119]

Hebrew identity, Hurston suggests, is socially constructed through an experience of ethnic or racial hatred. Hurston could draw on personal experience as well as her research with Boas (whose research attacked racism in anthropology) to make her point. But the experience of racism is not just a case in point for social constructionism; it transforms Moses into a revolutionary hero. After he kills the overseer and decides to help the Hebrews, Moses flees Egypt across the Red Sea, and Hurston's narrator reflects on his transformation: 'Moses had crossed over. He was not in Egypt. He had crossed over and now he was not an Egyptian. He had crossed over.'[120]

A similar transformation takes place in Hurston's autobiographical sketch, 'How it Feels to be Colored Me': 'I remember the very day that I became colored'.[121] When Hurston moves, at the age of thirteen, from an all-African-American town to Jacksonville, Florida, she 'becomes' colored: 'I was not Zora of Orange County any more, I was now a little colored girl. I found it out in certain ways.'[122] In a variation on this theme, Janie, the protagonist of *Their Eyes Were Watching God*, discovers she is 'colored' when she is six and sees herself in the mirror.[123] Like

---

116. Hurston, *Moses, Man of the Mountain*, p. 51. See also Blyden Jackson's Introduction to *Moses, Man of the Mountain*, pp. xiv-xv.

117. Hurston, *Moses, Man of the Mountain*, p. 86.

118. Hurston, *Moses, Man of the Mountain*, pp. 86-87.

119. Hurston, *Moses, Man of the Mountain*, pp. 92-93.

120. Hurston, *Moses, Man of the Mountain*, p. 104.

121. Hurston, 'How it Feels to be Colored Me', in *idem*, *Zora Neale Hurston: Folklore, Memoirs, and Other Writings*, p. 826.

122. Hurston, 'How it Feels to be Colored Me', p. 827. The link between Moses' identity and that of Hurston comes from a discussion with students in my course, Religion and Literature, Virginia Tech, 1999.

123. Zora Neale Hurston, *Their Eyes Were Watching God* (New York: HarperCollins, 1998), pp. 8-9.

Janie and her own account of becoming colored, Hurston's *Moses* depicts the leader in a state of becoming rather than being. By presenting traditional African-American dialect and imagery in this light, Hurston may be seen as practicing what Alain Locke, her friend and a key figure in the Harlem Renaissance, called 'minority jingo', a strategic use of stereotypes to counteract racism:

> minority jingo is the defensive reaction, sadly inevitable as an antidote, and even science has learned to fight poison with poison. However, for cure or compensation, it must be the right poison and in the right amount...minority jingo is good when it succeeds in off-setting either the effects or the habits of majority jingo and bad when it re-infects the minority with the majority disease.[124]

Locke, also an associate of Boas, shared Hurston's interest in reclaiming and celebrating distinctively African-American cultural forms.

Hurston's novel has been criticized for being inconsistent in its aims, tone, and depiction of Moses; Louis Untermeyer expressed disappointment in the character of Moses:

> The balance between his royal Egyptian breeding and his Hebraic adaptation is insufficiently adjusted; his growth from a warrior-prince to prophet and seer is weakly motivated; the paradox of his violence and his proverbial meekness is scarcely explicated...the book is a series of compromises between the plausible and the bizarre, between the legend as we know it and the legend as it has been transplanted and recolored.[125]

But it is precisely this doubling, this layering of characterization, that subverts stereotypical images of Moses. The doubling is also explicit in the novel, just before the scene in which Moses discovers his Hebrew identity: 'In short, he was everybody boiled down to a drop. Everybody is two beings: one lives and flourishes in the daylight and stands guard. The other being walks and howls at night.'[126] These doublings and inconsistencies also serve the purposes of 'minority jingo' by subverting and mixing commonly held images of Moses, a strategy apparently lost on Ralph Ellison, who wrote that the novel 'did nothing for Negro fiction'.[127] Hurston holds contradictory perspectives in tension: at once demystifying and remystifying Moses, her Moses represents both humanistic rationalism a magical worldview.

Hurston's Moses sounds like the humanist of modern great-man tradition when he feels 'sympathy for the oppressed of all mankind'.[128] In the course of organizing

124. Alain Locke, 'Jingo', cited in Ross Posnock, *Color and Culture* (Cambridge, MA: Harvard University Press, 1998), p. 197. Posnock links Locke's idea of minority jingo to the contemporary notion of 'strategic essentialism'.

125. Louis Untermeyer, Review of *Moses, Man of the Mountain* (*Saturday Review*; November 11, 1939), in Henry Louis Gates, Jr, and K.A. Appiah (eds.), *Zora Neale Hurston: Critical Perspectives Past and Present* (New York: Amistad, 1993), p. 27.

126. Hurston, *Moses, Man of the Mountain*, p. 82. Hurston describes Janie in similar terms: 'She didn't read books so she didn't know that she was the world and the heavens boiled down to a drop' (*Their Eyes Were Watching God*, p. 76).

127. Ralph Ellison, 'Recent Negro Fiction', *New Masses* 40 (August 1941), p. 25.

128. Hurston, *Moses, Man of the Mountain*, p. 92.

a political struggle, he upholds the values of non-violence, freedom, justice and equality.[129] On the other hand, Moses much prefers the life of contemplation, magic arts, passion, and marriage. A former Egyptian soldier who becomes a quiet and powerful mystic, Moses is reluctantly compelled (by Jethro and the God 'I AM WHAT I AM') into the political arena. Moses' power and magical training come from two unconventional sources: the storytelling stableman Mentu (a clear allusion to African-American storytellers like Uncle Julius and Uncle Remus[130]) and the secret Egyptian book of Thoth, which gives Moses power 'to command the heavens and the earth, the abyss and the mountain, and the sea'.[131] Before Moses ever encounters God in the burning bush, he is able to work all the magic signs and wonders ascribed to him in the Bible, even the parting of seas.[132]

The question the novel raises is whether the dual nature of Moses can be fully expressed on a social and historical scale. The scene where he received the first 'tables of testimony' suggests a synthesis of humanistic and magical worldviews:

> Moses stayed up on the mountain so long because it takes a long time to learn God's sacred words that have the power in them to make and to do. Moses learned ten words from God. So he took the ten words of power and he made ten commandments out of them. On the back side of the words there were seals and these seals had the power of all destructions.[133]

At once magical and humanistic, this original set of tables has the capacity to provide freedom and power to Israel and to the rest of humanity. But the golden calf episode destroys the tables and these hopes for freedom and power. In the aftermath of this scene, Moses resorts to strict and even violent discipline, and the new set of tables is hidden from view in the newly established Tabernacle. Like the biblical Fall from Paradise, the golden calf leads to punitive actions and lowered expectations. Moses gives up the hope of sharing his full wisdom and power with the people, and even though he has renounced violence, he later kills Aaron in order to eliminate corruption and dissent among the people.[134]

By the end of the novel, Moses has given Joshua most of his political power, and instead of crossing into the promised land, he wanders away to pursue the contemplative life he learned from Mentu:

> And what would he, Moses, do over there? What could he do for Israel that he had not already done? Nothing but live in a palace and wear a crown… No, he didn't want to rule that way. He wanted freedom. He wanted to ask God and Nature questions.
>
> …When he sickened and crumbled like ordinary men, what would become of his laws and statutes? No, Moses must not die among the Hebrews. They must not see him die.

129. Hurston, *Moses, Man of the Mountain*, pp. 93, 175, 190, 256.
130. Lowe, *Jump at the Sun*, pp. 219-23.
131. Hurston, *Moses, Man of the Mountain*, p. 154.
132. Hurston, *Moses, Man of the Mountain*, p. 103.
133. Hurston, *Moses, Man of the Mountain*, p. 281.
134. Hurston, *Moses, Man of the Mountain*, p. 336.

So Moses set to work to build a tomb on Nebo for himself... He would end in mystery as he had come.[135]

Moses rediscovers the lizard, a wise talking animal that connects Moses to his youth in Egypt, and therefore to his African heritage:

Under one stone he found an ancient lizard and asked him, 'What are you doing under there, old lizard?'
'Oh just resting from living and thinking about the time when my ancestors ruled the world'... [The lizard then sends Moses to another lizard, a keeper of memories, and he goes.] The voice of thunder leaped from peak to plain and Moses stood in the midst of it and said 'Farewell'. Then he turned with a firm tread and descended the other side of the mountain and headed back over the years.[136]

The death and birth of Hurston's Moses are surrounded by mystery. His authority is both divine and human. By quoting and yet undermining the great-man tradition, Hurston created a postmodern Moses before anyone heard of 'postmodernity'; the contradictory tendencies of Hurston's Moses do not harmonize or resolve. Rather, they subvert stereotypical expectations and present the reader with the question of how to reconcile the Moses of magic and violence with the Moses of traditional piety and humanism.

6. *Conclusion*

Steffens, Mann, and Hurston confront the myth of Moses as a great humanist and Romantic hero through various means. By making Moses at once contemporary and unfamiliar, their novels subvert the great man tradition and make it possible to retrieve the ambiguity and mystery of biblical tradition.[137] Steffens and Mann embed their retellings in the specific political contexts of socialism and fascism, combining familiar episodes with violence to shocking effects. Steffens is explicit about his political appropriation of Moses, but his book is more an essay than a novel, and its effect is somewhat didactic and simplistic. Mann seems to lose control of his satirical project in all the web of associations between Hitler, Moses, fascism, and romanticism. Hurston brings another political context—the African-American liberation struggle—to the story of Moses. In addition, she represents rich cultural traditions about the magical powers of Moses. In so doing, Hurston challenges not only standard anthropological views of magic, but also standard images of Moses as a pious, Romantic, or humanistic hero. Hurston's novel offers powerful critiques of her own political and intellectual culture without retreating to primitivism. Instead, she juxtaposes humanistic and magical worldviews in a single work, not out of literary failure but rather out of literary strategy that demonstrates unresolved cultural questions of identity, humanism, and magic.

135. Hurston, *Moses, Man of the Mountain*, pp. 348-49.
136. Hurston, *Moses, Man of the Mountain*, p. 351.
137. This critical retrieval of scriptural tradition corresponds to Benjamin's project of recovering the 'pure language' of sacred texts. See my *Walter Benjamin and the Bible*, pp. 51-66.

Chapter 2

DOUBLE-MOSES: GENDER AND THE SACRED IN MOSES FILMS

Popular fiction about Moses prepared the way for a wider-reaching form of mass culture: feature-length films, some of which were adaptations of the novels (e.g. *Moon of Israel* and *The Ten Commandments*). The mixture of religious tradition, scholarship, biography, and contemporary ideology common to the novels became more concrete in the cinema. Films added little substance to the gallery of fictional portraits, but they were compelled by the medium to picture Moses in new and vivid ways: creating panoramic recreations of ancient Egyptian monuments, depicting miracles, and representing God on the big screen. As film audiences grew, the budgets and ambitions of filmmakers did as well, and blockbusters like *The Ten Commandments* broke records for spending and acclaim, rising to the level of cultural monuments, reflecting and projecting some of the most powerful images of the day.

Like novels, films have been understood as a new or substitute form of religion, but unlike novels, films present sense impressions of physical reality to spectators in a lowered, dream-like state of consciousness. According to Walter Benjamin, film induces shock in the spectator, an effect that accompanies a decline in the aura and cult value of art.[1] Nevertheless, argues Benjamin, capitalists and fascists alike have ritualized the medium.[2] For Benjamin and Siegfried Kracauer, film contributes to the perceived secularization of modern culture, representing physical reality to a world made up of what Durkheim calls the 'ruins of ancient beliefs'.[3] This world lies beyond clear norms and ideology, cluttered by debris and fragments from previous worldviews.[4] The spectator's experience takes many forms, but according to Kracauer, 'film exposes to view a world never seen before, a world as elusive as Poe's purloined letter, which cannot be found because it is within everybody's reach'.[5] In this contemporary world, film viewers 'absorb not so much wholes as "small amounts of material life"'.[6]

---

1.   Walter Benjamin, 'The Work of Art in the Age of Mechanical Reproduction', in *idem*, *Illuminations* (trans. Harry Zohn; New York: Schocken Books, 1969), pp. 217-51 (224-26, 240). For a critical assessment of Benjamin's remarks on film and their later influence, see David Bordwell, *On the History of Film Style* (Cambridge, MA: Harvard University Press, 1997), pp. 143-46.

2.   Benjamin, 'The Work of Art', pp. 232, 241.

3.   Siegfried Kracauer, *Theory of Film: The Redemption of Physical Reality* (Princeton, NJ: Princeton University Press, 1997), pp. 287-88.

4.   Siegfried Kracauer, *Theory of Film*, pp. 294-98.

5.   Siegfried Kracauer, *Theory of Film*, p. 299.

6.   Siegfried Kracauer, *Theory of Film*, p. 303. Theories of secularization and the religious nature of mass culture are numerous and debatable, but one need not commit to a specific set of

The new cultural ground broken by film was 'religious' in some sense but also beyond or at odds with institutional religion. Where did this ambivalence leave feature films with religious subjects? Were they part of traditional religion or secular culture? Unlike Benjamin and Kracauer, Cecil B. DeMille saw film as a new vehicle for the message that religious institutions and traditions are important and relevant:

> For more than twenty years, and increasingly in the years since World War II, people had been writing to me from all over the world, urging that I make *The Ten Commandments* again. The world needs a reminder, they said, of the Law of God; and it was evident in at least some of the letters that the world's awful experience of totalitarianism, fascist and communist, had made many thoughtful people realize anew that the Law of God is the essential bedrock of human freedom.[7]

DeMille's religion blends mass entertainment with postwar American Protestant ideology. Biblical films could be described as civil religion, but this term usually refers to phenomena (such as patriotic celebrations) that are beyond the context of traditional religion so basic to DeMille's film.[8] Civil religion also fails to describe the cultural contradictions (e.g. between tradition and modernity) inherent to biblical films. In fact, the films about Moses straddle the categories of traditional religion, civil religion, and 'secular' culture. This ambiguity makes the films religiously and culturally unstable: they may be viewed as entertainment, ideology, or as an affirmation or challenge to traditional religious teachings. What follows is an attempt to describe this complexity in the context of biblical texts and traditions about Moses.

Like centuries of religious art preceding them, religious films create visual images of invisible realities such as God, religious experience, and revelation. The physical depiction of Moses entails a focus on his life as much as his work. Moses on film is Moses embodied in live action; hence the tendency to concentrate on his life in Egypt. Such was the case with the first major Moses film, the Vitagraph Company's 1910 *The Life of Moses*, which is devoted mostly to Moses' youth, the plagues, and the Red Sea crossing.[9] At one-and-a-half hours and a staggering production cost of $50,000, the Vitagraph *Moses* successfully converted religion to film.[10] In order to attract churchgoers who considered film to be a vice and a Sab-

such theories in order to agree that film is an influential new form of mass culture in the twentieth century, and that it lies outside institutional religion. As films like *The Jazz Singer* (1927) attest, film was sometimes even perceived as a form of entertainment competing against institutional religion. Like the 1923 version of *The Ten Commandments*, *The Jazz Singer* presents a conflict between traditional religion and the modern culture of the jazz age. While *The Ten Commandments* strikes a severe moral blow to modernity, however, *The Jazz Singer* vindicates modern culture, albeit through the transformation of Jolson's character into an assimilated Jew who wears blackface.

7.   Cecil B. DeMille, *The Autobiography of Cecil B. DeMille* (London: W.H. Allen, 1960), p. 376.

8.   Robert N. Bellah, 'Civil Religion in America', *Daedalus* 96 (1967), pp. 1-21.

9.   William Uricchio and Roberta E. Pearson, *Reframing Culture: The Case of the Vitagraph Quality Films* (Princeton, NJ: Princeton University Press, 1993), pp. 163-64.

10.   Uricchio and Pearson, *Reframing Culture*, p. 163.

bath violation, Vitagraph marketed the film as a Sunday school lesson and hired the Reverend Madison Peters as a consultant.[11] Drawing heavily from the imagery of nineteenth-century Bible illustration, the film sought to reach a large audience by finessing the differences between biblical literalists and non-literalists, as well as Jews and Christians. By its rich visual effects and its inoffensive treatment of the great lawgiver, the film achieved wide distribution and set the stage for future Moses films.[12]

Film was also the perfect medium to capture enthusiasm for such contemporary discoveries as Tutankhamun's tomb (1922). The lavish sets, props, and costumes of the Moses films ride the wave of popular archaeology, the most physical branch of biblical research. Thus, while DeMille paid careful attention to material culture, especially in the Egyptian context, he showed almost no awareness of the major trends in biblical studies from the nineteenth century on—historical-critical scholarship of the Bible itself (see Chapter 3).[13]

Paradoxically, the physically present Moses is far-removed from the Moses of the Bible. For the Bible offers almost no physical description of Moses, and his life story appears only in fragments, many of which undercut each other. One of the greatest achievements of the biblical Moses is his writing of the law, which comes to serve as a guide to the Israelites after his death (Exod. 34; Deut. 31–34). The biblical Moses is thus ultimately defined by his absence, while the Moses of film must necessarily be a figure of presence. The biblical Moses is always viewed retrospectively, from the standpoint of the writing of Moses: the writing of Moses is the medium through which the life of Moses can be read.[14] And since the Bible suggests a trade-off between the life of Moses and the writing of Moses, Moses must die in order for his writing to come to life.[15]

This chapter examines tensions between biblical tradition and modern mass culture in three films: *Moon of Israel* (1924), *The Ten Commandments* (1956), and *Prince of Egypt* (1998).[16] My thesis is that each of the films employs doubling techniques to express the ambiguous role and identity of Moses. These strategies of doubling display modern anxieties about religious, gender, and racial identity. But they also express the paradox that the Moses of written tradition can only exist in the absence of the 'real' Moses. Just as texts become fully scriptural only in their afterlife, so Moses becomes *Moses* only through his death and physical absence

11. Uricchio and Pearson, *Reframing Culture*, pp. 167-68.
12. Uricchio and Pearson, *Reframing Culture*, pp. 192-94.
13. Henry S. Noerdlinger, with an Introduction by Cecil B. DeMille, *Moses and Egypt: The Documentation to the Motion Picture The Ten Commandments* (Los Angeles: University of Southern California Press, 1956).
14. James Nohrnberg, *Like Unto Moses* (Bloomington: Indiana University Press, 1995).
15. Michel DeCerteau, *The Writing of History* (trans. Tom Conley; New York: Columbia, 1988), p. 322.
16. The films I consider here are all produced for a mass audience by the entertainment industry. The three I choose here span film history from silent era to the present. They represent a range of technologies and cultural contexts, and yet they are all significant examples of popular film. I leave aside the categories of educational films and those produced for limited audiences.

from the tradition.[17] Despite his physical immediacy, the Moses of film retains his biblical ambiguity and association with writing.

1. *Doubling*

The splitting or doubling of Moses in the films reflects the problem of film itself. Biblical traditions of Moses are ambiguous and 'fraught with background',[18] and they do not follow biographical conventions. But when Philo and Josephus created biographies of Moses, they depicted a central, consistent, and heroic figure against the background of anti-Jewish polemics. This Moses was heroic as well, and he would become a model for later portrayals, including DeMille's 1956 *The Ten Commandments*. Despite their radical departure from the biblical portrait, biographies in this Hellenistic tradition, from Philo down to historical novels, often transformed the complexities of the biblical Moses into contemporary terms. In the physically concrete medium of film more than in fiction, ambiguities of characterization tend to split or double the character of Moses. Whereas the Moses of written tradition can straddle boundaries of morality, personality, gender, and ethnicity, the cinematic Moses must be either masculine or feminine, Egyptian or Hebrew. Forced to disambiguate Moses more sharply than ever, films also tend to split him along lines (especially of gender) that preoccupy the audience.

In *The Analysis of Film*, Raymond Bellour identifies a pattern of 'narcissistic doubling between man and woman' in American cinema: 'this doubling rules the two sexes' relations of desire'.[19] Although Bellour works deep within the conceptual spheres of Freudian and Lacanian psychoanalytic theory, it is possible to benefit from his insight without rehearsing the theories in detail. In simple terms, Bellour shows (e.g. through close analysis of Hitchcock) that dynamics of viewing and representation in film express how men and women define themselves by looking at each other. When a man (or the camera) looks at a woman, she becomes a projection of his desires and individuation: hence, his double.[20] The pattern is clear in the three Moses films considered here, each of which combines the biblical story of Moses with romance and a coming-of-age plot.

There is another kind of doubling in the Moses films: the doubling of protagonist and antagonist, Moses and the Pharaoh. According to René Girard, rivalry arises when two parties desire the same object. This rivalry generates a mimetic relationship between the parties that sometimes takes the form (in literature especially) of

17. See Benjamin, 'The Task of the Translator', and 'The Art of the Storyteller', in *idem*, *Illuminations*, pp. 69-82 and 83-109, respectively; see also Nohrnberg, *Like Unto Moses*.

18. Erich Auerbach, *Mimesis*.

19. Raymond Bellour, *The Analysis of Film* (Bloomington: Indiana University Press, 2000), p. 12. A different but also Lacanian account of doubling in American film appears in Slavoj Žižek, *Enjoy Your Symptom!* (New York: Routledge, 2001), esp. pp. 124-28.

20. The implications of the camera as an instrument of the male gaze are far-reaching. Significant feminist and gender studies approaches to film include Laura Mulvey, *Fetishism and Curiosity* (Bloomington: Indiana University Press, 1996); and J. Cheryl Exum, *Plotted, Shot, and Painted: Cultural Representations of Biblical Women* (JSOTSup, 215; Sheffield: Sheffield Academic Press, 1996).

doubling.[21] For Moses and Pharaoh, there is a clear rivalry over the desire to command the Hebrews (and sometimes the Egyptians), and in *The Ten Commandments* and *The Prince of Egypt*, this rivalry generates the image of Pharaoh as Moses' *alter ego*.

It is no surprise that the Moses films avoid his death and have difficulty depicting him as a writer: film requires Moses' presence, and writing requires his absence. Yet in imagining Moses as a physically present figure, the films adopt some of the ambiguities of the biblical Moses. And while they tend to repress his activity as a writer, the films displace the act of writing onto another character in the story. In *Moon of Israel*, the narrator, Ana, is a scribe in the Egyptian court. In *The Ten Commandments*, a recurrent phrase is 'So let it be written; so let it be done', a formula given in Pharaoh's commands that returns at the end of the film in reference to the Bible itself. In *Prince of Egypt*, the most important plot transitions take place in an underground vault decorated with hieroglyphic writing, the most graphic of which is the depiction of drowning babies.

Despite the necessity of casting Moses as a specific person, all three films considered here depict Moses as racially—or ethnically—ambiguous: Is he Egyptian or Hebrew? In *Moon of Israel*, the ambiguity is symbolized by the forbidden love between the Hebrew Merapi (the female Moses figure) and the Egyptian prince Seti. In *The Ten Commandments* and *Prince of Egypt*—like the Moses sketched by Schiller two centuries earlier and typical of the novels (see Chapter 1)—Moses reaches a moment of truth at which he discovers his Hebrew identity and then affirms it in a heroic gesture of self-sacrifice. This is the turning point familiar from *Bildungsroman* and coming-of-age films. Moses' self-discovery also fits the modern ideology of racial and ethnic nationalism, which says that race is destiny. At the same time, Moses and the Hebrews transcend traditional racial boundaries, because they denote a universal history of salvation (for Christians). Moses' race generates anxiety because he must be particular and universal at the same time.

The Ten Commandments also addresses race and slavery in the exotic and voyeuristic scene of the Ethiopian tributes and by the inclusion of African servants in the Exodus party gathering at the Passover. In *Prince of Egypt*, the skin of Moses and the other characters is decidedly dark; slavery is roundly condemned; and the most highly touted song from the soundtrack, 'When You Believe', featured the first collaboration between African-American pop stars Whitney Houston and Mariah Carey.[22]

The cultural anxiety of these films also appears through the lens of gender. As Ann Douglas shows in *The Feminization of American Culture*, religion from the nineteenth century was associated with women and femininity.[23] The church was a

21.   René Girard, *Violence and the Sacred* (trans. Patrick Gregory; Baltimore: The Johns Hopkins University Press, 1977), pp. 79, 146-61.
22.   The filmmakers released three separate soundtrack albums, including one subtitled 'Inspirational' that targeted African-American audiences. Other featured artists included Boyz II Men and CeCe Winans.
23.   Ann Douglas, *The Feminization of American Culture* (New York: Knopf, 1977).

place where women could enjoy unprecedented leadership roles, and men in the ministry could behave affectively and with compassion. In addition, Moses was identified with Judaism, and Judaism was associated with femininity in the modern period.[24] Like Jesus, the modern Moses thus became a walking set of gender contradictions.[25] Strict but compassionate, masculine and yet maternal, the cinematic Moses tended to split into doubles along gender lines and roles.[26]

In his 1923 version of *The Ten Commandments*, DeMille juxtaposes the biblical story of Moses with a modern morality tale that teaches the importance of Mosaic law. In the story of a mother and her two sons, the mother, who reads to her sons from the Bible, is the figure of religious authority, that is, the Moses figure. In his 1956 remake of *The Ten Commandments*, DeMille creates a thoroughly masculine Moses, a red-blooded American hero who reduces Nefertiri and Sephora to passionate despair. But after the scene of the burning bush, Heston's Moses changes appearance and behavior: he resembles Michelangelo's statue and no longer has any interest in women, as Nefertiri and Sephora admit to each other: 'He has forgotten both of us. You lost him when he went to seek his god. I lost him when he found his god.' The post-theophanic Moses is not feminized, but he is de-sexualized. Meanwhile, the plot of liberating the Hebrews turns on the wrath of Nefertiri, a powerful woman scorned by Moses who boasts, 'Who else can soften Pharaoh's heart...or harden it?' While Moses transcends the realm of human passion, his alter-ego, Rameses, falls prey to it, a weakness that leads to his downfall. These gender-charged doublings of Moses drive the plot of *The Ten Commandments*.

The most obvious doubling of Moses appears in *Moon of Israel*, in which a Hebrew woman named Merapi performs many of the liberating actions usually ascribed to Moses. In *Prince of Egypt*, Moses is consistently portrayed as a sensitive, compassionate young man as opposed to the stubborn and violent temper of his 'double', Rameses. In a gesture toward gender equality, the DreamWorks filmmakers depict Zipporah and Miriam as especially strong leaders. In different ways, then, the three films displace the feminine qualities of Moses onto other characters.

The doubling of Moses and anxieties about race and gender reflect a deeper conflict between the physically present Moses on film and the more significant but physically absent Moses of tradition. As long as Moses is alive, we might say, his story (i.e. the Torah) remains unwritten. Only when he is dead can Moses emerge as a writing and written figure of tradition. The films repress the death of Moses and tropes of writing in order to show Moses in the flesh. This repression surfaces in the cultural anxieties of race and gender, as well as in traces of writing. Thus, in their uniquely vivid depiction of Moses, the films practice the narrative eclipse of the biblical text.

24. Sander Gilman, *Difference and Pathology: Stereotypes of Sexuality, Race, and Madness* (Ithaca, NY: Cornell University Press, 1985).

25. Colleen McDannell, *Material Christianity* (New Haven: Yale University Press, 1995), pp. 180-97.

26. See Søren Kierkegaard, *The Concept of Anxiety* (trans. Reidar Thomte; Princeton, NJ: Princeton University Press, 1980).

In plot and characterization, films about Moses resemble other modern portrayals. One can find the influence of biblical tradition, Egyptian archaeology, Hellenistic biography, art history, and biblical scholarship, but modern novels about Moses are the closest counterparts to the popular films. For novels and films, the critical question is how modern culture balances the claims of history, tradition, and entertainment. The following analysis of three films shows how traditional Mosaic distinctions (between life and written tradition, for instance) find expression in this new cultural form. My approach deals selectively with issues that arise particularly because of the medium of film: gender, race, religion and secularization, and doubling in the characterization of Moses.

2. The Ten Commandments *(1956)*

No Moses film is better-known or more heavily researched than DeMille's 1956 version of *The Ten Commandments*.[27] Critics have analyzed the film's cinematography, historical context, ideological content, and religious purpose since it was released in 1956. DeMille himself documented the making of the film with painstaking detail in his autobiography and in a book-length survey (written by Henry Noerdlinger under DeMille's supervision) of research for the film.[28] Running close to three hours and surpassing previous films in scale, budget, and ambition, the film continues to find large audiences through regular network telecasts and wide video distribution. No account or image of Moses since 1956 has made a similar impact on popular impressions of Moses. Charleton Heston, whose supposed resemblance to Michelangelo's Moses was memorialized in a portrait in which he posed with the statue, has become synonymous with Moses in the popular imagination.[29]

---

27. Film and television versions of the Moses story since *The Ten Commandments* (1956) are still judged against that standard. Instead of duplicating the great American story of liberty, these versions have identified niches or angles of their own. Burt Lancaster's 1975 *Moses* (RAI/ITS Incorporated Television Company Ltd) makes no attempt to reproduce the spectacular epic dimensions of DeMille's. Instead, this television version offers a very spare, even harsh, kind of realism; many of the scenes are graphically violent. Costumes and sets are simple, emphasizing the real conditions of life in villages and deserts. Lancaster's *Moses* is quiet but intense, disheveled and rough in comparison to his brother Aaron. The film takes a naturalistic approach to the signs and wonders; the plagues are presented as natural disasters in vivid, rapid succession. It presents manna as the resin of the tamarisk tree and offers a plausible account of the quail miracle.

Ben Kingsley's *Moses* (Turner Broadcasting, 1996) is more jocular and vulnerable. Filmed in warm tones and completed with a lush soundtrack, this production includes a number of scenes in which Moses doubts his God and his mission. Kingsley's Moses stutters and hesitates; he also shouts with joy after the crossing of the Red Sea and the giving of the Ten Commandments.

28. DeMille, *The Autobiography of Cecil B. DeMille*. Noerdlinger, *Moses and Egypt*. In a typically American spirit of pragmatism, Noerdlinger's study addresses material culture and Egyptian history, elements that would be crucial to the costumes, sets, and design of the film, but it ignores the basic challenge of documentary scholarship, that is, the historicity of the Bible itself (see Chapter 3).

29. DeMille, *The Autobiography of Cecil B. DeMille*, p. 380.

That DeMille's Moses is the epitome of a heroic great man borne of American Protestant, Cold War culture is self-evident. The place of the film among Hollywood spectaculars, with its impressive special effects, sets, costumes, and blend of high purpose and entertainment is well-established. But what does the cultural position of the film reveal about its relationship to biblical tradition? How does DeMille's paradigm reflect and shape the cultural images of Moses?

In *Theory of Film*, Kracauer distinguishes between films that corroborate and those that debunk popular views of the world. Corroborative films, he says, 'are as a rule called upon not to authenticate the truth to reality of an idea but to persuade us into accepting it unquestioningly'.[30] These images 'are intended to make you believe, not see. Sometimes they include a stereotyped shot which epitomizes their spirit: a face is so photographed against the light that hair and cheek are contoured by a luminous line intimating a halo. The shot has an embellishing rather than revealing function.' Kraucauer illustrates, 'Remember the ostentatious happiness of the collective farmers in Eisenstein's *Old and New*, the enraptured crowds hailing Hitler in the Nazi films, the miraculous religious miracles in Cecil B. DeMille's *The Ten Commandments*, etc. (But what an incomparable showman was DeMille, alas!).'[31]

Building on stereotypes and reinforcing preconceptions of reality, films such as DeMille's fail to challenge viewers or show reality in unexpected ways. Aside from his striking juxtaposition of *The Ten Commandments* with Nazi propaganda, it is worth noting how Kracauer links religiosity to corroborative film through the mention of haloes and religious miracles. Kracauer's three examples also run an ideological gamut from Soviet socialism to German fascism, with DeMille's ideology implied but not defined. Films saturated with religion and ideology, Kracauer seems to say, tell us what we already know. Corroborative films may draw from an impressive array of special effects, but they dazzle to divert, not to reveal anything new.

Yet Kracauer's comment on DeMille's showmanship qualifies the negative judgment. Writing soon after the release of *The Ten Commandments*, Kracauer seems ambivalent about a film at once so spectacular and so banal. Even viewers who find the acting pompous and the plot unoriginal cannot deny the impressive detail with which Egyptian costumes, objects, and buildings are rendered in the film, not to mention the drama and scale of the miracle scenes and the signs and wonders. And if *The Ten Commandments* is a sham corroboration of reality built on the ruins of ancient beliefs, it is a fact that remains hidden from all but a few critics. DeMille was criticized by some for too little pious literalism and by others for too much, but his message of American freedom and faith won overwhelming support among viewers and has become, as Gerald Forshey and Sumiko Higashi argue, a part of American culture.[32] By 1959, three years after its release, the film had been seen by

30. Kracauer, *Theory of Film*, p. 306.
31. Kracauer, *Theory of Film*, p. 306.
32. Gerald E. Forshey, *American Religious and Biblical Spectaculars* (Westport, CT: Praeger, 1992), pp. 137-40; Sumiko Higashi, 'Andimodernism as Historical Representation in a Consumer

98.5 million people.[33] Today the film holds a regular place in American Easter and Passover observance with annual Sunday evening network broadcasts.[34]

Higashi describes the project of DeMille's two versions of *The Ten Command-ments* as 'antimodernism'. Echoing Kracauer's view that the films corroborate rather than debunk images of reality, Higashi views the film as a conventional reflection of American culture:

> Ultimately, DeMille contributed not only to the secularization of evangelical Protestantism, but also to its reification as spectacle for mass consumption... DeMille's practice of reifying religious spectacle as a commodity—a strategy that influenced advertisers who preached spiritual uplift through consumption—ulti-mately proved that the custodians of culture were justified in their concerns about the debasement of traditional art.[35]

Split between religiosity and entertainment, convention and spectacle, DeMille's 1956 epic embodies Mosaic tensions and distinctions in a compelling way. Under the constraints of genre conventions, systems of production and distribution, as well as the physical realities of the medium itself, films about Moses display and concretize Mosaic distinctions between enchantment and disenchantment. Put in other terms, DeMille's genius is his balance of piety and profanity. DeMille's Moses embodies more complexity of gender, race, and traditional piety than at first meets the eye. Heston's Moses is undeniably masculine, but he transforms into an asexual holy man after the burning bush episode. In terms of the plot, Nefertiri and Rameses are also his doubles.

The film's opening credits signal its religious purpose by suggesting that viewers will take a 'pilgrimage'. In the film's prologue, DeMille steps from behind a curtain (a kind of revelation, etymologically speaking) and addresses the audience directly. Noting how unusual the introduction is, he claims:

> we have an unusual story—the story of the birth of freedom; the story of Moses... The theme of this picture is whether men ought to be ruled by God's law or whether they are to be ruled by the whims of a dictator like Rameses. Are men the property of the state or are they free souls under God? The same battle continues throughout the world today. Our intention was not to create a story but to be worthy of the divinely inspired story created three thousand years ago: the five books of Moses.

Determined that his audience will get the film's didactic point, DeMille becomes a master of ceremonies to introduce it. The son of a playwright who considered a

Culture: Cecil B. DeMille's *The Ten Commandments*, 1923, 1956, 1993', in Vivian Sobchack (ed.), *The Persistence of History* (New York: Routledge, 1996), pp. 91-112 (107-108).

33. DeMille, *The Autobiography of Cecil B. DeMille*, p. 379 n. 1. Also in Ilana Pardes, 'Moses Goes Down to Hollywood: Miracles and Special Effects', *Semeia* 74 (1996), pp. 15-32 (15).

34. Higashi, 'Antimodernism', p. 107. There is little research on the impact of the film on American culture, but see Purnima Mankekar, *Screening Culture, Viewing Politics* (Durham, NC: Duke University Press, 1999), for an excellent study of televised epic dramas in India.

35. Higashi, 'Andimodernism', p. 98.

career in ministry, DeMille considered his filmmaking a kind of ministry.[36] His fierce determination to make this film, at age 73, was borne out by his return to the set one day after a heart attack, against his doctor's advice.[37] But DeMille does not simply retell the biblical story: with the help of Philo and Josephus, he supplements it by filling in the thirty-year period of his early life.[38] In the 1923 production, the biblical story serves to preface a modern tale with an unmistakable moral lesson. And even in the much-expanded 1956 version, DeMille seems compelled to guide the viewer's interpretation. Perhaps to forestall competing images of Moses (as a proto-socialist or totalitarian figure, for instance[39]), DeMille declaims his film's meaning with the same kind of stentorian voice that Heston will use to deliver the law.

As Alan Nadel observes, the need to supplement a sacred text with secular materials is a clear paradox; it can either sanctify the supplement or profane the sacred text.[40] On the one hand, DeMille seeks to harmonize the piety of ancient Israel and modern Christianity with the Enlightenment principle of human liberty. At the same time, the pageantry and choreography of the tributes from Ethiopia, the light frivolity of the Egyptian women bathing, and the epic grandeur of Moses' orchestrated raising of an obelisk offer viewers state-of-the-art visual pleasures. DeMille's pious purpose never interferes with what Kracauer calls his showmanship. As such, *The Ten Commandments* is a monument to a number of tensions inherent in epic films about religious tradition: the challenge of piety and pleasure together. In order to accomplish this balance, DeMille adopts the well-established strategy of concentrating on Moses as an Egyptian hero whose story of personal development draws the liberation of Israel in its wake. His opening credits cite Dorothy Clark Wilson's *Prince of Egypt* (1949) (along with the more heavily Christian novels of Southon and Ingraham) as a source for the film, and the influence is clear: the film shares the novel's genre of historical romance and a great deal of its plot as well.

The most distinguishing features of the film are its scope and attention to detail, which is richly documented in Noerdlinger's book about the research behind the film. Matching the most advanced technology and large-scale Hollywood production resources with the archeological discoveries of ancient Egypt, the film remains one of the most ambitious and successful in history. Unlike the 1923 version (also very ambitious for its time), the 1956 film clothes its moralism and piety in dramatically compelling and visually stunning (though almost completely humorless) garments. But how do piety and entertainment interrelate? As a genre,

36. Alan Nadel, 'God's Law and the Wide Screen: *The Ten Commandments* as Cold War "Epic" ', *PMLA* 108 (1993), pp. 415-30 (426).
37. DeMille, *The Autobiography of Cecil B. DeMille*, pp. 392-93.
38. Nadel, 'God's Law and the Wide Screen', p. 417.
39. Ernst Bloch, *The Principle of Hope* (trans. N. Plaice, S. Plaice, and P. Knight; 3 vols.; Cambridge, MA: MIT Press, 1986), III, pp. 1230-31. See also the discussion of Mann, Steffens, and Hitler in Chapter 1.
40. Nadel, 'God's Law and the Wide Screen', pp. 417-18

historical romance clashes with the Bible. The book of Exodus is not primarily the story of Moses, especially not the moral and personal development of a solitary individual. Only by exploring the thirty-year period on which the Bible is silent can the genre reach its objective. DeMille's supplement to the Bible thus enjoys the freedom to create an entertainment suited to his own purposes without losing the authority of biblical tradition.

When the baby Moses arrives in the basket, he is wearing a red-and-black striped cloth; years later, this 'Levite cloth' will become the sign and evidence of Moses' Hebrew identity: it is produced in the scene where Moses learns with certainty who he is, and he later wears it with pride as leader of the Hebrews. This secret of Moses' identity is controlled by women. When the spiteful Egyptian servant, Memnet, reveals the fact to Nefertiri, Nefertiri kills her and shares the secret with Moses. Stunned by the possibility that he may be a Hebrew, Moses thwarts Nefertiri's plan to keep the secret between them as a bond of their love, insisting, 'Love cannot drown truth'. Moses questions his Egyptian mother, Bithia, who manages to calm him temporarily, but later, when Moses comes upon Bithia and his true mother, Jochebel, in a heated discussion, Moses discovers the truth, and the Levite cloth offers physical evidence. Like Rosebud in *Citizen Kane*, the Levite cloth is an artifact that lends meaning to Moses' life by continuity to his childhood, especially to his real mother.[41] (The recognition scene gains impact from the fact that Moses had providentially rescued Jochebel from being crushed in an earlier scene at a construction site.)

But Moses separates from both his mothers at this point. Seizing his identity from the group of women who had conspired to keep it secret, Moses sets out in a passionate quest for meaning, against the plea of the ever-lovesick Nefertiri. He joins the Hebrews and quickly learns to hate slavery. In an act of violence that mirrors Nefertiri's killing of Memnet, Moses kills an overseer who is thrashing Joshua for protecting a Hebrew woman (Lillia—later an object of villainous desire by Dathan and in the golden calf scene). Dathan, the negatively stereotyped 'Jew' (played by the only Jew in the leading cast, Edward G. Robinson[42]), betrays Moses to Pharaoh. Seti decides at that point that Rameses will be his successor and Nefertiri his queen. Rameses makes his first official act the exile of Moses, explaining that Moses and Nefertiri will suffer more intensely in their separation if he can live. He sets out into the wilderness with a staff and clothing made from the Levite cloth.

For all his masculinity, then, Moses' fate is tied closely to the world of women. In two elaborate scenes, Moses is discovered by women near water: first in the basket, and second by Sephora at the Midianite well. These women 'save' Moses in a sense, though he reciprocates (and readjusts the power differential) by protecting and liberating them in return. Depicted as weak and sexualized, the power of these women is fleeting but necessary to the survival of Moses, their masculine counterpart.

---

41. In *Prince of Egypt* this purpose is served by the lullaby which Moses dimly remembers when Miriam sings it to him as an adult.
42. Nadel, 'God's Law and the Wide Screen', p. 427.

Moses has three doubles in the film: himself, Nefertiri, and Rameses. The radical change in appearance after the burning bush episode marks a change of personality, a kind of second Moses—no more a lover, military leader, and industrial builder of empire, he is now a holy man whose face (and hair color) is suffused with the light associated with theophany (Exod. 34.29-35). Unlike the Moses of the Egyptian court, this Moses shows no capacity for spontaneity or intimacy. Charleton Heston's performance after the burning bush is majestic and almost robotic, a figure who lacks personal initiative or human passion. When he returns to Egypt, he resists Nefertiri's advances: 'The Moses who loved you was another man'. The burning bush marks the point in the film where DeMille's invention meets biblical tradition: entertainment gives way to edification, personality is replaced by piety.

Moses' rival and same-sex double in the film is Rameses, played by the exotic (i.e. un-American) Yul Brynner. Their resemblance lies in their shared desire for Nefertiri and the Hebrews. In Girard's terms, the antagonism is mimetic, since they both want the same thing, and this 'doubling' makes them prone to violence. The pattern changes, however, when Moses becomes a holy man. At that point he no longer fights his double 'man to man'. Indifferent to Nefertiri and even Sephora, the post-burning bush Moses represents the hardest and most stoic ideal of manhood. Free at last from the feminine comforts of the Egyptian court, and tested in the desert wilderness, Moses seems incapable of passion for any man or woman. Rameses, meanwhile, is consumed by human passion—the love of Nefertiri and the jealous hatred of Moses. Though he strives to be a strong ruler, Rameses betrays his weakness by allowing this passion to guide his actions. In a novel explanation of an age-old biblical puzzle, Nefertiri boasts to Moses that she can soften or harden Pharaoh's heart as she wishes, and Moses concedes her part in God's plan: 'Yes, you may be the lovely dust through which God will work his purpose'. Pharaoh is thus unmanned not by Moses but by his passion for Nefertiri, a passion that destroys the lives of the firstborn and the Egyptian army in the Red Sea.

In a plot that makes Moses the epitome of stereotypical masculinity, Nefertiri enjoys wider influence than any other character, even saving Moses' wife and son (Sephora and Gershom) from the wrath of Pharaoh. In this way she represents what Bellour calls the 'narcissistic double' of Moses. Like Merapi in *Moon of Israel*, Nefertiri is a beautiful woman whose desirability drives the plot—including the liberation of the Hebrews—forward. If Nefertiri, like Merapi, embodies the exotic Orient, then she is also a female projection of Moses—a necessary but ultimately dispensable part of Moses; a more ancient, worldly, perhaps Jewish Moses who must be replaced by a masculine and Christian Moses. At the level of genre, the female Moses is the Moses of historical (and Orientalist) romance. As such, she is not so easily dispensed with. DeMille's film thus merges the genres of romance and biblical epic in a symbiosis of plots and subplots that makes Nefertiri and Moses doubles of each other.

The tension between piety and entertainment in *The Ten Commandments* is inherent to all the Moses films. Is there such a thing as biblical romance, or is this term an oxymoron? If film is the medium most wedded to the physical world, a modern and secular form of entertainment, then what impact does it have on a

religious story? There are no simple answers to the question. Benjamin and Kracauer view film as a secular phenomenon that bears distinct traces of religiosity. As
such, religious films bring the tension between piety and entertainment to the
surface. The tension is expressed through the clash of Egyptian and Hebrew culture, and even more basically, through a conflict between male and female characteristics. The contradictions inherent in popular religious film find expression in the
characterization of Moses, particularly with respect to his ethnicity and gender. *The
Ten Commandments* replicates biblical tradition even by reinventing it.

3. Moon of Israel

Moon of Israel (1924) is based on the 1918 novel of that name by popular writer H.
Rider Haggard, a British lawyer, politician, and author who lived in South Africa.
Haggard wrote other historical romances and adventure stories, including *King
Solomon's Mines*, a novel about African exploration (1885), *She* (1887) and *Cleo-
patra* (1889). Haggard dedicated *Moon of Israel* to the Orientalist Egyptologist
Gaston Maspero, and his friend Rudyard Kipling praised the book (see Chapter
1).[43] The film was produced in Austria, where intellectual and cultural life were
flourishing despite post-war political and economic upheaval. As Hitler's *Mein
Kampf* (1925–27) notoriously shows, post-War Austria was a place where questions of race, nationalism, and Judaism were familiar and highly charged. The film
was directed by Michael Curtiz, who later emigrated to the United States and
became one of the most successful directors in Hollywood's history. His directorial
credits include *Cabin in the Cotton* (1932), *Casablanca* (1942), *Life With Father*
(1947), *White Christmas* (1954), and *Francis of Assisi* (1961).[44] Seen by American
film producers as a rival to DeMille's *The Ten Commandments*, Paramount studios
purchased American rights to *Moon of Israel*, and it was never released in the
United States.[45]

  Moon of Israel is not ostensibly the story of Moses at all; it centers on a Hebrew
slave named Merapi, who performs many of the narrative functions played by
Moses in the book of Exodus. But the film includes Moses and parallels Exodus,
thus creating several oppositions between Merapi, the supposed witch, and Moses
the prophet. Merapi kills a Hebrew to save her Egyptian love, Prince Seti, whereas
Moses (though this scene is not part of the film) kills the Egyptian overseer to save
a Hebrew. Merapi is engaged in the illicit love of an Egyptian; while Moses (again
in the biblical account but not in the film) engages in illicit love of a Cushite.
Before Moses inflicts the plagues on the Egyptians, Merapi demonstrates the power
of her God in a contest with the Egyptian gods. Moses causes the death of Pharaoh
Meneptah at the crossing of the Red Sea, while Merapi sacrifices her own safety,

---

  43.   Haggard's African novels have received more critical attention than *Moon of Israel*. See,
e.g., Gail Ching-Liang Low, *White Skins/Black Masks* (London: Routledge, 1996); and Norman
Etherington, *Rider Haggard* (Boston: Twayne, 1984).
  44.   This list was prepared with the use of WorldCat, a database of university libraries around
the world.
  45.   Facets Multimedia Center, online at <http.//www.facets.org/>.

her child, and her own life for the love of Seti. When she is injured earlier in the story, Merapi is carried across a small body of water by Seti. Finally, by the pity evoked at her death by crucifixion, Merapi seems to ensure that Seti, rather then being killed by an angry mob, will become the next pharaoh.

Moon of Israel, I suggest, is a story of gender reversal between Moses and Merapi. Both play the role of liberator, but by splitting Moses from Merapi, the film allows Moses to remain pious, distant, and masculine, while Merapi can be feminine, veiled (as in the contest scene), transgress the boundary of sexual and religious taboo to marry Seti—and die tragically at the end. (Their child dies in the plague as well, a signal that their relationship is not divinely sanctioned.) When Moses appears, he is usually seen from a distance, silhouetted against the sky and standing above the people. With a long beard, staff, stout build and stern demeanor, he resembles the Moses of Claus Sluter's 1405 sculpture (see Chapter 4). Moses and the Bible stand in the background; Merapi and her story of romance are in the foreground. The scriptural tradition of Moses as author and main character is thus figuratively pushed aside for a literary one in which the Egyptian servant Ana is the author; he is introduced in the credits as *der Romanschreiber*. In *Moon of Israel*, romance prevails over biblical epic.

Merapi first appears in a scene of the prince (in disguise) and Ana looking at the buildings and Israelite slaves. The two men observe a stout, bearded Moses talking to the slaves; he tells them that God hears their pleas, and they then bow in worship. The film then cuts to a scene (with titles) of Merapi (daughter of Nathan, a Levite) in a ragged and revealing dress (cut well above the knee and showing cleavage). An Egyptian overseer flirts with her; she refuses; he then becomes violent toward the other slaves, killing one. Merapi weeps; Seti and Ana retaliate against the overseer, and when Seti reveals his identity (from under a hood), everyone bows. At the public trial of the overseer, Merapi testifies in her own defense. Seti says there will be no killing of Israelite slaves and sends the overseer away; Merapi thanks him.

Seti next sees Merapi on a trip to Goshen. Though he is married to the princess Userti, he clearly loves Merapi, and when he and Ana see her bathing, they overhear her praying for help in her hopeless love for Seti. When Seti and Ana reveal themselves, she falls, and Seti bandages and carries her, marking the second time he saves Merapi. In his visit to the Hebrew camp, Seti learns that Merapi is engaged to Laban. He attends a Sabbath service that features typical Jewish imagery of prayer, bowing, Hebrew inscriptions, a menorah, and prayer shawls. In his ignorance, Seti unveils the Ark of the Covenant, leading the shocked Hebrews to call for his death. But Merapi saves him from a Hebrew ambush; Seti and Ana shoot arrows at the Hebrews while their African chariot driver runs ahead for help. In her second and most shocking rescue of Seti, Merapi kills a Hebrew who is about to kill him. With this she has turned away from her own people. Merapi has sacrificed racial and religious identity for the forbidden love of Seti.

Merapi moves into the palace, and Seti asks how he can repay her. His wife, Userti, looks on jealously. The Hebrews, meanwhile, ask Merapi to intercede for them. In a scene that precedes and outdoes the signs of Moses, Merapi invokes

Jehovah in a challenge between her God and the Egyptians'; hail, smoke, and wind overwhelm the court, and the statues of the Egyptian gods collapse.

Against the background of a succession struggle and Moses' demands to release the Hebrews, Merapi and Seti seal their love with a kiss and later a baby (shown cradled by a dark-skinned African). Though his love for Merapi and weakness lose him the throne, Merapi calls Seti her king. Their baby dies in the final plague, and Merapi appeals to Seti to help the Hebrews, but the new pharaoh rebuffs Seti, and the Red Sea scene follows.

Still near the Red Sea, Seti sends for Merapi to flee from Egypt, but she is captured by vengeful Egyptians who call her a witch, bind her, and carry her away. Meanwhile, Seti dreams she is in trouble and sets out to rescue her. When he arrives on the scene, Merapi has been hung on a cross-like structure surrounded by fire. Seti takes her down from the cross and embraces her, Ana proclaims Seti the new pharaoh. The villain responsible for Merapi's fate, an evil magician, is placed on the cross and prepared for the fire. But Merapi is dying: 'Hold me fast', she says, and in the final scene of the film, he kisses her.

Merapi's doubling and displacement of Moses resolve the challenge of filming Moses. By placing the biblical narrative and its main character literally in the background, the film preserves the distant antiquity, the *scriptural* dimension, of the story. By remaining marginal to *Moon of Israel*, the Bible and Moses retain the aura of ancient tradition, thus avoiding the tendency of film to render their subjects so immediate as to seem trivial. At the same time, Merapi's role as a kind of female Moses continues the biblical tradition of Moses as a focus of polemic. Modern anxieties of gender and race concentrate in a heroine who is part exotic damsel in distress, part warrior, part prophet, and part martyr. She fits the racial stereotype of the Jewess as an exotic, dark beauty ('Moon', 'witch'), but she transcends her racial identity for the love of Seti. Though she dies tragically, Merapi is vindicated as a martyr. On the level of meta-narrative, Merapi also vindicates the genre of Orientalist romance—its stock message that love conquers all relegates the biblical story of Moses to the background. Yet by its bold transpositions, *Moon of Israel* illuminates the paradoxes of writing and identity in Moses tradition.

4. Prince of Egypt

Prince of Egypt presents DeMille's old song in a new key; the technology of contemporary animation allows it to rival the special effects of the 1956 film, still considered impressive today.[46] With an estimated budget of $75 million, the animated feature follows DeMillle's narrative formula: the Egyptian youth and early career of Moses. The values and message also mirror DeMille's concerns for faith (in the song 'When You Believe') and freedom. Like DeMille, Jeffrey Katzenberg, the film's producer, made a public show of approaching scholars and religious authorities for the making of the film:

46. The film cost over $13 million. See DeMille, *The Autobiography of Cecil B. DeMille*, p. 379.

Mr. Katzenberg has consulted about 700 bible scholars, Egyptologists, divinity school teachers and religious leaders including the conservatives Jerry Falwell and Pat Robertson. They were consulted on everything from the costumes to the compression of the story into 90 minutes to making sure the Bible tale was being retold in a way that would not offend Christians, Muslims, or Jews.[47]

Nevertheless, David N. Freedman, one of the biblical scholars consulted by the filmmakers, said 'People like me are the window dressing… They invite us to come in to look and they don't really listen to us.'[48]

New elements of the plot reflect a more liberal, post-Cold War ethos.[49] Rameses is driven not by jealousy over a woman but by the hunger for approval from his stern father, Seti. Early in the film, when Moses and Rameses destroy large monuments under construction during a chariot race, Seti admonishes Rameses (his heir) harshly: 'One weak link can break the chain of a mighty dynasty!' When Seti rebuffs Rameses' effort to explain, Moses intercedes: 'All he cares about is your approval; I know he will live up to your expectations. All he needs is the opportunity.' The scene is filled with ironic prefiguration, since Rameses will bring down the dynasty precisely by living up to his father's expectations, that is, by continuing to oppress the Hebrews. Showered with love and approval as a young boy, Moses adjusts to the challenges of his biblical call, while Rameses grows up to be a pharaoh blinded by anger toward his dead father.

The theme of the bully starved for fatherly approval was already a staple of films in the 1980s such as *Breakfast Club* and *Parenthood*, and it has roots in the popularization of Freudian theory by such works as Arthur Miller's *Death of a Salesman*. *Prince of Egypt* thus affirms the motif of the love-deprived bully, with its sentimental lesson on the need for fathers to show love for their sons, as an icon of American culture. Moses and Rameses become Girardian doubles by their rivalry over the father Sethi (as well as the Hebrews), though here, as in *The Ten Commandments*, Moses transcends the 'man-to-man' confrontation with Rameses as a biblical prophet.

Prince of Egypt signals a more culturally, religiously, and racially pluralistic vision of society than *The Ten Commandments*. The message of liberation applies more broadly and explicitly to various groups (though DeMille reached clumsily toward that goal). *Prince of Egypt* also expands the roles of Miriam and Zipporah to prominent and strong figures. Miriam, who saves Moses' life at the beginning and triggers his self-recognition later, represents the virtue of faith. Zipporah, who first appears in a scene as a slave, is humiliated and then set free by Moses; her independence and pluck symbolize freedom.

47. *The New York Times* (14 December 1998).

48. James Sterngold, 'Just Like Real Life? Well, Maybe a Little More Exciting—Scholars Get Cameo Roles as Film Consultants', *The New York Times* (26 December 1998), p. A23.

49. See Erica Sheen, '*The Ten Commandments* and *The Prince of Egypt*: Biblical Adaptation and Global Politics in the 1990s', *Polygraph* 12 (2000), pp. 85-99. See also Jennifer Rohrer-Walsh, 'Coming-of-Age in *The Prince of Egypt*', in Richard Walsh and George Aichele (eds.), *Screening Scripture: Intertextual Connections Between Scripture and Film* (Harrisburg, PA: Trinity Press, 2002), pp. 77-99.

By its use of animation and pop star soundtracks, the film seems to embrace American popular culture even more firmly than *The Ten Commandments* did, though the difference may only reflect changes in the film industry. But *Prince of Egypt* clearly differs from *The Ten Commandments* on the portrayal of gender roles: Miriam and Zipporah are strong and morally good at the same time (though both, especially Zipporah, are sexualized), and Moses is depicted throughout in a gentle, almost feminine light. His face and voice typically register surprise and wonder rather than the sternness of Heston. His tenderness toward Rameses remains undiminished even at the end of the story. The burning bush episode combines *mysterium tremendum* with a heavy dose of *mysterium fascinans*: the fear and surprise of the commission scene are replaced by a reverie sequence in which Moses appears to hurtle through space with a wide-eyed and satisfied expression on his face. The angel of death and Red Sea crossings, likewise scenes of awesome theophany, are balanced against the joyful scenes of victory that immediately follow them. The image most reminiscent of DeMille's masculine Moses comes in the final scene, depicting Moses with the tablets, but he is shown from behind and only as a kind of afterword.

As the opening scenes of *Prince of Egypt* make clear, Moses and Rameses grow up together and share a close friendship. Their eventual antagonism will result from Moses' new role as liberator of the Hebrews and Rameses' heart, hardened by his resolve to realize his father's wishes. When Moses returns to Egypt, Rameses welcomes him warmly; they embrace and laugh. But when Moses explains his mission, the atmosphere changes. The brothers' separation is dramatized in a musical scene against the backdrop of the plagues. While the horrors and suffering of the plagues are shown in succession to the music of a chorus singing in the style of Carl Orff's *Carmina Burana*, Moses and Rameses face off in the following duet:

Moses:	Once I called you brother,
	once I thought the chance to make you laugh was all I ever wanted,
	and even now I wish that God had chosen another serving as your
	foe on his behalf;
	it's the last thing that I wanted.
	This was my home;
	all this pain and devastation,
	how it tortures me inside—
	all the innocent who suffer from your stubbornness and pride.
	You who I called brother,
	why must you call down another blow?
	'Let my people go', thus saith the Lord.
Rameses:	You who I called brother,
	how could you have come to hate me so?
	Is this what you wanted?
	Then let my heart be hardened.
	And never mind how high the cost may grow.
	This will still be so.
	I will never let your people go.
Moses (with Rameses):	Thus saith the Lord, 'Let my people go'.
Rameses:	I will not let your people go.

This back-and-forth exchange recalls the Greek tragic technique of *stichomythia* ('the exchange of insults and accusations that corresponds to the exchange of blows between warriors locked in single combat'), which Girard associates with the violent conflict between doubles.[50] As the song comes to an end, the darkened profiles of Moses and Rameses face each other, merge in a superimposed image, and then split again. The brothers are doubles split apart by their respective destinies. Rameses, embittered by his disapproving father, has hardened his heart; Moses, compelled by a divine 'father', must renounce the comforts and corruption of Egypt to lead his people to freedom. Yet as the scene makes clear, Moses continues to care for Rameses; it is this love that feminizes him and creates dramatic tension. The conflict of this scene is resolved after the Red Sea crossing, at which Moses bids Rameses farewell. At this point the dramatic tension dissolves, and the remainder of the film—the celebration and the brief sequence of Moses standing on Sinai with the tablets—has the structure of an epilogue. In another sense, since Miriam and Zipporah represent this duty, drawing Moses away from Egypt and toward his new role, it is women who separate the two men from each other. The change makes Moses more masculine (as husband and protector rather than intimate of Rameses) but less so as well (submissive to women's will).

With *The Ten Commandments*, on the other hand, Moses is consistently masculine but linked to his feminine double Nefertiri. The macho Moses of the first part of the film is an all-American lover, symbolized by Nefertiri's cooing 'Oh Moses'; the macho Moses of the later half is Michelangelo's, a powerful and ascetic holy man divorced from human attachments. After the burning bush episode, Moses does not return Nefertiri's desirous gaze, and yet his imperviousness only increases his masculine power. Like Wilson's *Prince of Egypt*, *The Ten Commandments* retains the elements of historical romance; the plot is driven by the love triangle of Moses, Nefertiri, and Rameses.

The animated Moses, by contrast, continues to gaze at Rameses even after the Red Sea divides them; here, he finally separates from Rameses, not Nefertiri, in order to deliver his people to freedom. *Prince of Egypt* depicts a kinder, gentler, more feminine Moses surrounded by strong women and a brother figure (Rameses) wounded by his father's disapproval. Despite these distinctively 1990s turns, *Prince of Egypt* preserves the doubling structure and major plot elements of *The Ten Commandments*. *The New Yorker* put it with humorous succinctness:

> The picture is O.K. The picture is *fine*. The cast is packed. The prince is Kilmer. The brother is Fiennes. The squeeze is Pfeiffer. (The dance is hubba-hubba.) The trouble is scale. The trouble is bombast. The predecessor is DeMille. The mood is tumescent. The music is nuts. Look. The thing is this. The cutting-edge computer-generated imagery is white-hot new. The movie is old-fashioned. The story is forever. The movie is for the holidays. The choice is yours.[51]

This pithy review captures the paradox of tradition and innovation in *Prince of Egypt*: it seems at once original and completely unoriginal. A similar paradox

50. Girard, *Violence and the Sacred*, pp. 150-51.
51. *The New Yorker* (28 December 1998–4 January 1999), p. 140.

applies to the relationship between the medium of film and the Bible as written tradition. While writing and texts are linked to Moses in the Pentateuch, they appear
mostly in the Egyptian context in the films. In *Prince of Egypt*, pivotal scenes take
place in the underground vault whose walls are covered with hieroglyphics that
depict scenes of Egyptian courtly history. The film shows the room three times: first
in a dream Moses has just after learning his Hebrew identity. This sequence, one of
the most visually spectacular of the film, shows the drowning of the Hebrew babies
in the Nile. The hieroglyphics are rendered vividly, and they become animated
during the dream. Soon afterward Moses discovers the image from his dream in the
vault itself; Seti finds him there and admits that the terrible infanticides did take
place. Much later, just before the killing of the firstborn, Moses and Rameses meet
there for the last time; while Moses warns Rameses to relent, Rameses' son enters,
asking what Moses is doing there. Hieroglyphics thus function as a kind of script
for the film itself.

5. *Conclusion*

Films about Moses necessarily make him physically present. But in their attempts
to reconcile the ambiguities of biblical tradition, the films double Moses into male
and female, the familiar and the other, reflecting contemporary anxieties about
gender and race. In the tradition of heroic biographies of Moses extending back to
Philo and Josephus, the films largely ignore the structure and even contents of the
biblical accounts of Moses. With sensory impact and mass appeal unthinkable just
a hundred years earlier, Moses films eclipse biblical tradition more emphatically
than any other medium. If the biblical Moses is essentially scriptural, he is also
essentially posthumous, a writer who emerges only after his own death. Like
Benjamin's storyteller, who merges (through death) with his story, the biblical
Moses is a figure of writing rather than a figure of speech and action. Nevertheless,
the figure of the writing Moses, so decisively repressed by post-biblical tradition,
does return in the films: the doubling of Moses, by demonstrating the virtual impossibility of rendering *any one* Moses on screen, exhibits the complexities of biblical
writing. In addition, each of the films brings writing into the story—not the writing
of Moses, but the writing of Egypt (the hieroglyphics in *Prince of Egypt* and the
narrator/scribe Ana in *Moon of Israel*), and in the case of *The Ten Commandments*,
the fiery writing of God on the tablets of the law and the recurring line 'So it is
written; so it shall be done', which applies first to Egypt and later to the Bible.
Forced by the medium and conventions of film to show Moses in heroic action, the
movies nevertheless gesture, through doubling and references to writing, to a more
biblical Moses, a Moses of tradition and writing.

Chapter 3

LEGEND AND HISTORY
IN MODERN SCHOLARLY PORTRAITS OF MOSES

The traditional story of Moses is simple, but its original form in the Bible is not. This discrepancy did not escape the notice of modern scholars, but they sometimes failed to recognize it. Even when they doubted the historicity of the Moses story, scholars approached the subject with the model of traditional biography, asking themselves whether to describe the biblical account as legend or history. More often than not, biblical scholars projected images of Moses as a popular hero onto the biblical text. This chapter identifies these patterns in modern scholarship, particularly through the category of legend (*Sage*).[1]

The search for the historical Moses never rivaled the search for the historical Jesus, but it did concern scholars for whom Moses is the central figure of the Pentateuch. This pursuit of historicity led scholars to the hypothetical source documents and cultural settings of the Bible. Through scientific methods of analysis and reasoning, they examined evidence from the Bible and from other ancient documents and human artifacts. When Julius Wellhausen published his *Geschichte Israels* in 1878, historical research on the Pentateuch, including the hypothesis on multiple sources, was already well-established. Wellhausen gave a rigorous and detailed history of the Pentateuch and its sources, and he is still credited with gaining widespread scholarly acceptance for the documentary hypothesis.

A separate branch of biblical scholarship, known today as form criticism, developed around the turn of the century. Unlike the source critics of the Wellhausen school, Hermann Gunkel and Hugo Gressmann sought to isolate the narrative (not documentary) traditions hidden within the Pentateuch. Myth, folktale, legend, and history were their objects of study, and they pursued them with the same confidence as Wellhausen sought the documentary sources.[2]

Form critics and source critics divided the Bible into ever-smaller units. Through a process Mario Liverani calls 'rationalistic paraphrase', they also analyzed biblical

---

1.   The term *Sage* can be translated 'legend' or 'story', despite the cognate term *Legende*. See, though, Gunkel's more specific terminology in John J. Scullion, Translator's Introduction to Hermann Gunkel, *The Stories of Genesis* (Berkeley: BIBAL Press, 1994), p. xvii.

2.   While modern archaeological discoveries of Egyptian, Mesopotamian, Hittite, and Ugaritic texts and artifacts played a key role in the story of modern biblical scholarship, they play a secondary role here, since the five scholars and the subject of Moses traditions deal mainly with evidence internal to the Bible.

texts to fit contemporary notions of historical plausibility.[3] A simple example of 'rationalistic paraphrase' appears in William Albright's *The Biblical Period From Abraham to Ezra*. In this survey of historical-critical and archaeological scholarship, Albright retells the biblical story of Moses as an inspired hero and brilliant leader: 'As against the decadence of contemporary Egyptian and Canaanite religion, Moses drew inspiration from the simple traditions of his own Hebrew people and the stern sexual code of the nomads, among whom he spent much of his early manhood before the Exodus'.[4] Such scholarship demystified narrative traditions into a rationalized account of human history and development. Hans Frei is correct to observe that historical-critical research diminished or eclipsed biblical narrative. Atomizing the Pentateuch to reconstruct the history behind it shifted attention away from the shape and meaning of its stories: 'the realistic or history-like quality of biblical narratives, acknowledged by all, instead of being examined for the bearing it had in its own right on meaning and interpretation was immediately transposed into the quite different issue of whether or not the realistic narrative was historical'.[5] But historical criticism did not completely extinguish the narrative flame of the Bible.[6] In fact, the new historical research tended to intensify and reify biblical narrative by its drive to define biblical history and narrative strata. Wellhausen, whose *Prolegomena zur Geschichte Israels* (1883 [an expanded version of *Geschichte Israels*]) is often cited as a seminal classic of historical criticism, idealizes biblical legend with the same fervor as his Romantic predecessors Herder and Goethe. For Wellhausen and the other historians surveyed here, narrative enjoys a privileged position unnoticed by Frei. This narrative, often characterized as legend (German *Sage*, from the verb *sagen*, 'to speak', sometimes translated 'story' or 'saga'[7]), bears the stamp of German idealist thought.

Biblical scholars were rarely as explicit about narrative models as Elias Auerbach, who wrote (in 1953):

> Moses was without doubt the most powerful genius brought forth by Israel. He was in his own time a solitary figure of greatness. The human material on which he

3.   Mario Liverani, 'Storiografia politica hittita—II: Telipinu, ovvero: della solidarietà', *OA* 16 (1977), pp. 105-108, cited in Niels Peter Lemche, 'Rachel and Lea. Or: On the Survival of Outdated Paradigmas in the Study of the Origin of Israel, II', *Scandinavian Journal of the Old Testament* 1 (1988), pp. 39-65 (53). See also Lemche, 'On the Problem of Studying Israelite History Apropos Abraham Malamat's View of Historical Research', *BN* 23 (1984), pp. 94-124.
4.   William Albright, *The Biblical Period From Abraham to Ezra* (New York: Harper & Row, 1963), p. 18. See also Albright, *Archaeology and the Religion of Israel* (Baltimore: The Johns Hopkins University Press, 1968).
5.   Hans Frei, *The Eclipse of Biblical Narrative*, p. 16.
6.   I allude to Walter Benjamin, 'The Storyteller': 'The storyteller: he is the man who could let the wick of his life be consumed completely by the gentle flame of his story', pp. 108-109. Benjamin's intertwining of storyteller and story (*Erzähler and Erzählung*) captures a dimension of the biblical portrait of Moses often neglected by biblical scholars. See Rudiger Lux, 'Der Tod Moses als "besprochene und erzählte Welt" ', *ZTK* 84 (1987), pp. 395-425.
7.   Ronald M. Hals analyzes this terminological confusion in 'Legend', in George W. Coats (ed.), *Saga Legend Tale Novella Fable* (JSOTSup, 35; Sheffield: JSOT Press, 1985), pp. 45-55 (45-49). A further confusion is the cognate term *Legende*.

worked was primitive, just awakening out of man's primeval period, still lacking any history, and only awakened to its own self-consciousness by him… In the work of man, Moses was, through the grace of God, the artist who saw in the rough block not only the hidden, the perfect form; impatiently and patiently, he struck it out of the stone with a heavy hammer and smoothing chisel.[8]

Auerbach stands at one extreme of the scholarly spectrum, making no secret of his evaluative commitments to the figure of Moses. Yet Auerbach is equally emphatic in his loyalty to historical scholarship: 'Even the oldest account has to be used with the greatest caution if the recovery of a historical portrait of Moses is to result. All that we learn about Moses is clothed in the form of legends and miracle stories. Not one word of these stories goes back to Moses himself.'[9] Building on Gressmann's analysis of Moses legends, Auerbach sees no apparent contradiction between historical rigor and hero-worship.

At the other extreme of scholarship on Moses was the view held by Martin Noth (and Eduard Meyer before him[10]) that Moses did not exist, at least not as described in the Bible. Noth can hardly be accused of uncritically endorsing narrative stereotypes, and yet I intend to show, perhaps deconstructively, how he did just that. By his commitment to certain views on traditional narratives such as legend, saga, and myth, Noth stands closer to Auerbach than might at first appear. Like most other modern scholars, Noth and Auerbach shared the goal of uncovering the kernels of historical truth under the husks of legend and multiple sources. Though their conclusions were different, they shared a methodology based on the opposition between legend (however defined) and history. And behind this notion of legend stood the image of Moses as a charismatic hero.[11]

This chapter seeks to demonstrate that modern scholars engaged in the narrative eclipse of the biblical text by their common commitment to ideas of legend and history and the opposition between them.[12] This commitment took different forms (evolutionary anti-Jewishness in Wellhausen and Jewish humanism in Buber, for instance) and led to different conclusions, but it produced remarkable agreement on

8. Auerbach, *Moses*, pp. 215-16.

9. Auerbach, *Moses*, p. 9.

10. Eduard Meyer, *Die Israeliten und ihre Nachbarstämme* (Halle: Max Niemeyer, 1906).

11. See, e.g., Max Weber's famous definition of 'prophet' as 'a purely individual bearer of charisma, who by virtue of his mission proclaims a religious doctrine or divine commandment', *The Sociology of Religion* (trans. Ephraim Fischoff; Boston: Beacon Press, 1963), p. 46. Weber's work first appeared in 1922, and thus may have influenced Noth, von Rad, and Buber; I cite it only to illustrate an idea that circulated widely in the modern period.

12. My survey covers some of the same ground as Eva Osswald's *Das Bild des Mose in der kritischen alttestamentlichen Wissenschaft seit Julius Wellhausen* (Berlin: Evangelische Verlaganstalt, 1962); Rudolf Smend's *Das Mosebild von Heinrich Ewald bis Martin Noth* (Beiträge zur Geschichte der Biblischen Exegese, 3; Tübingen: J.C.B. Mohr, 1959); and Douglas A. Knight's *Rediscovering the Traditions of Israel* (Missoula, MT: Society of Biblical Literature, 1975), all three of which are excellent and thorough reviews of historical scholarship on Moses. Osswald and Knight concentrate on historical issues and methods, and Smend places biblical research into a larger intellectual context (e.g. citing Troeltsch and Weber), my purpose is different and more specific: to explore the concepts of 'history' and 'legend' as narrative categories in research about Moses.

the biblical story of Moses (whether they believed it was true or not). Scholars did not perpetuate myths about Moses as openly as modern novelists and filmmakers did, but their claims to scientific standards made the stakes different and arguably higher. Five highly influential and distinctive scholars are examined here: Julius Wellhausen (1844–1918), Hugo Gressmann (1877–1927), Martin Noth (1902–68), Gerhard von Rad (1901–71), and Martin Buber (1878–1965).[13] Though these scholars sought to distinguish legend from history in very different ways, they reinforced non-biblical images of Moses that go back as far as Philo and Josephus.

1. *Myth, Legend, and History*

Moses is focal to questions of history in part because of his place in the biblical canon. Genesis is admittedly a collection of diverse legends that are scarcely subject to historical verification. The books immediately following the Moses story, Joshua through Kings, deal with a later period of settlement and monarchy, much of which is consistent with external sources. The stories of Exodus, Numbers, and Deuteronomy, however, resist easy labeling as legend *or* history. The account may correspond to Egyptian history, but the exact period is unknown. The narratives of migration, identity formation, and settlement of a small people may be accurate in broad outlines, but they are filled with textual problems, miracles, and stories of a leader who seems much too godlike to be real.

While some responded to the ambiguities of Moses by following the long-standing tradition of elaborating and retelling his story, modern scholars set themselves the task of getting at the historical truth behind the story. But in order to do so, they distinguished between legend and history without examining the meaning of their terms. Scholars thus operated in accordance with long-held assumptions about the nature of legend and myth laid down in the nineteenth century.[14] According to this distinction, legend and myth are typically oral forms of tradition, while history is generally written. Myths and legends are very brief, and they communicate a single message.

These assumptions about oral and written tradition reflect larger patterns of nineteenth-century thought which I will describe broadly as German idealism.[15]

---

13.   One could argue that other scholars were more influential: for instance, Ernst Sellin, whose *Mose und seine Bedeutung für die israelitisch-jüdische Religionsgeschichte* (Leipzig: A. Deichertsche Verlagsbuchhandlung, 1922) provided the basis for Freud's *Moses and Monotheism*. Nevertheless, Sellin is a relatively minor figure among biblical scholars. He makes no appearance in the Moses studies of Noth and von Rad, and Buber disparages his research: *Moses: The Revelation and the Covenant* (Atlantic Heights, NJ: Humanities Press, 1989), p. vii n. 2. All five of the scholars discussed here continue to influence scholarship. An example of Noth's influence, for instance, is Herbert Schmid, *Mose: Überlieferung und Geschichte* (Berlin: Alfred Töpelmann, 1968), which challenges Noth's dismissal of Moses' historicity (see esp. pp. 112-13).

14.   See Bruce Lincoln, *Theorizing Myth: Narrative, Ideology, and Scholarship* (Chicago: University of Chicago Press, 1999), and Robert Oden, *The Bible Without Theology* (Urbana: University of Illinois Press, 1987), pp. 40-70.

15.   My use of the term coincides with that of Karl Ameriks, who understands German idealism broadly as a set of cultural and philosophical trends in the late eighteenth and nineteenth centuries:

One characteristic of idealist thought is an emphasis on the individual as the embodiment of such ideals as passion, rationality, and integrity. Like the Romantic heroes of German and British literature, this type of individual stands at the center of idealist thought, as a model of self-determination and strength in adversity; Schiller's portrait of Moses as the hero who decides to save the people (often an ethnically defined *Volk*) is an example.[16] A second strand of idealist thought is the search for an idealized past. To this way of thinking, ancient history, especially in Israel, is noble, pure, and a basis for ethical claims in the present. Thinkers as diverse as Locke, Herder, Rousseau, Hamann, and Humboldt valorized the past and sought to uncover it, and biblical scholars continued this search. A third pattern of idealist thought is the view of history as following a logical developmental process; evolutionary models of history, Hegel's developmental logic, and the historiography of Herder, Humboldt, and Ranke are familiar forms of this pattern.[17]

Biblical studies followed these intellectual currents along with its more immediate counterparts, folklore studies (e.g. in the early nineteenth-century collections of the Grimms), classical studies, which had literary and philosophical links to contemporary literature (e.g. Goethe's neoclassicism), and philosophy (e.g. Nietzsche's *Birth of Tragedy*). With the emerging consensus that the Pentateuch was a combination of distinct sources, it was important to establish methods of identifying the parts that made up the whole. Since these parts must have come from oral traditions, it followed that they were relatively smaller and earlier than the written sources, which combined them. The search for short, orally transmitted legends within biblical tradition proved useful to form critics and traditio-historical critics alike.[18] This line of thinking meant that it was no longer possible to speak of the biblical text itself as any kind of integrated narrative. The Pentateuch was rather a series of fragments whose only unity lay either in the constituent documentary sources or in the legends, heroes (like Moses), and *Volk* (i.e. Israel) behind them. What is astonishing about this emerging consensus on the nature of biblical legend is its epistemological boldness: in effect, modern scholars were claiming that the radical fragmentation of the Bible was visible to them for the first time, despite centuries of transmission, reading, and commentary. In the face of this fragmentation, German idealist thought offered ways of understanding the origins and nature of ancient Israel, its religion, and especially its leader, Moses.

'Introduction: Interpreting German Idealism', in *idem* (ed.), *The Cambridge Companion to German Idealism* (Cambridge: Cambridge University Press, 2000), pp. 1-17.

16. Schiller, *Die Sendung Moses*, XVII, pp. 377-413 (389).

17. See Oden, *The Bible Without Theology*, pp. 8-16. For Hegel's discussion of Moses and Judaism in dialectical context, see his *Lectures on the Philosophy of Religion: One-Volume Edition, The Lectures of 1827* (ed. Peter C. Hodgson; trans. R.F. Brown, P.C. Hodgson and J.M. Stewart; Berkeley: University of California Press, 1988), pp. 371-74.

18. See Frank Moore Cross' analysis of the romantic roots of Gunkel's notion of *Sage* as a primitive and short unit of narrative, shared at one time by Homeric scholars: 'There is in Gunkel's application of his method no reckoning with a long and continuous tradition of epic singers and epic cycles, mythic cycles and hierophants' (*From Epic to Canon* [Baltimore: The Johns Hopkins University Press, 1998], pp. 35-36).

2. *Julius Wellhausen*

It is tempting to view Wellhausen's work either as a creative paradigm shift or as the result of the Durkheimian effervescence[19] of nineteenth-century thinkers, but neither scenario is fully accurate. His research had roots in the eighteenth century work of Jean Astruc and Gottfried Eichhorn and the early nineteenth-century scholarship of Karl Heinrich Graf and Wilhelm DeWette.[20] Unlike the leading idealist thinkers of a generation before, Wellhausen was not a great scholar, poet, and philosopher. Nevertheless, his debt to the idealist tradition was clear even to himself: 'Histories have been stimulated, from Hegel and Schleiermacher, although they came from de Wette. We are more indebted to Herder and Goethe on the one hand and the French foundational philosophy of language on the other.'[21]

In his *Prolegomena zur Geschichte Israels* (1883), Wellhausen valorizes the earlier Jehovistic tradition as 'naïve' and 'natural'. The Priestly tradition, which he considers to be the latest in the Hexateuch, is by contrast legalistic, abstract, artificial, and lifeless: 'The Jehovist still lives in the spirit of the legend, but the Priestly Code is strange to that spirit (*Dem Geiste der Sage...entfremdet*), and does violence (*Zwang*) to the legend, by treating it from its own point of view, which is quite different from the old one'.[22] Since Moses appears in early and late sources of the Hexateuch, according to Wellhausen, he appears in more than one guise. The contrast between Jehovistic and Priestly tradition thus emerges clearly in the composite portrait of Moses. In the earlier Jehovistic strand, Moses is a man of God who delivers and cares for his people: 'Here all is life and movement: as Jehovah Himself, so the man of God, is working in a medium which is alive; is working practically, by no means theoretically, in history, not in literature'.[23] The priestly Moses, by contrast, is 'clearly defined and rounded off... It is detached from its originator (*Urheber*) and from his age: lifeless itself (*selber unlebendig*), it has driven the life out of Moses and out of the people, nay, out of the very Deity'.[24] This anti-Priestly polemic runs consistently through the *Prolegomena* and culminates in a denigration of Judaism itself, a religion 'estranged from the heart' in which 'Worship no longer springs from an inner impulse'.[25]

---

19. By applying a term Durkheim uses to describe 'elementary' religious life to modern scholarship, I wish to suggest that social and literary context are relevant to the study of scholars as well as cultures. See Emile Durkheim, *The Elementary Forms of Religious Life* (trans. Karen Fields; New York: Free Press, 1995), p. 218.

20. Ernest Nicholson, *The Pentateuch in the Twentieth Century* (Oxford: Clarendon Press, 1998), pp. 4-6.

21. Fr. Bleek, *Einleitung in das Alte Testament* (rev. J. Wellhausen; Berlin, 1878), p. 655, cited in Lother Perlitt, *Vatke und Wellhausen* (Berlin: Alfred Töpelmann, 1965), p. 186 (my translation).

22. Julius Wellhausen, *Prolegomena to the History of Israel* (Atlanta: Scholars Press, 1994), pp. 336-37; German edition: *Prolegomena zur Geschichte Israels* (Berlin: Georg Reimer, 1899), p. 341. See also Wellhausen, *Prolegomena* (English), pp. 61, 77, 342-43, 347.

23. Wellhausen, *Prolegomena*, p. 346 (English).

24. Wellhausen, *Prolegomena*, p. 347 (pp. 430-31 of the German edition).

25. Wellhausen, *Prolegomena*, pp. 424-25: 'Aus innerem Trieb erwächst der Kultus nicht mehr, er ist eine Übung der Gottseligkeit geworden', Wellhausen, *Prolegomena* (German), p. 430.

Wellhausen illustrates the contrast between J and P at length in his analysis of the 'bridegroom of blood' episode (Exod. 4.24-26), which he attributes to J. The purpose of this story, says Wellhausen, is to explain why Hebrews circumcised their boys: 'the circumcision of male infants is here explained as a milder substitute for the original circumcision of young men before marriage'.[26] The Priestly account of this tradition in Genesis 17, by contrast, imposes an alien style on the narrative of Abraham and Isaac: 'This institution completely throws into the shade and spoils the story out of which it arose.'[27] Wellhausen continues with generalizations: 'The law (*Kultusgesetz*) purifies the legend (*Kultussage*), that is to say, denies all its main features and motives (*Grundzügen und Trieben*)... The whole material of the legend is subordinated to legislative designs: the modifying influence of the law on the narrative is everywhere apparent.'[28]

Wellhausen's contrast between priestly religion and its more authentic antecedents combines Christian theology with early Romantic thought. The criticism of priestly law echoes the gospels' depiction of Pharisaism and Paul's contrast between law and gospel: 'The Pharisees killed nature by statute.'[29] The idealization of early, oral tradition, on the other hand, echoes the Romantic tendency to idealize early sources as natural and authentic.[30] As Lothar Perlitt shows, the affinity for early biblical tradition is explicit in Herder, and it reflects the Romantic bias toward the earliest phases of history, a theme found also in Rousseau, for instance.[31] Wellhausen credits Goethe with a pre-critical version of this position, quoting Goethe's *Israel in der Wüste*:

> 'These last four books of Moses have been made quite unreadable by a most melancholy, most incomprehensible (*höchst traurige, unbegreifliche*), revision. The course of the history is everywhere interrupted by the insertion of innumerable laws, with regard to the greater part of which it is impossible to see any reason for their being inserted where they are.' The dislocation of the narrative by these monstrous growths (*ungeheuren Auswüchse*) of legislative matter is not, as Goethe thinks, to be imputed to the editor; it is the work of the unedited Priestly Code itself, and is certainly intolerable (*unerträglich*).[32]

See Lou H. Silberman, 'Wellhausen and Judaism', *Semeia* 25 (1983), pp. 75-82. See also Rudolf Smend, 'Wellhausen und das Judentum', *ZTK* 79 (1982), pp. 249-82. Smend's study is very thorough if somewhat apologetic.

26.   Wellhausen, *Prolegomena*, p. 340.

27.   Wellhausen, *Prolegomena*, p. 340.

28.   Wellhausen, *Prolegomena*, p. 341 (p. 345 of the German edition).

29.   Wellhausen, *Die Pharisäer und Sadducäer* (Greifswald, 1874), p. 19, cited in Perlitt, *Vatke und Wellhausen*, p. 208 (my translation). Another striking passage is Wellhausen's remarks on Chronicles and other books as a form of midrash, which paradoxically preserves and twists tradition; Wellhausen, *Prolegomena*, p. 227. See also Perlitt, *Vatke und Wellhausen*, pp. 210, 243.

30.   See the discussion of Wellhausen's view of oral tradition in Douglas A. Knight, 'Wellhausen and the Interpretation of Israel's Literature', *Semeia* 25 (1983), pp. 30-31.

31.   Perlitt, *Vatke und Wellhausen*, pp. 211-12.

32.   Wellhausen, *Prolegomena*, p. 342 (p. 347 of the German edition).

For Goethe as for Wellhausen, pure narrative—legend and history together—constitutes the true and original record of biblical tradition. Law is not only secondary but also 'melancholy', extraneous, 'monstrous', and 'intolerable'. Even though
Wellhausen declares his purpose to be historical, that is, to show that J is earlier
than P, the overwhelming argument is that J is not just earlier but *better*—more
natural, spontaneous, and authentic—than P.[33]

There is, to be sure, a counterveiling impulse in Wellhausen that views the history of biblical tradition as progress. Like Hegel and Darwin, Wellhausen sometimes suggests that the development of law out of legend is necessary and
important.[34] The Bible evolves from myth, which precedes ancient Israel, to legend
and history, which is then followed by law. This process, he avers, actually anticipates modern science:

> The mythical mode of view is destroyed by the autonomy of morality; and closely
> connected with this is the rational view of nature, of which we find the beginnings
> in the Priestly Code. This view of nature presupposes that man places himself as a
> person over and outside of nature, which he regards as simply a thing. We may
> perhaps assert that were it not for this dualism of Judaism, mechanical natural
> science would not exist.[35]

The evolutionary development of biblical tradition may be inevitable and culturally
productive. But insofar as Wellhausen shares the romantic nostalgia for origins
found in Herder and Goethe, this progress is bittersweet. And from the standpoint
of the integrity of ancient legend, at least, the imposition of the Priestly law is
destructive and unnatural.

Rooted in early tradition but claimed by the Priestly editors as one of their own,
Moses stands uncomfortably on the cusp of this divide between narrative and law.
The Jehovist Moses is the spontaneous, living, and natural guardian; his Torah is
'nothing but a giving of counsel, a finding the way out of complications and difficulties which had actually arisen'.[36] The Priestly Moses, by contrast, is a false and
distant echo of the original, shaped by an overwhelming urge to impose law. He is

> a religious founder and legislator, as we are accustomed to think of him. He re-
> ceives and promulgates the torah, perhaps not as a book—though, when we come to
> think of it, we can hardly represent the transaction to ourselves in any other way—

---

33. Wellhausen, *Prolegomena*, p. 296. Another idealist influence on Wellhausen's view of
Moses traditions may be Freiedrich Schelling's *Philosophie der Mythologie* (edited manuscripts
and lecture notes from 1837 and 1842) (ed. Klaus Vieweg and Christian Danz; Munich: Wilhelm
Fink, 1996), esp. pp. 62-65. Genesis, especially the mythic materials of chs. 1–11, evinces an especially descriptive contrast between J and P; in J, says Wellhausen, there is 'a kind of antique
philosophy of history, almost bordering on pessimism: as if mankind were groaning under some
dreadful weight, the pressure not so much of sin as of creaturehood. We notice a shy, timid spirit,
which belongs more to heathenism' (Wellhausen, *Prolegomena*, p. 314).

34. See Perlitt, *Vatke und Wellhausen*, pp. 80-85.

35. Wellhausen, *Prolegomena*, p. 315; for other descriptions of the Priestly Code as a sign of
progress, see pp. 307, 337.

36. Wellhausen, *Prolegomena*, p. 346.

but certainly fixed and finished as an elaborate and minutely organised system, which comprises the sacred constitution of the congregation for all time to come... The people is there for the sake of the law, not the law for the sake of the people.[37]

Authentic Moses narratives, simply stated, should be *about* Moses, his actions, and the events of his career, not the law. Like biographical narratives from the Hellenistic tradition to the nineteenth century, the Jehovist tells this story while the Priestly editor smothers it with law.

The tension between the Jehovist and the Priestly tradition leaves a number of issues unresolved. If the Priestly Moses is not authentic, then can we know about him from the Jehovist, who after all is also a kind of redactor? What is the status of the earliest layers of tradition *as history*, and what are its defining characteristics, besides being less systematic than the Priestly source? At times Wellhausen speaks of the Jehovist redaction as 'legend' (*Sage*), and at other times as history. In the opening of his chapter on the Hexateuch, he contrasts the 'historical books' to the Hexateuch:

> When the subject treated is not history but legends about pre-historic times, the arrangement of the materials does not come with the materials themselves, but must arise out of the plan of a narrator... This, however, is not the place to attempt a history of the development of the Israelite legend. We are only to lay the foundation for such a work, by comparing the narrative of the Priestly Code with the Jehovistic one.[38]

The Hexateuch is thus not primarily history but legend, unlike the later historical books of the Bible. Wellhausen's task, only partially completed here, is to develop the 'history of tradition' (*eine Geschichte der Überlieferung*).[39] Wellhausen seeks to establish the historical circumstances of the legendary sources, not the events they record.

Elsewhere, though, Wellhausen describes the Jehovist source as 'originally a pure history-book'.[40] Wellhausen also implies that the Jehovist legends are more accurate and closer to historical reality, because they lie closer in time to the events: 'This precipitate of history [the Priestly Code], appearing as law at the beginning of the history, stifles and kills (*erdrückt und tötet*) the history itself'.[41] It is not clear, then, what if any distinction Wellhausen makes between legend and history. Legend is clearly understood as a genre of ancient tradition, but 'history' seems to connote both a genre ('history-book') as well as a truth-status. In addition to leaving the question of legend and history unresolved, Wellhausen also fails to provide a rich account of legend. This project became the focus of the history of religions school under Gunkel and Gressmann (see below).

In an article on Israel for *Encyclopedia Britannica*, written later than the *Prolegomena*, Wellhausen seems to amplify his claims to the history of Moses: 'He

---

37. Wellhausen, *Prolegomena*, p. 346.
38. Wellhausen, *Prolegomena*, p. 196 (p. 296 of the German edition).
39. Wellhausen, *Prolegomena*, p. 13 (p. 13 of the German edition).
40. Wellhausen, *Prolegomena*, p. 345.
41. Wellhausen, *Prolegomena*, p. 347 (p. 352 of the German edition).

undertook the responsibilities of their leader, and the confidence of success which he manifested was justified by the result. But it was not through any merit of his that the undertaking (of which he was the soul) prospered as it did… One whom the wind and sea obeyed had given him His aid.'[42] This Moses is presented simply as a matter of historical fact, with very little mention of documentary traditions and legends. He also appears to take on some of the trappings of the Priestly source so derided by Wellhausen in the *Prolegomena*. As the 'originator of the Torah in Israel', Moses 'gave a definite positive expression to their sense of nationality and their idea of God'.[43] The Moses of Pentateuchal history (as opposed to law) is 'manifestly trustworthy, and can only be explained as resting on actual facts'.[44] The Moses of Wellhausen's *Britannica* article seems not to suffer from the division between J and P.

At times Wellhausen seems to blur the distinction between legend and history or simply does not make it at all. The dominant dichotomy in his work, in any case, is the contrast between legend (or history) and *law*. Moses lies between the two, though Wellhausen seeks to recover the Jehovistic Moses, a great leader and founder of Torah, from the lifeless abstraction of Priestly codes. He speaks of this earlier Moses as a figure of legend and history, claiming always that he is more original than the Priestly Moses, and at times that he is historically factual (even though this claim goes beyond his own methodological boundaries).

Wellhausen's *Prolegemona* shaped generations of documentary scholarship primarily by its cogent and well-argued division of the Hexateuch into documentary sources. But it also reflected ideas about legend, history, and law that were common in Christian tradition and German idealism. Wellhausen was not only a clear-eyed proponent of a new approach to the Bible; he was also a partisan of Jehovist's narrative against the Priestly Code. In this way, Wellhausen's biases toward legend and against law challenge Frei's claim that historical scholarship looked past biblical narrative. Frei's dichotomy between history and narrative, in fact, resembles Wellhausen's contrast between law and legend: both oppositions prize narrative over forms that destroy it.

3. *Hugo Gressmann*

Hugo Gressmann's *Mose und seine Zeit* (1913) was an early and influential example of form-critical research on biblical legends, or the history of religions (*Religionsgeschichte*) school, as the work of Gressmann and Gunkel was sometimes described. Unlike Wellhausen, Gressmann placed an idealized, heroic Moses at the center of his project, even though he would subdivide the tradition into twenty-nine main traditions.[45] The book, whose subtitle is *A Commentary on the Moses-Legends*, follows a comparative method, linking the birth of Moses to legends of Sargon,

---

42. Wellhausen, 'Israel', in *Prolegomena*, pp. 429-548 (433).
43. Wellhausen, 'Israel', p. 434.
44. Wellhausen, 'Israel', p. 438.
45. Lemche suggests that Gressmann's portrait reflects 'imperial Germany's ideal of a public servant' ('Rachel and Lea', p. 45 n. 22).

Gilgamesh, and Osiris, for instance.[46] By analyzing the legends in this way, Gressmann (like Gunkel) believed he could make inferences about later literary history (e.g. *Sagensammlungen* and *Sagenkränze*) as well as the actual history of ancient Israel.

Gressmann sought to uncover the earliest sources of each legend, but he did not attempt to reintegrate them in a single narrative. At the same time, he accepted the broad outlines of the Pentateuch as historically accurate.[47] Although he derided Wellhausen's literary criticism for failing to reach the deepest layers of tradition,[48] he adopted Wellhausen's framework for identifying pentateuchal sources, even echoing his assessment of P as lifeless as compared to J: on the narrative of Moses' death, he writes, 'The Jahwist's description of Moses' death, as opposed to the spiritless legends (*geistlosen Sage*) of the Priestly redactor, sparkles with the living colors of popular storytelling'.[49]

In his effort to identify the historical kernel of biblical narrative through the analysis of legend (*Sage*), Gressmann embraces the methodological paradox of seeking fact through fiction. Beneath the biblical text lie the documentary sources, and beneath them lie the original legends which offer the best record of original events. Under the strain of all these layers, his analysis rests finally on the strength of creative analogies, vast erudition, and heuristic observations. His criteria for classifying and dating narrative material, however, suggest a simple evolution (common in German idealism and the other historians surveyed here) that moves from fairytales and myths to legends and history. In his discussion of Josephus' version of Moses' birth, for example, Gressmann writes,

> One can doubt whether old tradition is still present here; but if it should concern an earlier version, then it is certain that one has returned to the original. The received story has replaced the folktale motif (wise sayings of a new ruler) with a historical one (the weakening of the Hebrew people). But the heavy weight of the birth legend (*Geburtssage*), which carries a thoroughly folkloric (*märchenhaften*) character, is forced with its inner logic into conflict with the historical tendency (*historischen Zuges*), which would be felt like a foreign body and today still works that way.[50]

Gressmann's distinction between folktale, legend, and history thus forms a continuum from fiction to fact, as well as from shorter units to longer ones. In the case of Moses' birth, he says, we have not folktale but legend, because 'a historical person appears in the place of the folk hero'.[51] Here Gressmann appears to reach a

---

46.   H. Gressmann, *Mose und seine Zeit: Ein Kommentar zu den Mose-Sagen* (Göttingen: Vandenhoeck & Ruprecht, 1913), pp. 8-14.

47.   Douglas A. Knight, *Rediscovering the Traditions of Israel* (Missoula, MT: Scholars Press, 1975), pp. 85-6.

48.   H. Gressmann, *Albert Eichhorn und die Religionsgeschichtliche Schule* (Göttingen: Vandenhoeck & Ruprecht, 1914), pp. 31-37.

49.   Gressmann, *Mose und seine Zeit*, p. 343 (my translation).

50.   Gressmann, *Mose und seine Zeit*, pp. 6-7.

51.   Gressmann, *Mose und seine Zeit*, p. 7. See Benjamin's similar distinction between fairytale (folktale) and legend, which he attributes to Ernst Bloch ('The Storyteller', p. 103). Benjamin

historical conclusion with the same historical assumption—namely, that Moses is a historical person. The criterion for distinguishing folktale from legend and history is history itself rather than a set of formal criteria, though his comparative analysis of motifs and traditions suggests many possibilities. Legends are tied to specific historical persons and places, while a folktale 'can wander as an ownerless good from people to people'.[52]

Gressmann was not alone in his comparative study of biblical legends: he credited Eduard Meyer and Hermann Gunkel, as well as the psychologists Otto Rank and Wilhelm Wundt, as authorities. In a long essay on the directions in Old Testament research written over a decade after *Mose und seine Zeit*, Gressmann articulated the program and methods for the *Literaturgeschichte* school initiated by Gunkel and to which he belonged. The object of this research was the literary genre or form (*Gattung*), the basic unit underlying the collection of writings in the Bible. Gressmann insists that *Gattungsgeschichte* has little to do with folklore studies; rather, it studies 'the various forms of narrative and history-writing, lyric and prophecy, law and wise sayings according to their essence, situation, form, contents, tone, and history'.[53] The related field of story history (*Stoffgeschichte*), however, deals primarily with legend and folklore, and Gressmann observes that the boundary between *Stoffgeschichte* and world literature and folklore studies is blurred.[54]

In this self-conscious statement of method, Gressmann retains his grasp on historicity as the goal of *Literaturgeschichte* as well as the criterion according to which literary forms are classified. Yet he admits that the historical goal of this research remains unclear: Is it the people and events of biblical tradition or literary forms common to many ancient cultures? Is it written collections of legends or oral folk traditions?[55] These questions remain unanswered in the article, and they are rarely raised in *Mose und seine Zeit*. The historical conclusions toward which Gressmann reaches follow mainly from the assumption that the Moses story is comprised of many distinct legends, a genre that lies between folktale and history on a continuum of historicity.

Although by today's standards Gressmann may seem naïve and unrigorous, the *Religionsgeschichte* he and Gunkel developed sprang from the insight that ancient cultures and their literary forms are fundamentally different from modern ones. Gressmann criticized Wellhausen as well as the theological school of Ritschl for failing to recognize the distinctiveness and depth of ancient cultures.[56] In this way,

---

also distinguishes between fairytale and myth: 'The fairy tale tells us of the earliest arrangements that mankind made to shake off the nightmare which the myth had placed upon its chest' ('The Storyteller', p. 102).

52. H. Gressmann, 'Sage und Geschichte in den Patriarchersählungen', *ZAW* 28 (1910), pp. 1-34 (12, my translation).

53. H. Gressmann, 'Die Aufgaben der alttestamentlichen Forschung', *ZAW* 42 (1924), pp. 1-33 (26).

54. Gressmann, 'Die Aufgaben der alttestamentlichen Forschung', p. 28.

55. Gressmann, 'Die Aufgaben der alttestamentlichen Forschung', p. 29.

56. Gressmann, *Albert Eichhorn und die Religionsgeschichtliche Schule*, pp. 30-33, 48-50.

he contributed to the formation of religious studies as a discipline independent from Christian theology. Yet, like his contemporaries Wilhelm Dilthey and Ernst Troeltsch, Gressmann struggled with the epistemological implications of historical and cultural research. For Gressmann, the recognition of legends and folklore in the Bible led to rich comparative insights but also to historical arguments that could only be circular.

4. *Martin Noth*

In *A History of Pentateuchal Traditions* (*Überlieferungsgeschichte des Pentateuch*, 1948), Martin Noth dealt swiftly with the biblical Moses: except for the death and marriage episodes, no story about him can be considered authentic. Like Wellhausen, Noth analyzed the text into documentary sources, and although he placed P earlier than Wellhausen did, he echoed Wellhausen's description of the Priestly narrative: 'Its author lacks any direct connection with a narrative tradition that is still fresh and alive'.[57] Along with Gerhard von Rad, Noth studied with Albrecht Alt and became one of the most influential Pentateuch scholars of the twentieth century.

Like Wellhausen, Gressmann, and Alt before him, Noth sought to uncover the history behind the biblical text. He developed, for instance, the widely accepted theory that pre-monarchic Israel was divided into a federation ('amphictyony') of twelve distinct clans.[58] Though the goal of his research was to uncover history, he is primarily a scholar of the text. Most of his evidence is internal to the Bible, and most of his conclusions deal with the history of the text rather than the people and their land.[59] Key to Noth's research, therefore, were methods and criteria for distinguishing early materials from later ones, and history from legend. Though these methods were by no means original to Noth, they bear mentioning in the context of Moses' historicity: 'Only in the course of the elaboration and compilation of the Pentateuchal narrative did Moses gradually achieve the commanding position [*Herrschaft*] which he now holds in it... Outside of, and independent of, the Pentateuchal narrative, his name is mentioned with striking infrequency [*nur auffällig spärlich*] in the Old Testament.'[60] When he restates the point later, Noth makes it more strongly, saying it plays a 'negligible' role [*keine nennenswerte Rolle spielt*]

---

57. Martin Noth, *Exodus* (Philadelphia: Westminster Press, 1962), p. 16. The J narrative, by contrast, *is* 'fresh and alive' (*Exodus*, p. 15).

58. Nicholson, *The Pentateuch in the Twentieth Century*, p. 58.

59. One of the harshest criticisms of Noth's work is Thomas L. Thomson, 'Martin Noth and the History of Israel', in Steven McKenzie and M. Patrick Graham (eds.), *The History of Israel's Traditions* (JSOTSup, 182; Sheffield: Sheffield Academic Press, 1994), pp. 81-90, which accuses Noth of being a logician and theologian who wrote history without evidence. According to Thomson (pp. 85-87), Noth's work aspires to the same form-critical goals as Gunkel and collapses under its failure to define provide evidence for biblical *Sitze im Leben* and *Gattungen*.

60. Martin Noth, *A History of Pentateuchal Traditions* (trans. Bernhard W. Anderson; Chico, CA: Scholars Press, 1981), p. 156 (first published in German as *Überlieferungsgeschichte des Pentateuch* [Stuttgart: W. Kohlhammer, 1948], p. 172).

in the Old Testament.[61] Noth proceeds with a skeptical survey of Moses' role in several Pentateuchal 'themes', that is, major narrative divisions he distinguishes in the text.

Noth begins with the theme of 'revelation at Sinai'. Layer by layer, he strips this tradition of its latest versions (e.g. Deuteronomy), taking Moses away at the same time. In its earliest form, the E passages in Exod. 24.1-2, 9-11, Noth argues that since the seventy elders stand with Moses at Sinai, the narrative must have added Moses later, though he makes his argument by placing the burden of proof on the view that Moses was original: 'it cannot be maintained that the theme "revelation at Sinai" could never have been narrated without the figure of Moses'.[62] In other words, Moses can only be original to a tradition if he is essential to it, if the story could not be told without him.

Other criteria for authenticity emerge from the denial that Moses was original to the 'guidance out of Egypt' theme. First of all, Noth denies that Moses' Egyptian name or birth story indicates he was a primary part of the story. An Egyptian name could easily be assigned by later tradition (though Noth omits that the name is given a Hebrew etymology in Exod. 2); and the birth story, as Gressmann had shown, was stock in trade for ancient heroes. Noth's boldest and most ingenious point on this score, though, comes from an often-overlooked fact that certain leaders of the Hebrews ('foremen' or 'supervisors', שֹׁטְרִים) dealt with Pharaoh without Moses and 'fully sufficed in this theme as the spokesmen of the Israelites before Moses stepped into the position of leadership [*Führerstellung*] in the tradition'.[63]

The same kind of reasoning applies to the themes of 'guidance [*Führung*] in the wilderness', 'revelation at Sinai', and 'guidance into [*Hineinführung*] arable land'. In each case, the originality of Moses is dismissed because he is 'simply the spokesman of the people and the mediator of the divine answers, functions which he had to take on once he was on the point of assuming the general role of leader [*Führerrolle*]'.[64] On the other hand, Noth suggests that Moses may be an early or original part of the 'mountain of God' theme (which he separates from the Sinai theme), because this theme is closely tied to the stories of Moses' marriage to a Midianite, a story that is 'so little separable from his person that here at last we actually hit upon an original *Moses* tradition'.[65]

Two distinct processes—each of which is theoretically loaded—are assumed here by Noth: first, in order to be authentic, a legend must be so closely tied to its central character that it would not be possible without him or her. Second, traditions such as ancient Israelite religion and their attendant texts (i.e. the Pentateuch) ascribe greater and greater status and centrality to legendary figures as they develop. If real charismatic leaders did not exist, they must be invented.

61. Noth, *A History of Pentateuchal Traditions*, p. 159 (p. 175 of the German edition).
62. Noth, *A History of Pentateuchal Traditions*, p. 162.
63. Noth, *A History of Pentateuchal Traditions*, p. 163 (p. 180 of the German edition).
64. Noth, *A History of Pentateuchal Traditions*, p. 166 (p. 182 of the German edition). Indeed, if there is a common thread to the Moses traditions challenged by Noth, it is the role of Moses as a powerful leader [*Führer*].
65. Noth, *A History of Pentateuchal Traditions*, p. 168.

The second Moses tradition that Noth considers authentic (even though it appears only in D and P) is his burial, which because Moses is essential to it and because it includes the place name of Beth-Peor, strikes the 'bedrock of a historical reality [*geschichtlichen Sachverhaltes*] which is absolutely original'.[66] Since Moses must actually have died and been buried outside the arable land, Noth argues that the explanations for Moses' death as premature were secondary, and that he was never an essential part of the tradition: 'the more concrete information concerning the location of the grave site had priority over the general assertion that Moses did not enter the promised land... Moses entered into this narrative because his grave site lay on the path of the Israelites who were occupying the land.'[67]

At the heart of Noth's almost vehement dismissal of Moses seems to be a deep suspicion of legends and legendary figures.[68] Yet while he deprives the Moses legends of their historicity, he indirectly affirms their power. The kind of narrative he dismisses (and yet affirms) is much more like Hellenistic biographies and legends of great men than biblical narratives. Eva Osswald is thus right to derive from Noth's research the image of Moses as a 'charismatic leader' (*charismatischen Führer*) whose stature had a 'great ability to absorb' (*gewaltige Absorptionskraft*) later traditions.[69] Despite what Noth considered their inauthenticity, biblical tradition inventively and energetically ascribed the leadership of the people, from the Exodus to the settlement, to one individual. Though Moses didn't exist, the Israelites had to create him. Noth thus implies that religious traditions such as ancient Israel need strong human leaders. By defining authentic stories as those to whom the main figure is essential, Noth further reifies the category of legend, leaving out the possibility that the Bible could have its own characteristic narrative forms in which a human figure is present but not central, or in which human agency is joined to divine agency. Noth's history overwhelms legend only by making legend a basic human need for narrative coherence and human leadership.

5. *Gerhard von Rad*

For Gerhard von Rad, like Noth a student of Albrecht Alt, the pursuit of ancient Israelite history led to theology. His form-critical study of the Hexateuch, published in 1938, led him to focus increasingly on how source traditions came together to

---

66. Noth, *A History of Pentateuchal Traditions*, p. 173 (p. 190 of the German edition).
67. Noth, *A History of Pentateuchal Traditions*, p. 173. This reading also compels Noth to emend the text of Deut. 34.5-6 to read 'they buried' or 'he was buried' (see p. 172 n. 482).
68. Like Wellhausen, Noth distinguishes between myth and legend. In his commentary on the Moses birth story, which he regards as legend, he claims that the 'mythical element' is missing from this story. He further distinguishes the legend from history: 'The story certainly only arose once the historical figure of the man Moses had taken a firm place in the ancient Israelite tradition' (Noth, *Exodus*, p. 27).
69. Osswald, *Das Bild des Mose*, p. 340. Though Osswald accepts Noth's conclusions, she claims that 'Moses himself appears in the tradition, though raised above it by legend, as a form full of blood and life, whose character becomes accessible through certain somewhat increasingly connected themes' (p. 340, my translation).

serve a central theological purpose.[70] While von Rad's project remained historical, he expressed frustration with the source-critical approach alone.[71] He looked beyond the tension between legend and history with the category of *Heilsgeschichte*, a term he applied to the theological purposes of the Bible. For von Rad, the Hexateuch was a story of faith beginning with creation and reaching fulfillment with the settlement of land in Joshua. Indeed, the Old Testament as a whole deals primarily with 'Jahwe's relationship to Israel and the world…as a continuing divine activity in history'.[72]

Von Rad accepts the prevailing view that it is impossible to reconstruct the historical Moses.[73] More importantly, Moses is the glue holding together the narrative traditions of the Hexateuch. Nevertheless, each of the three documentary sources reflects a distinct theological perspective on Moses.[74] In the earliest strand of tradition, 'the Jahwist', Moses is a central figure, and yet, observes von Rad, 'it is striking how, *vis-à-vis* Jahweh and his action, Moses retires right into the background… Even at the miraculous crossing of the Red Sea, once Moses has intimated what is about to happen, he merely looks on with the rest of the Israelites (Exod. XIV.13 f).'[75] For J, Moses was 'no worker of miracles, no founder of a religion, and no military leader. He was an inspired shepherd whom Jahweh used to make his will known to men.'[76] But Moses grows in stature with the other documentary sources: in E he is a miracle worker and prophet; in P he is a holy man 'set apart for intercourse with Jahweh alone' (Exod. 24.34).[77] D presents the 'most rounded portrait of Moses, and probably has the most emphatic theological stamp upon it'. D also considers Moses to be a suffering mediator (Deut. 1; 3–4; 9; 34; Num. 12).[78]

By combining history with theology, von Rad resolves some difficulties and creates others with respect to Moses. On the one hand, he retains much of the scientific rigor of the traditio-historical school. And the advantage of *Heilsgeschichte* is that its claim to validity does not depend solely on historicity. In other words, theology offers an alternative to the disintegration of a biblical text that has been radically subdivided and labelled historically untrue. On the other hand, the commitment to theology, even as a term applied to the text, opens von Rad up to a number of harsh criticisms, such as an evolutionary theory of religion, an implied bias toward Christianity and credalism, an unwarranted level of abstraction, and

70. D.G. Spriggs, *Two Old Testament Theologies* (London: SCM Press, 1974), pp. 6-7.

71. Spriggs, *Two Old Testament Theologies*, p. 7.

72. Von Rad, *Old Testament Theology* (trans. D. Stalker; 2 vols.; New York: Harper & Row, 1962), I, p. 106. See the survey of von Rad's biblical theology in Leo Purdue, *The Collapse of History: Reconstructing Old Testament Theology* (Overtures to Biblical Theology; Minneapolis: Fortress Press, 1994), pp. 45-68.

73. Von Rad, *Old Testament Theology*, I, p. 291.

74. Von Rad, *Old Testament Theology*, I, p. 289.

75. Von Rad, *Old Testament Theology*, I, pp. 291-92.

76. Von Rad, *Old Testament Theology*, I, p. 292.

77. Von Rad, *Old Testament Theology*, I, pp. 293-96.

78. Von Rad, *Old Testament Theology*, I, pp. 294-95.

worst of all, the anachronistic projection of contemporary standards of history and theology onto the ancient world.[79]

The most basic problem of von Rad's historical theology is the relationship between history and theology. This tension emerges vividly in the discussion of Moses in the introduction to *Old Testament Theology* (1957):

> Historical investigation searches for a critically assured minimum—the kerygmatic picture tends towards a theological maximum. The fact that these two views of Israel's history are so divergent is one of the most serious burdens imposed today upon Biblical scholarship. No doubt historical investigation has a great deal that is true to say about the growth of this picture of the history which the faith of Israel painted: but the phenomenon of the faith itself, which speaks now of salvation, now of judgment, is beyond its power to explain.[80]

Even when the historian challenges biblical accounts, the theologian can make a coherent account of the faith statements of the people. The very act of combining literary sources and traditions, however flawed in historical terms, bears witness (kerygma) to the faith of Israel.

For von Rad, the development of ancient history-writing represents a remarkable step in the progress of human civilization, 'since its effects on the spiritual development of the whole of the West are incalculable'.[81] Like other biblical scholars, von Rad viewed history as a more advanced and extensive form in contrast to earlier traditions of 'miracle stories' (*Wundererzählungen*), which were episodic and disconnected from an overall history.[82] Biblical narrative, unlike critical scholarship, bears the traces of these stories, but von Rad insists on the historical value of the Bible nonetheless:

> The means by which this historical experience is made relevant for the time, the way in which it is mirrored forth in a variety of pictures, and in sagas in type form (*typisierenden Sagen*), are those adapted to the possibilities of expression (*Ausdrucksmöglichkeiten*) of an ancient people…in these traditional materials the historic and factual can no longer be detached from the spiritualising interpretation which pervades them all.[83]

Though the legends and miracle stories that infuse biblical narrative admittedly lack historicity, von Rad insists on their historical value in another sense—as records of Israel's faith.

The tension between history and theology plays out in von Rad's analysis of Moses:

---

79. Spriggs, *Two Old Testament Theologies*, pp. 44-54. Similar charges, especially evolutionism and a Christian theological bias, were levelled at Wellhausen; see Perlitt, *Vatke und Wellhausen*, pp. 153-57.

80. Von Rad, *Old Testament Theology*, I, p. 108.

81. Von Rad, *Old Testament Theology*, I, p. 50.

82. Von Rad, *Old Testament Theology*, I, p. 50; *Theologie des Alten Testaments* (2 vols.; Munich: Chr. Kaiser Verlag, 1987), I, p. 64.

83. Von Rad, *Old Testament Theology*, I, p. 108 (p. 121 of the first volume of the German edition).

> In practically all the accounts of the period from the sojourn in Egypt down to the
> arrival in the land east of the Jordan, the reader encounters Moses… If the reader
> were not constantly meeting with him, the renowned leader, the man of God, the
> warrior, etc., the whole of what is presented to us in the documentary sources as a
> connected narrative would disintegrate into a series of rather incoherent episodes
> (*ziemlich beziehungslosen Episoden*).[84]

Von Rad concedes that this narrative continuity may be the later result of 'a
confessional arrangement of different complexes of tradition'. He refers pointedly
to Noth's conclusion that Moses may not be original to most Pentateuch traditions,
but he responds as follows:

> It is not possible to examine this thesis here—indeed, the very nature of the case
> no longer admits the possibility of any exact answer to the question. But even
> those who believe that the historical element can be regarded as broader and more
> firmly founded than this are, for all that, far from gaining the picture of Moses as
> the founder of a religion so urgently sought by the modern reader. In every case
> they only reach very ancient individual traditions (*sehr alte Einzelüberlieferungen*)
> which are difficult to reconcile with one another. Here too it is a constant surprise
> to observe how greatly interest in the sacral function of Moses, his 'office', out-
> weighs interest in his person; and along with this, the old narrators are already
> haunted by an interest directed mainly to something relevant to their own time
> (*etwas ihnen gegenwärtiges*) and not merely to the historical or biographical.[85]

Instead of challenging Noth's conclusions directly, von Rad brackets the question
of historicity. The focus of his research becomes the confessional (i.e. theological)
structure of the Hexateuch. From this point of view, it is the 'sacral function' and
'office' of Moses that count. The questions of whether Moses lived, who he was,
when he lived, and what he did, are 'merely' historical and biographical.

Here von Rad shifts from history to the theological process of drawing sources
together. With this he gives up—partly at least—the search for the historical
Moses, a cherished goal of scholars since the eighteenth century as well as of 'the
modern reader'. The origins of Moses (and, by implication, ancient Israel itself) lie
beyond the scope of historians, despite the Romantic pursuit of origins. The more
interesting issue, suggests von Rad, is how these ancient traditions were combined
in the theological service of *Heilsgeschichte*.

Von Rad and Noth agree that the historical Moses lies beyond the reach of biblical research and that his roles and importance increase with the formation of the
Pentateuch (or Hexateuch). Where Noth and von Rad differ is how they evaluate
this uncertainty. For Noth the point seems to be the critical debunking of unques-
tioned tradition. The high level of suspicion of toward Moses legends yields the
suggestion that with Moses, and indeed the Pentateuch itself, we have a mixture of
incongruous sources and traditions: 'Now, since the sources were combined through

---

84. Von Rad, *Old Testament Theology*, I, p. 13 (p. 27 of the first volume of the German
edition).

85. Von Rad, *Old Testament Theology*, I, p. 14 (p. 28 of the first volume of the German
edition).

a purely literary procedure of addition, it is clear that the result was simply a compilation in which not only the narrative materials but also the theological concerns
are juxtaposed and interwoven with one another just as plainly and incongruously
as the individual sources had presented them'.[86] Like the Moses traditions, the
Pentateuch itself fails to meet the standards of coherence and historical authenticity.

Von Rad's account of the Moses traditions meets the challenge of historical
uncertainty and incoherence with the notion of *Heilsgeschichte* and the history of
its formation. By concentrating on the formation of biblical tradition rather than its
origins, von Rad anticipated the canonical criticism of Brevard Childs, whose work
also combines theological and historical interests.[87] In this way, von Rad resolved
the tension between legend and history, but it was quickly replaced by the new and
equally vexing tension between theology and history.

6. *Martin Buber*

Martin Buber's *Moses* (1944/46) diverges from the scholarly projects discussed
thus far, and yet it directly addresses the challenge of legend and history. In fact,
Buber begins his Preface with the question of Moses' historicity. Quoting Eduard
Meyer's 1906 claim that Moses was not a historical figure, Buber writes:

> It is precisely this, the description of Moses as a concrete individuality and the
> demonstration of what he created and what his historical work was, that I have
> made my purpose in this book; on the, to me, obvious basis of unprejudiced criti-
> cal investigation, dependent neither on the religious tradition nor on the theories of
> scholarly turns of thought.[88]

Buber's claim to an 'unprejudiced critical investigation' suggests the scientific rigor
of the historical-critical scholars, but his next phrase undercuts that assumption.
The study of Moses will not depend on religion or 'theories of scholarly turns of
thought'. In fact, Buber's study is a unique hybrid of his own philosophical and
biblical research applied to the biblical texts about Moses. In structure and method,
the book recalls Gressmann more than the other scholars considered here, dividing the Moses traditions into twenty-one distinct sections. Yet Buber is critical of

86. Noth, *A History of Pentateuchal Traditions*, p. 250. Noth concedes that the juxtaposition
of sources in the Pentateuch is 'admirably compact', and the juxtaposition of sources can sometimes be 'theologically significant', as in the case of the two creation stories of Genesis, but the
overall whole is not greater than the sum of its parts (pp. 250-51). The tone of Noth's commentary
on Exodus is, however, a bit more congenial: here he speaks of Exodus as part of a larger whole,
even at the stage of oral transmission. As for the distinct sources within Exodus, he describes the
book 'as it were a fabric, skillfully woven from a series of threads, and the only satisfactory way of
analysing a fabric is to keep firmly in sight the threads of which it is made up' (pp. 10, 12, 18).
87. John Barton makes this point in 'Gerhard von Rad on the World-View of Early Israel',
Journal of Theological Studies 35 (1984), pp. 301-23 (310).
88. Martin Buber, *Moses*, p. vii. See Buber's acknowledgment of Auerbach's *Moses*, which he
reviewed in manuscript before his book was published (see pp. x-xi).

Gressmann's book, which 'exhausted itself in an analysis, which frequently led to entirely erroneous results, of the various strata of saga-growth'.[89]

Like von Rad, Buber concedes that the continuity of biblical narrative is impossible in light of historical scholarship. Buber admits that each of the traditions he presents stands alone. 'Nevertheless', he writes, his study 'could endeavour to indicate a certain temporal sequence in connection with Biblical composition. Though this may not afford any pragmatic connection, it does offer the picture of a sequence of events, in which a great process of the history of the spirit manifests itself as though in visible members.'[90] Against the powerful tide of documentary fragmentation, Buber offers a fragile, even spiritual 'picture' of a sequence.

What emerges from Buber's studies, in fact, is the image of a heroic individual. Moses is a tragic hero, a brilliant mythmaker, and writer: 'If we take away all the legendary traits of Moses we must still recognize him as the spiritual force in which the Ancient Orient concentrated itself at its close and surmounted itself'.[91] While this portrait itself is not highly original, Buber's reflections on method are, especially in the context of the tension between legend and history. In his first chapter, 'Saga and History', Buber presents a set of meta-historical reflections that challenge the distinction between legend and history.[92] In a survey of scholarship on the nature of 'saga', Buber agrees that historical scholarship must be critical and reductive: 'It must remove layer after layer from the images as set before it, in order to arrive at the earliest of all'.[93] Once uncovered, this early layer of tradition reveals not 'what really happened' but rather how some event affected a group of people: 'we become conscious of the saga-creating ardour with which the people received the tremendous event and transmitted it to a moulding memory'.[94]

The implications of Buber's method for biblical tradition are significant: 'whether Sinai was a volcano cannot be determined historically, nor is it historically relevant'. But the biblical tradition of Sinai, including Moses, God, and covenant,

> is essentially a historical process, historical in the deepest sense; it is historical because it derives from historical connections and sets off fresh historical connections. When faced by such tales it is wrong to talk of a 'historicization of myth'; it might be preferable to describe them as a mythisation of history, while remembering that here, unlike the concept familiar in the science of religion, myth means nothing other than the report by ardent enthusiasts of that which has befallen them.[95]

89. Buber, *Moses*, p. vii. See Benyamin Uffenheimer, 'Buber and Modern Biblical Scholarship', in Haim Gordon and Jochanon Bloch (eds.), *Martin Buber: A Centenary Volume* (New York: Ktav, 1984), pp. 163-211 (166-68).

90. Buber, *Moses*, p. viii. In some ways, Buber's approach anticipates George W. Coats' more recent attempt to find unity within textual diversity by describing the Moses narratives as heroic saga: George W. Coats, 'The Moses Narratives as Heroic Saga', in *idem* (ed.), *Saga Legend Tale Novella Fable*, pp. 33-44; and *idem*, *Moses: Heroic Man, Man of God* (JSOTSup, 57; Sheffield: JSOT Press, 1988).

91. Buber, *Moses*, p. 85; see also pp. 59, 127.

92. The title echoes Gressmann's 'Sage und Geschichte', pp. 1-34.

93. Buber, *Moses*, p. 16.

94. Buber, *Moses*, p. 16.

95. Buber, *Moses*, p. 17.

Buber's task, then, is to recognize which layers of tradition are closest to the events that generated them and which come from later attempts to elaborate them, for while historical method makes it nearly impossible to verify the events themselves, the layers of saga are potentially available to critical analysis. In this way, his approach echoes Wellhausen's and Gressmann's, though Buber directs his book against their most positivistic followers. Buber's humanism and holism differ from theirs, but the debt to German idealism is clear.

Buber's approach becomes clear, for example, in the discussion of the plagues. In an echo of his preface, Buber rejects two opposing approaches: 'that of the person accepting traditions entire, holding that everything written here records something that has happened in fact in some specific place at some specific time; and that of the self-assured professional scholar who proposes to treat everything recorded here as literature pure and simple'.[96] Buber's alternative, a kind of *via media* between these extremes, is to ask what events might have triggered the long process of tradition-formation that yielded the narrative as it appears in the Bible: 'It is certainly not a chronicle which we have to work on, but it is equally not imaginative poesy; it is a historical saga'.[97]

Buber wishes to make Moses relevant to the present; Moses is a 'living and effective force at all times; and that is what places him thus afresh in our own day [1944], which possibly requires him more than any earlier day has ever done'.[98] As he argues at length in his 1936 essay, 'People of Today and the Jewish Bible', which he published in a collection about the translation of the Bible into German,[99] the Bible offers a solution to the rootlessness and religious disintegration of modern life. Buber proposes a process of reading the Bible as if for the first time, correlating its reports of revelation, creation, and redemption to the personal experience of the reader.[100]

The process Buber describes closely follows the hermeneutical method of his teacher, Wilhelm Dilthey. For Dilthey, it was possible to transcend one worldview (*Weltanschauung*) by encountering another; the bond between the two was experience. Beyond the fragmentation of historical scholarship, promised Dilthey, lay the possibility of genuine understanding (*Verstehen*). Dilthey was also a leading influence on von Rad's biblical theology of actualization, the capacity of biblical texts to remain present and vital for successive generations.[101] According to this

96. Buber, *Moses*, p. 61.
97. Buber, *Moses*, p. 61.
98. Buber, *Moses*, p. x.
99. M. Buber and Franz Rosenzweig, *Die Schrift und ihre Verdeutschung* (Berlin: Schocken Books, 1936).
100. See Brian Britt, 'Romantic Roots of the Debate on the Buber-Rosenzweig Bible', *Prooftexts* 20 (2000), pp. 262-89.
101. A. Josef Greig, 'Some Formative Aspects in the Development of Gerhard von Rad's Idea of History', *Andrews University Seminary Studies* 16 (1978), pp. 313-31 (324-30). James Groves, however, attributes the concept of actualization mainly to Herder, failing to note what is arguably the more immediate influence of Dilthey (*Actualization and Interpretation in the Old Testament* [Atlanta: Scholars Press, 1987], pp. 13-16).

view, YHWH's words and actions constitute a message 'so living and actual for each moment that it accompanied her [Israel] on her journey through time, interpreting itself afresh to every generation, and informing every generation what it had to do'.[102] For Buber and von Rad, the hermeneutics of Dilthey offered a bridge between the ancient biblical world in the experience and understanding of the individual subject. But insofar as their projects were historical as well as hermeneutical, questions of evidence remained unanswered. Buber and von Rad made the Bible compelling for modern readers, but they did not convincingly account for the past to the present. Conceding to Noth and others that the historical Moses lay beyond contemporary view, von Rad and Buber reconstructed him, arguably in their own images, out of theology and legend.

7. Conclusion

Like centuries of believers before them, Buber and von Rad sought to bring Moses and the Bible into the present, but to do so they faced the challenge of historical scholarship, which had decisively fragmented and historicized the Bible. Their Diltheyan efforts to make the ancient tradition speak to the present would appear to set them apart from Wellhausen, Gressmann, and Noth, whose declared purpose was to discover the historical roots of the Bible. But even these historians—inadvertently perhaps—made the Bible contemporary by their assumptions, methods, and conclusions. They shared the general portrait of Moses found among German idealists, which depicted him as a solitary individual and legendary hero who delivered his people and gave them the law, a figure closer to the Moses of Philo and Josephus than the Bible.

All five scholars distinguished between history and legend and offered similar accounts of the two categories. History represents the discipline of uncovering real events and the narrative that reports it. Legend is a more primitive form that comprises one of the building blocks of biblical tradition. Legend combines folklore (or myth) and history to relate the great deeds of the hero of a particular people (*Volk*). As the pivotal figure between Genesis and the history books, Moses combines myth and history to epitomize the German idealist hero. Moses is the lynchpin of biblical tradition, a liminal figure *par excellence*.[103] For biblical scholars, Moses embodies legend itself. Whatever their status *vis-à-vis* history, legends of Moses present him as the central figure in a specific, heroic narrative. Recognizing the literary fragmentation of the Pentateuch, the scholars discussed here sought in different ways to recover the legendary strata within its component parts. Although Buber and von Rad attempted more holistic approaches, it was not until the development of canonical criticism, especially under Brevard Childs, that the final shape of biblical texts became the primary object of modern scholarly study.

---

102. Von Rad, *Old Testament Theology*, I, p. 112.
103. Compare Jan Assmann's idea of 'Mosaic distinction', in *idem*, *Moses the Egyptian* (Cambridge, MA: Harvard University Press, 1997).

Interlude

BIBLICAL TEXT,
BIBLICAL TRADITION

Chapter 4

CONCEALMENT, REVELATION, AND GENDER:
THE VEIL OF MOSES IN THE BIBLE AND IN CHRISTIAN ART*

Written texts are not the only or best carriers of tradition. From late antiquity on-
ward, images based on the Bible proliferated to form an important body of interpretive traditions. Many scholars of literature and history have turned recently to
the study of images; Mieke Bal, for instance, argues that reading and seeing are
closely related, and that images are 'texts'. Visual details, such as the nail and hole
in a painting by Rembrandt, can call 'attention to the work of representation' and
prompt a narrative process of 'reading'.[1] Long before film and mass printing, visual
images of Moses constituted a kind of popular culture that both eclipsed and preserved biblical tradition.

This chapter examines several texts about Moses' veil (Exod. 34.29-35) in the
Bible and in Christian art. I argue that the veil of Moses presents a compelling
model of revelation neglected and even avoided by religious traditions. My analysis
begins with the ancient Hebrew text, continues to Paul and post-biblical interpretation, and then shifts to images in Christian art that depict Moses and two female
figures: Synagogue and Nature. While the Exodus story seems to concern divine
communication through the prophet Moses, Christian interpreters (following Paul)
associate the veil with Jewish blindness to the gospel. In visual art, the veil of
Moses is sometimes associated with a more common image: the allegorical female
Synagogue, who wears a blindfold. Few interpreters in Jewish or Christian tradition
have explored the religious richness of Moses' veil, a biblical episode that alternates between presence and absence, concealment and revelation.

To 'read' the veil in writing and images is thus to 'read' texts about revelation.
Worn after his conferences with God and the people of Israel, the veil signifies
Moses' work as a prophet. But if the face is essential to personal identity,[2] then the
veil dissociates Moses from his prophetic office. For post-biblical tradition, this
separation was too high a price to pay for fidelity to biblical tradition. The veil was

* A version of this chapter, bearing the same title, originally appeared in *Religion and the Arts* 7.3 (2003), pp. 227-73.

1. Mieke Bal, *Reading Rembrandt: Beyond the Word-Image Opposition* (New York: Cambridge University Press, 1991), pp. 3-4. The view is echoed by W.J.T. Mitchell, *Picture Theory*
(Chicago: University of Chicago Press, 1994), pp. 94-95: 'all arts are "composite" arts (both text
and image)'; see also his *Iconology* (Chicago: University of Chicago Press, 1986).

2. Excerpt from Emmanuel Levinas' *Time and the Other*, in Seán Hand (ed.), *The Levinas
Reader* (Cambridge: Basil Blackwell, 1989), pp. 37-58 (44-49).

either ignored, removed, or marked as a punishment. Through a survey of these traditions of the veil, I will suggest that the repression of the veil entails a repression
of text and textuality, and that the repressed veil and the text nevertheless resurface
in transformed ways, especially in veiled female figures.[3]

It seems odd for an episode so striking and central in the Bible—the giving of the
law and renewal of covenant after the golden calf episode—to find so little mention
in commentaries and religious art.[4] The omission is particularly strange for Christian art, which includes many images of the horns or beams of light on Moses' face,
a topos from the same passage of Exodus. The veil episode, as I have argued elsewhere, can be linked to other biblical stories about the concealment or restraint of
the prophet during a covenantal crisis.[5] Yet, with the exception of a few Jewish
commentaries, most written and pictorial references to the veil of Moses follow
Paul's reference in 2 Corinthians 3, which opposes Moses and Jesus in a brilliant
typological move:

> Now if the ministry of death, carved in letters on stone, came in glory so that the
> people of Israel could not gaze at Moses' face because of the glory of his face, a
> glory now abolished, how much more will the ministry of the Spirit come in
> glory?... Since we have such a hope, we are very bold, not like Moses, who put a
> veil [κάλυμμα, Lat. *velamen*] over his face to keep the people of Israel from gazing
> at the end of the glory that was being set aside. But their minds were hardened; for
> to this day, when they hear the reading of the old covenant, that same veil remains
> unlifted [μη ἀνακαλυπτόμενον, Lat. *manet non revelatum*], because only through
> Christ is it abolished. Yes, to this day whenever Moses is read, a veil lies over their
> minds; but when one turns to the Lord, the veil is removed. (2 Cor. 3.7-16)

Though there are debates on specific elements of this passage,[6] the general point is
clear: Jesus and his followers, through their spiritual boldness, surpass the Jewish

---

3.   Let me define text as any phenomenon subject to reading, where reading is a set of de-
coding and interpretive practices rooted in Western literary traditions. This notion has roots in the
biblical idea of Torah as life (Deut. 32.47), Renaissance ideas of the 'Book of Nature', Wilhelm
Dilthey's hermeneutics, and Roland Barthes' landmark essay, 'From Work to Text' (in Josué
Harari [ed.], *Textual Strategies* [Ithaca, NY: Cornell University Press, 1979], pp. 73-81). 'Text' in
this sense is the center of much work in religion and literature, and it includes pictures, music,
films, and television broadcasts. See my 'Apology for the Text', *Literature and Theology* 14
(2000), pp. 412-29.

4.   My survey of commentaries includes the following textual databases: CETEDOC, Latin,
and Greek, as well as several rabbinic sources and recent scholarship. My survey of art comes
primarily from the iconographic files of the Index of Christian Art in Princeton, which includes
about eight card catalogue drawers on images of Moses. The Index includes works from the first to
the fourteenth centuries. I have also searched the Jerusalem Index of Jewish Art, edited by Bezalel
Narkiss. In addition, I have searched scholarly and iconographic resources at Harvard University,
the University of Virginia, and Virginia Tech.

5.   See my 'Prophetic Concealment in a Biblical Type Scene', *CBQ* 64 (2002), pp. 37-58,
where I argue that prophetic concealment is a narrative element in many biblical episodes of covenant crisis and prophetic recommissioning. The elements of this type scene are: crisis, theophany
and recommissioning (or commissioning) of the prophet, and divine plan and its implementation.

6.   See, e.g., Linda Belleville, *Reflections of Glory: Paul's Polemical Use of the Moses-Doxa
Tradition in 2 Corinthians 3.1-18* (JSOTSup, 52; Sheffield: JSOT Press, 1991), pp. 13-23.

tradition of Moses and the law. When commentaries and other Christian works cite this scene, the Pauline message remains fairly stable and clear. But artistic depictions of the veil of Moses have a vividness that may inadvertently reflect the spirit of Exodus more than Paul's letter.

Of the few documentary and artistic renderings of Moses' veil, most of them, following Paul, take the veil off, so to speak. Why is there such reluctance to show Moses with a veil on his face? If I am correct that the central concern of the Exodus episode is Moses' role as prophet, then the veil introduces an element of silence and disempowerment at the very moment when Moses is supposed to be reinstating the covenant and his own authority as a prophet. Whatever the veil means, my assumption is that its role in Exodus and subsequent tradition reflects significantly on ideas of revelation. I suggest that the avoidance of the veil by interpreters and artists bespeaks anxiety before the veil. In Christian art, this anxiety takes a number of forms, especially the preference to show the veil only partly covering Moses' face, as well as an apparent preference to depict the Pauline veil on the female allegorical figure of Synagogue. In short, most accounts of Moses' veil either disparage him or the Israelites; few consider the possibility that the veil is part of a process of revelation.

1. *The Exodus Episode*

The wearing of a veil by Moses in Exod. 34.29-35 has received much less attention from commentators and scholars than the well-known glowing (or disfigured) face in the same scene.[7] There has been little analysis of the text's literary structure and even less attention to the veil. But in the context of narrative traditions about prophecy, the episode plays on the dynamics of writing and speaking, as well as revealing and concealing, in divine–human communication. These dynamics call attention to the larger issue of revelation.

Exodus 32–34 is exceptional among other scenes of theophany in Exodus. In Exod. 3.6, Moses hides his face, 'for he was afraid to look at God'. And while Moses and the elders do see God in Exodus 24, their vision seems to be limited to the feet and pavement. After that moment, only Moses continues up the mountain where he sees the fiery appearance of God. In Exodus 32–34, by contrast, Moses speaks to God 'face to face, as one speaks to a friend' (33.11, though see the contrary implication in 33.21).[8]

---

7. The famous problem of Moses' shining or disfigured face, which was also misunderstood by Jerome and others to mean 'horns of light', has overshadowed the equally vexing issue of the veil or mask. Hugo Gressmann and others have traced the veil back to cultic mask traditions, though others have noted how the text's present form rules out such a reading (*Mose und seine Zeit*, pp. 246-47). In all the discussion of these obscure references, though, there has been little analysis of the text's literary structure and even less attention to the veil. For a thorough review of the literature, see William H. Propp, 'The Skin of Moses' Face—Transfigured or Disfigured?', *CBQ* 49 (1987), pp. 375-86 (375 n. 1).
8. The phrase is repeated in Deut. 34.10.

Following the scenes of the golden calf and the reinscription of the tablets, the veil episode is part of the reordering of the community and the renewal of the cove-nant.[9] The frightening and miraculous transformation of Moses' face, and its subsequent concealment by a veil, constitute a kind of theophany. Just as the face of God is usually off-limits to Moses (with the exceptions of Exod. 33.11 and Deut. 34.10), so the face of Moses is sometimes off-limits to the people. Like the Mesopotamian stories of heavenly ascent, the episode presents a person transformed by contact with the divine.[10] A number of texts (e.g. Num. 6.25; Eccl. 8.1; Pss. 31.17; 67.2) describe divine favor idiomatically as causing the face to shine (הֵאִיר פָּנָיו).[11] While these parallels may not bear directly on Moses' transformed face, they offer suggestive evidence that theophany and divine enlightenment can appear on the human face. The entire episode concerns revelation and covenant between God and people through the mediation of Moses; the episode of the veil compresses these issues into a stunning narrative of speech, concealment, and revelation.

By dwelling more on *how* revelation takes place than on *what* is revealed, the episode calls attention to the written and spoken communication between God, Moses, and Israel. The episode is thus predominantly about revelation in speech and writing. The veil serves to set apart prophetic speech, and it suggests the routinization of theophany and a dynamic of revealing and concealing.

The purpose of the veil is not obvious. Its presence can hardly be overlooked, since biblical narrative makes very sparing use of description to make the story or characters more vivid. Unlike some scenes of theophany, there is no respectful or protective barrier between Moses and YHWH (cf. Exod. 19; 24). Nor does the veil divide the speaking prophet from people. The text clearly states that Moses removes the veil when he speaks with YHWH or the people. It is thus difficult to suggest, as some have done, that the veil is a kind of cultic mask (like the horns of Zedekiah in 1 Kgs 22.10-12) worn to signify the prophet's work.[12] Unlike Parson Hooper in Hawthorne's 'The Minister's Black Veil', Moses wears the veil when he

---

9. See Thomas Dozeman, *God on the Mountain* (Atlanta: Scholars Press, 1989), p. 172. Dozeman (n. 58) also suggests that the shining face is a mirror of divine כָּבֹד ('glory'). See also Dozeman's more recent treatment in: 'Masking Moses and Mosaic Authority in Torah', *JBL* 119 (2000), pp. 21-45.

10. 'Similar imagery was in use in ancient Mesopotamia, where an encompassing, awe-inspiring luminosity known as *melammu* was taken to be characteristic attribute of divinity' (Nahum Sarna, *Exodus: The Traditional Hebrew Text with the New JPS Translation* [Philadelphia: Jewish Publication Society of America, 1991], p. 221). See Menahem Haran, 'The Shining of Moses' Face: A Case Study in Biblical and Ancient Near Eastern Iconography', in W. Barrick and John Spencer (eds.), *In the Shelter of Elyon* (JSOTSup, 31; Sheffield: JSOT Press, 1984), pp. 167-68.

11. See, e.g., Eccl. 8.1. See C.L. Seow, *Ecclesiastes: A New Translation with Introduction and Commentary* (AB, 18C; Garden City, NY: Doubleday, 1997), pp. 277-78 n. 1. See also Hab. 3.4.

12. Gressmann, *Moses und seine Zeit*, pp. 249-51. On Zedekiah's horned mask, see Paul Dion, 'The Horned Prophet (1 Kings 22.11)', *VT* 49 (1999), pp. 259-60. The most exhaustive recent study of Moses' veil is Thomas Dozeman, 'Masking Moses and Mosaic Authority in Torah', *JBL* 119 (2000), pp. 21-45. Dozeman's argument considers the religious function of the veil or mask in the biblical and cultic context, whereas my emphasis lies on the significance of the veil for ideas of revelation and scripture in biblical and post-biblical settings.

is *not* performing his duties. The biblical narrator implies that the veil is designed to counteract the Israelites' fear of Moses' transformed face, but since the veil is removed when Moses addresses them, the fear would be allayed only some of the time.

The narrator makes it clear that the veil is worn when Moses is 'in his capacity as a private individual', as Nahum Sarna puts it, or off-duty, so to speak.[13] It divides times when Moses performs as a prophet from other times. The veil is thus a temporal rather than a spatial barrier between the sacred and the ordinary. When he wears the veil, there is no prophecy, no divine revelation.[14] The covered prophet is a silent prophet.

A close look at the episode reveals a focus on speech and patterns of repetition:

> 27: YHWH said to Moses, 'Write these words; in accordance with these words I have made a covenant with you and with Israel'.
> 28: And he was there with YHWH forty days and forty nights; he ate no bread and drank no water; and he wrote on the tablets the words of the covenant, the ten words.
> 29: Moses came down from Mt Sinai. As he came down from the mountain with the two tablets of the testimony in his hand, Moses did not know that the skin of his face shone because he had been speaking with YHWH.
> 30: When Aaron and all the Israelites saw Moses, his face was shining, and they were afraid of him.
> 31: But Moses called to them; and Aaron and all the leaders of the congregation returned to him, and Moses spoke to them.
> 32: After that all the Israelites gathered, and he commanded them everything that YHWH had said to him on Mt Sinai.
> 33: And when Moses had finished talking to them, he put a veil on his face.
> 34: But when Moses would come before YHWH to speak with him, he removed the veil until he came out; and he would go back and tell the Israelites what he had been commanded.
> 35: And when the Israelites saw that the face of Moses was shining, Moses returned the veil to his face until he came to speak to him.

The episode may be schematized as follows:

1. Theophany, speech and writing, and return (vv. 27-28)
2. Shining face (קרן עור) linked to speech (בדברו אתו) (v. 29)
3. Shining face (קרן עור) seen (v. 30)
4. Speech (vv. 31-32)
5. Veil (מסוה) linked to speech (vv. 33-34)
6. Shining face (קרן עור) seen (v. 35, echoing v. 30)
7. Veil (מסוה) linked to speech (v. 35, echoing vv. 33-34)

The turning-point in the episode comes when Moses puts on the veil in v. 33. Like the theophany in 1 Kings 19 and a number of other biblical scenes in which the prophet is concealed, the veil lies at the center of the episode, framed before and

13. Sarna, *Exodus*, p. 221.
14. Cf. Ezek. 3–4.

after by speech.[15] The shining face and the veil are arguably secondary, however, to the ongoing speech among Moses, God, and people; by marking and ritualizing the people's fear of Moses' face, the veil serves to continue the communication (vv. 33-35). The veil and the shining face are interwoven with speech, a juxtaposition that suggests they are intrinsic to the process of revelation. The episode fits the traditional hero narrative pattern of withdrawal and return, with a particular focus on communication. Having ascended the mountain, Moses returns to renew and implement the covenant. The veil and shining face may draw attention away from these communicative tasks, but they are emphasized in the text through repetition.[16]

2. *Post-Biblical Legacy/History of Interpretation*

a. *Jewish Interpretation*

The most important post-biblical mention of the veil is 2 Corinthians 3, where Paul contrasts the veil of Moses to the bold unveiling effected by Christ.[17] While it is easy to see why most subsequent Christian references more or less paraphrase Paul's brilliant re-reading, it is less clear why Jewish interpreters make so little reference to the veil. Linda Belleville suggests that because מסוה is a *hapax legomenon* in the Bible, it stimulated very little of the verbal association so essential to rabbinic discourse.[18] This explanation is certainly plausible, but I will also suggest that the veil has been an unappealing puzzle because it alienates and silences Moses in ways that seem less tied to morality than to the ambiguous dynamics of divine–human communication.

Philo makes no mention of the veil and neither does Josephus, but Pseudo-Philo (in *Biblical Antiquities*) mentions the veil just before the golden calf incident. In this retelling, the reason for the veil is unclear, since bright light only makes Moses difficult to recognize. Terror is not mentioned: 'And Moses came down…the light of his face overcame the brightness of the sun and moon and he knew it not. And it was so, when he came down to the children of Israel, they saw him and knew him not.' (The failure to recognize Moses here evokes the story of Joseph.) 'And it

15. See my 'Prophetic Concealment in a Biblical Type Scene'.

16. Repetition can be a vehicle of meaning in the Bible: see Burke O. Long, *1 Kings with an Introduction to Historical Literature* (Grand Rapids: Eerdmans, 1984), p. 202; and my 'Deut. 31–32 as a Textual Memorial', *BibInt* 8 (2000), pp. 358-74. See Chapter 5 for a discussion of whether Moses' speaking ability, described as limited in Exod. 4, is restored by the ophany in Exod. 34 (note the role of Aaron in both texts).

17. The Septuagint (LXX) translates מסוה as κάλυμμα, which is also the term used for a tabernacle screen (מסך) in Exod. 27.16. The curtain of the temple, however, is indicated by another term: פרכת, which becomes καταπέτασμα in LXX (Exod. 26.31). Incidentally, Philo uses both terms to describe the screen in Exod. 27 (*Moses*, p. 492). This is the term used for the temple curtain that tears in the New Testament passion narrative (Mk 15.38). In Latin, however, both Greek terms (κάλυμμα and καταπέτασμα) are translated as *velamen*, which would make the typological link between the veil of Moses and the veil of the temple easy. The veil also becomes a symbol of Jewish–Christian separation: for example, the temple curtain, found in Bonaventure. See Benjamin E. Scolnic, 'Moses and the Horns of Power', *Judaism* 40 (1991), pp. 569-79 (578).

18. Belleville, *Reflections of Glory*, p. 69 n. 1.

came to pass after that, when Moses knew that his face was become glorious, he made him a veil to cover his face.'[19]

Numbers Rabbah, an early rabbinic text, suggests that the veil is a form of punishment (awe) for sin: 'As long as a man refrains from sin he is an object of awe and fear. The moment he sins he is himself subject to awe and fear... As soon as they had sinned, however, they could not even look at the face of the intermediary.'[20] A similar tone prevails in another early midrash, *Pesikta Rabbati*:

> Even as a man cannot look at the sun as it rises, so no man could look at Moses, until Moses put a veil over his face... But then there was resentment in Israel. They said: 'Because we did that deed, we were on the way down in disgrace, and hence Moses was told to take the way down from the Mount. Now that the Holy One, blessed be He, is reconciled with us and has forgiven our sin, the glory of your person is restored, while our glory remains lowered.'[21]

A more oblique midrashic reference has the angels of God turning away from Moses' shining face when his veil is removed.[22]

These three midrashic sources neglect the use of the veil in the text, asking no searching questions about its meaning, origins, or religious significance, and making no interesting comparisons with likely analogues (e.g. the covering of Elijah's face in 1 Kgs 19.13); instead they explain the veil in moral terms. Like Paul, these sources seem to concentrate on the fear of the Israelites and the exalted state of Moses.

In the Samaritan tradition, which exalts Moses even more highly, the veil somehow magnifies the heavenly glory: '[Moses] dwelt in the cloud and wore the shining light for which was prepared a great veil from on high to magnify it, terrifying the minds of Israel so that they might not look upon the face'.[23] A source of mystery and wonder rather than concealment, this veil radiates heavenly glory and inspires fear in the Israelites, whereas the biblical veil conceals the shining face and mitigates the peoples' fear.

b. *Christian Interpretation*

The most influential Christian interpretation of the veil of Moses is Paul's typological contrast between Moses and Christ in 2 Corinthians 3, quoted above. Belleville's excellent study of the passage has established that Paul's reading is original but applies elements from rabbinic and Hellenistic tradition to the rhetorical task.

---

19. Pseudo-Philo, *Biblical Antiquities* (trans. J.R. James; New York: Ktav, 1971), p. 110. Josephus makes no mention of the veil, and the Targums add nothing to the sparse biblical account: 'All merely state that the people feared to approach him' (Belleville, *Reflections of Glory*, p. 30).

20. *Num. R.* 11.3, *The Midrash Rabbah* (ed. H. Freedman; trans. J.J. Slotki; London and New York: Soncino Press, 1977), p. 419.

21. *Pesikta Rabbati* (trans. William Braude; 2 vols.; New Haven: Yale University Press, 1968), pp. 180-81; also see *Midrash HaGadol*, cited in Belleville, *Reflections of Glory*, pp. 69-70, which is basically a paraphrase of this passage.

22. *Midrash HaGadol*, in Belleville, *Reflections of Glory*, p. 70.

23. Belleville, *Reflections of Glory*, p. 51.

Contrary to Scott Hafemann's argument that Paul's reading of the veil is a serious exegesis of Exodus 34, Belleville argues convincingly that 2 Corinthians 3 is a polemical rendering of the veil to express a message about the boldness of Christians in contrast to their non-Christian Jewish counterparts at that time. According to Sze-Kar Wan, Paul's text is a polemical exegesis that makes use of Hellenistic mystical traditions of Moses and challenges somewhat his personal and textual authority on the basis of mystical experience.[24] Taken together, the work of Belleville and Wan presents Paul's text as a polemic against pro-Jewish Christians who, like Philo and Josephus, perceived Moses as a sort of Hellenistic hero.

Most other Christian interpretations paraphrase Paul in homiletic rather than exegetical contexts, paying little attention to the shape of the text. Origen, for example, quotes and closely paraphrases Paul in a homily on Exodus 34: 'Who would not marvel at the magnitude of the mysteries? Who would not greatly fear the sign of a dulled heart? Moses' face was glorified, but "the sons of Israel" were not able "to look at the appearance of his countenance"; the people of the Synagogue were not able "to look".'[25] (Note the early juxtaposition of Moses and Synagogue, two figures that are linked in later art history, here.)

One striking exception to this interpretive pattern is a poetic homily by the fifth/sixth century Syriac Bishop Jacob of Serugh: 'This is what the veil on Moses' face symbolizes:/ that the words of prophecy are veiled'.[26] With these words, Jacob takes Paul's reading of the veil one step beyond biblical notions of revelation. The veil of Moses contrasts with the disclosure brought about by Christ, but it also applies to scripture in general: 'That veil of Moses openly cries out to the entire world/ that the words of scripture are likewise veiled./ Moses is the model of all that is uttered in prophecy,/ providing a type for the veiled character of the Old Testament.'[27] Typological associations between Moses and Christ take up the bulk of the poem, which runs to 460 lines. Jacob ties them so closely together that it is Christ who speaks through the veil of Moses: 'This was the reason why the veil was required,/ so that the Son of God might be veiled from onlookers'. With the advent of Christ, the veil is removed and Moses' stammering speech is healed: 'the doctor has arrived to loosen the stammerer's tongue,/ Moses' words, that had formerly been halting, are now restored'.[28]

Jacob's typological reading clearly builds on Paul's, but by globalizing the veil to symbolize the Old Testament, it makes explicit the link between the veil and revelation that I argue is implicit in Exodus 34. The veil is a typological symbol of revelation, and although Jacob's reading is highly anti-Jewish, it shows unusual

24. Sze-Kar Wan, 'Charismatic Exegesis: Philo and Paul Compared', *The Studia Philonica Annual* 6 (1994), pp. 54-82 (72-79).

25. Origen, *Homilies on Genesis and Exodus* (trans. R. Heine; Washington: Catholic University Press, 1981), pp. 367-68.

26. Sebastian Brock, 'Jacob of Serugh on the Veil of Moses', *Sobornost* 3 (1981), pp. 70-85 (72).

27. Brock, 'Jacob of Serugh', p. 74.

28. Brock, 'Jacob of Serugh', p. 80.

attentiveness to the details of the Old Testament text, acknowledging the veil, the stammering, and many other textual details of the Moses story.[29]

A fascinating but often overlooked interpretation of Moses' veil is Nathaniel Hawthorne's 1836 story, 'The Minister's Black Veil'.[30] While Hawthorne's engagement with the biblical veil of Moses is glancing at best, the story and other writings demonstrate a sophisticated understanding of the dynamics of veils in a religious context.[31] Like the veil of Moses, Hooper's veil is effective for preaching, but it is worn at all times and eventually destroys him. Like *The Blithedale Romance*, 'The Minister's Black Veil' is not an allegory but a meta-allegory with greater depth and reflexivity than Paul or Bunyan.[32] Hawthorne's reader must choose between the coherent moral vision of a veiled Hooper and the more complex and distanced perspective of the author. Without commenting directly on biblical texts, the story thus engages the interpretive complexity of the veil of Moses.

So, in the history of interpretation, we have at least four types of response to the veil: silence, paraphrase, modest moral interpretations (rabbinic sources), and bold, expansive interpretations (Paul, Jacob, and Hawthorne). For the rabbis and Paul,

29.   See Nohrnberg, *Like Unto Moses*, pp. 348-49 n. 3, on the shining of Moses' as a burn.

30.   According to Judy McCarthy, 'That Hawthorne was deeply aware of the complexity of Moses as an archetypal character (both in the Old and New Testaments) has been amply demonstrated' (J. McCarthy, '"The Minister's Black Veil": Concealing Moses and the Holy of Holies', *Studies in Short Fiction* 24 [1987], pp. 131-38 [131-32]). McCarthy reads the veil as a symbol of interpretation in the story, pointing both toward concealment and revelation (pp. 137-68). According to Lawrence Berkove, the story creates an inverse relationship between Moses' veil and Hooper's; citing 2 Cor. 3, Berkove argues, 'Insofar as Mr. Hooper's veil suggests Moses, therefore, it does so not as a foreshadowing but as an overshadowing of Christ' (Lawrence Berkove, '"The Minister's Black Veil": The Gloomy Moses of Milford', *The Nathaniel Hawthorne Journal* 8 [1978], pp. 147-57 [151]).

31.   Consider the following excerpts from Hawthorne's journals: 'In a grim, weird story, a figure of a gay, laughing, handsome youth, or a young lady, all at once, in a natural, unconcerned way, takes off its face like a mask, and show the grinning, bare skeleton face beneath' (Jullan Hawthorne, *Nathaniel Hawthorne and his Wife: A Biography* in the *Works of Nathaniel Hawthorne* [Boston: Houghton Mifflin & Co., 1891], XIV, p. 498).

A second excerpt reads: 'The dying exclamation of the Emperor Augustus, "Has it not been well acted?" An essay on the misery of being always under a mask. A veil may be needful, but never a mask. Instances of people who wear masks in all classes of society, and never take them off even in the most familiar moments, though sometimes they may chance to slip aside' (*The American Notebooks*, in *The Centenary Edition of the Works of Nathaniel Hawthorne* [21 vols.; Columbus: Ohio State University Press, 1972], VIII, p. 23).

Hawthorne's comments on Michelangelo's Moses appear in his 1858 Italian Notebooks (date of 'The Minister's Black Veil' [1836]) 'I found it [the statue] grand and sublime, with a beard flowing down like a cataract; a truly majestic figure, but not so benign as it were desirable that such strength should be... The whole force of this statue is not to be felt in one brief visit, but I agree with an English gentleman who, with a large party, entered the church while we were there, in thinking that Moses has "very fine features",—a compliment for which the colossal Hebrew ought to have made the Englishman a bow' (N. Hawthorne, 'Passages From the French and Italian Notebooks', in *The Works of Nathaniel Hawthorne* [24 vols.; Boston: Houghton, Mifflin & Co., 1883], X, pp. 164-65).

32.   See my 'The Veil of Allegory in Hawthorne's *The Blithedale Romance*', *Literature and Theology* 10 (1996), pp. 44-57.

the veil is a barrier required not by the presence of God but by the failings of the people. For Paul and later Christians, these human failings reside specifically in the Jewish people. Beside the notion of the veil as punishment for religious disobedience or weakness, post-biblical interpretations recognize the veil as a communication barrier rooted in the holy function of prophetic speech. Here the case of Jacob of Serugh stands out, but the idea appears in the background of rabbinic and Pauline traditions as well.

In all, very few interpreters have explored the full possibilities of Moses' veil as a symbol of revelation. What does it mean, after all, for a story about a prophet to highlight not only presence but absence, not only action but inaction, not only the uncovered face that speaks but the covered face that sits in silence? The veil remains ambiguous and mysterious in the biblical text and the reticent history of interpretation.[33]

3. *Images*

a. *Early Images (Ninth–Twelfth Centuries)*

Images of Moses' veil are few and diverse. They show no sustained pattern of mutual influence: some of them illustrate the book of Exodus, and others have a stronger link to Paul or a post-biblical theological tradition. Like their counterparts in biblical commentary, most of the images avoid the complete covering of Moses' face. Nevertheless, there is something uncanny about these images that affirms the Exodus story's dynamic of revelation and concealment. Eight images of Moses with a veil are discussed here; six of them actually show Moses with his face at least partly covered.

The earliest veiled Moses image I have found comes from the ninth century *Vivian Bible* (a Carolingian illustrated Bible from Tours—846 Paris Bibliothèque Nationale[34] [see Fig. 1, next page]), long before the horned Moses iconography appeared in the eleventh century.[35] This image pairs the unveiling of Moses by the four personified evangelists with another image above that shows the scene from Rev. 5.6 of the opening of the book. Playing on the Pauline opposition of veiling and revelation (*velamen et revelatio*), the image also suggests a dichotomy between old and new covenants. The book of Revelation appears above the unveiled Moses, suggesting a clear hierarchy as well as the fulfillment (also from Paul) of the promised unveiling of Moses by the coming of Christian time. In a way that anticipates the iconographic program of Abbot Suger in the twelfth century (see below), this image of Moses' veil is explicitly based on the Pauline text, though expanded in scope to include Revelation.[36]

---

33. Note the link to the concealment of Moses at his birth, after the murder in ch. 2, and upon in the burial scene of Deut. 34.6.

34. See Konrad Hoffmann, 'Sugers "Anagogisches Fenster" in St. Denis', *Wallraf-Richartz-Jahrbuch* 30 (Cologne: M. Dumont Schauberg, 1968), pp. 57-87.

35. See Ruth Mellinkoff, *The Horned Moses in Medieval Art and Thought* (Berkeley: University of California Press, 1970), p. 5.

36. By its theological source, Victorinus of Pettau. See Hoffmann, 'Sugers "Anagogisches Fenster" in St. Denis', p. 59.

Figure 1. Vivian Bible *(Paris Bibliothèque Nationale, 846 CE) in Hoffman, 'Suger's 'Anagogisches Fenster' in St-Denis', Plate 47*

Another feature of this image is obvious but important to note—the veil is removed. Moses is shown without it. Unlike the window at St-Denis (Fig. 4), where the veil is in the process of coming off, here it has come off, and Moses sits as if enthroned, surrounded by the evangelists and the arc of the veil over his head.

Whether it is deliberate or inadvertent, the result is a Christian composition that appears to glorify Moses. As most of these images attest, the depiction of Moses with a veil can be less theologically stable than Paul's text.

The second-earliest instance of Moses with a veil comes from an eleventh-century manuscript page from a liturgical book (Fig. 2). In this illustration, the veil of Moses only partly conceals his face. The scene is one of three on the page. The largest scene, on top, depicts Christ in a mandorla with Peter at his right and Moses to his left—the inscription for Peter reads, 'Moses, to whom Jesus gives the tablets of the laws...' On the bottom left is a scene of Moses commissioning Aaron as a priest; and on the right is the veiled Moses.

Like most other images in this survey, Moses' face is covered only partially: his right eye and more than half of his face can be seen by the viewer. His left hand holds the veil. Above his head, in his right hand, he holds the tablets of the law.

Figure 2. *Städelsches Kunstinstitut, Inv. 622, Folio XI*
in Swarzenski, Die Illuminierter Handschriften, *Plate v*

Below him on either side are people with hands raised facing him. The position of
these people is ambiguous; does the partial covering of the veil hide Moses' face
from them? Their gaze is directed above Moses' face, at the tablets of the law.
Moses' right eye, meanwhile, looks toward the viewer: the pupil is larger than any
of the others on the page, including Christ's. A distinction is thus drawn between
the Hebrews *in* the image and the (implied) Christian viewer *of* the image.

Figure 3. Farfa Bible, *Catalan text (eleventh or twelfth century),*
*Vatican Library 5729, fol. 6vo (*Pamplona Bibles *1.352 [Fig. 105a])*

The only image of Exodus 34 (Fig. 3 [previous page]) that shows Moses with a mask rather than a veil comes from the Catalan *Farfa Bible* of the eleventh or twelfth century[37] (which is also roughly when images of Moses with horns began to appear). The mask bears some resemblance to the face of God.[38] From left to right, the illustration depicts God with a nimbed head, seated within a mandorla. His right hand is raised in apparent blessing, and his left holds the tablets of the law. Moses is shown to the right of God, kneeling and receiving the tablets in his hands, which are covered with a decorated cloth. In the next episode of the continuous narrative, Moses stands to the right facing a group of six people with tablets in his right hand and what may be a rod in his left. He stands on swirling waves of cloud or water. Moses' body and mask face right, but his face is turned partly toward the viewer at an angle of about 45 degrees. Below the six Israelites are four animal heads, one with a horn (Egyptian horses or Israelite livestock?), and to their right is another figure, probably Aaron, holding aloft a rectilinear object that tapers at the bottom. It is likely that these elements depict the offerings and ritual objects outlined in Exodus 35 and following.

Some elements of this image seem obvious: Moses receives the law directly from God. He then delivers the law to the Israelites. The two scenes resemble each other: Moses bows or kneels before a God who stands above him surrounded by a double nimbus, and the people bow (though less deeply) before a Moses who stands slightly above them with cloud or water swirling at his feet. One difference, however, is that the gaze of Moses in the first scene is directed upward, toward the face of God, while the people gaze ahead or downward, perhaps in awe of Moses' face. At least one of the Israelites seems to be looking directly at one of the animal heads, perhaps an allusion to the golden calf episode. The effect of this 'two-faced' depiction is again that the Christian viewer is able to see the face of Moses, while the Israelite viewer cannot.

Unlike later images of Moses that depict him with horns of light coming from his face, no obvious change is shown here. Yet the mask and the averted gaze of the Israelites clearly depict the scene in which Moses' face is transformed. Whatever change the Israelites see, it is not shown to the viewer of this illustration. Yet viewers of this image *do* see something the Israelites do not: the real face of Moses behind the mask. By seeing what the Israelites do not, the viewer of the image enjoys the privilege of knowing what Moses' face really looks like.

But what is it that makes Moses' face so frightening to the people? Perhaps the transfiguration is an illusion visible only to them. Like Moses himself, who must serve as a mediator between people and God, the edifying transmission of God's law seems to require an additional barrier between Moses and the people. Perhaps because the law is so holy, or perhaps as a result of their faithless worship of the golden calf, the face of Moses becomes so frightening to the people that he must wear a mask. Or it could be that the mask itself frightens the people; if so, the artist

---

37. In F. Bucher (ed.), *Pamplona Bibles* (2 vols.; New Haven: Yale University Press, 1970), I, p. 352 (Fig. 105a).

38. Thanks to Ann-Marie Knoblauch for this suggestion.

would have taken considerable liberties with the text, presenting the mask as a cause of fear rather than a way to alleviate it. But whether the fear is illusory or caused by the mask, the moment has passed, and as Paul says in 2 Corinthians, for Christians there is no longer a need for fear. Whether this image of Moses is Pauline and typological, however, is not easy to know with certainty. Typological images of Moses, including the Vivian Bible and others, date back as far as the ninth century.[39]

Typology is also obvious in the image from a stained glass window at St-Denis (twelfth century) (Fig. 4), which depicts Christ unveiling Moses:

Figure 4. *Drawing, Anagogical Window, St-Denis (twelfth century), Glencairn Museum, Academy of the New Church, Bryn Athyn, PA*

Unlike several other images in which the viewer can see most of Moses' face, this image shows only part of the face. Holding the tables of the law in his right hand, Moses stands with his head almost completely covered. Jesus stands next to him, on the right, removing the veil with his right hand. Moses and Jesus have similar clothing and features: both are bearded and of the same height and build, but Moses wears an ornamental belt. Three other men look on, hands raised in apparent wonder at the scene; they wear what appear to be priestly hats or turbans, possibly to represent the sort of Jewish leaders criticized by Paul in 2 Corinthians and elsewhere. Around the image is a caption, written by Abbot Suger, the mastermind of the art of St-Denis; it reads: 'What Moses veils the doctrine of Christ unveils. They who despoil Moses lay bare the Law.'

---

39. Archer St Clair, 'A New Moses: Typological Iconography in the Moutier-Grandval Bible Illustrations of Exodus', *Gesta* 26 (1987), pp. 19-28.

The allusion to 2 Corinthians is clear. Abbot Suger, a contemporary of Bernard and Abailard, may be one of the best-documented designers of his time. His own detailed plans for the art of his abbey offer tremendous insights into the administrative and creative processes of the twelfth century. Unfortunately, the window itself was destroyed or lost in 1799, and there are problems with its reconstruction and arrangement.[40] The window we have now was reconstructed from a drawing and from Suger's mention of the window 'where the veil is taken off the face of Moses'.[41]

The other medallions in this 'anagogical' window depict the unveiling of Synagogue by Christ (Fig. 5), the apocalyptic opening of a book with lion and lamb, the mystic mill of Paul (a typological image in which the grain of the old covenant is ground into the flour of the new), the ark of the Covenant, and a scene of Mary with Christ crucified in the foreground:[42]

Figure 5. *Moses and Synagogue, Anagogical Window (Detail),*
St-Denis (twelfth century), in Panofsky, Abbot Suger, *Fig. 16*

40.   See Erwin Panofsky, *Abbot Suger on the Abbey Church of St.-Denis and its Art Treasures* (Princeton, NJ: Princeton University Press, 1979), pp. 201-203.

41.   *The Book of Suger, Abbot of St.-Denis, on What Was Done Under his Administration* (trans. Erwin Panofsky), in Panofsky, *Abbot Suger*, p. 75; Jane Hayward, 'Stained Glass at Saint-Denis', in Sumner Crosby *et al.* (eds.), *The Royal Abbey of St.-Denis in the Time of Abbot Suger* (New York: Metropolitan Museum of Art, 1981), pp. 61-71 (61-67).

42.   Jane Hayward, 'Stained Glass at Saint-Denis', p. 69, fig. 24.

Suger described some of the windows, such as the ark and cross, in his plans:

> On the Ark of the Covenant is established the altar
> with the Cross of Christ;
> Here Life wishes to die under a greater covenant.

Despite the problem of how much the current window resembles the original, the St-Denis window clearly presents the veil of Moses in Paul's version, with Jesus removing it as an obstruction to Revelation. It is less clear whether the influence of Pseudo-Dionysus, the neo-Platonic Christian writer of the fifth–sixth centuries, can be seen here.[43] At the same time, by its juxtaposition with the image of Christ removing the blindfold from Synagogue, the image represents an early association between the veil of Moses and the blindfolded Synagogue. It would be too tidy to say that Synagogue displaces the veiled Moses, but here at least is evidence that the two are linked in the Christian visual imagination.

The Anagogical window illustrates the ambiguity of allegorical expression. Correspondences between Old and New Testaments suspend the question of their relative status—one can assign priority to either or see them as equivalent. The allegorical move opens up a whole set of possible interpretive meanings. As Walter Benjamin shows in his study of German tragic drama, allegory relativizes the symbolic process.[44] Simply stated, if Moses corresponds to Jesus, then Jesus corresponds to Moses, and either can eventually correspond to anyone else. In other words, allegorical systems have a logical tendency to unravel (or deconstruct) themselves, and the potency of the Pauline reading of Moses' veil is undercut by the knowledge that Pauline tradition associated the veil with Judaism and spiritual blindness *and* that other interpretive possibilities exist.

The Pauline reading of the veil may also change meaning simply by the shift from the words of 2 Corinthians to the image of Jesus lifting the veil from Moses in St-Denis. Paul's text is verbal and grounded in a rhetorical and theological context

43. According to Panofsky, Abbot Suger was influenced by the thought of Pseudo-Dionysius the Areopagite, a fifth–sixth century Christian and neo-Platonic writer, who wrote the following on Moses as a hierarch whose spiritual ascent captures the mystery of revelation: 'It is not for nothing that the blessed Moses is commanded to submit first to purification and then to depart from those who have not undergone this… He sees the many lights, pure and with rays streaming abundantly. Then, standing apart from the crowds and accompanied by chosen priests, he pushed ahead to the summit of the divine ascents. And yet he does not meet God himself, but contemplates, not him who is invisible, but rather where he dwells… But then he [Moses] breaks free of them, away from what sees and is seen, and he plunges into the truly mysterious darkness of unknowing. Here, renouncing all that the mind may conceive, wrapped entirely in the intangible and the invisible, he belongs completely to him who is beyond everything. Here, being neither oneself nor someone else, one is supremely united by a completely unknowing inactivity of all knowledge, and knows beyond the mind by knowing nothing' (*The Mystical Theology*, in *Pseudo-Dionysius: The Complete Works* [trans. Colm Luibheid; New York: Paulist Press, 1987], pp. 136-37; cf. Gregory of Nyssa's similar account in *The Life of Moses*, pp. 152-70). See Erwin Panofsky, *Abbot Suger*, pp. 18-22. See also John Gage, 'Gothic Glass: Two Aspects of a Dionysian Aesthetic', *Art History* 5 (1982), pp. 36-58.

44. See W. Benjamin, *The Origin of German Tragic Drama* (trans. John Osborne; London: New Left Books, 1977), p. 175.

that circumscribes its meaning. The window in St-Denis, on the other hand, invites a whole range of interpretive responses, even though it stands firmly in the context of ecclesiastical art, surrounded by other 'anagogical' scenes.

What are some of these possible associations? One would be to see the clear resemblance between Moses and Jesus as a statement on their similarity, mirror-relationship, or even equivalence. Is Jesus unveiling an earlier version of himself in this scene? Is Moses a kind of Jesus *in nuce*, only released from the shell of the law by Jesus in a later manifestation? For less erudite viewers, the gesture of Jesus itself may be ambiguous: Is he covering or uncovering? Is the gesture an act of respect, mercy, affection, or hostility? The image of the veil does not project the same kind of supersessionist or hierarchical relationship between Jesus and Moses that we have in the case of 2 Corinthians. Rendered in the edifying medium of stained glass, the veil of Moses takes on a vividness missing from Paul's text, the effect of which is an increased range of interpretations.

Another possible association is the sense in which the image feminizes Moses. Like a groom unveiling a bride, Jesus, standing close to Moses, lifts the veil from his face. While this association may have been missing from the original window, it is unavoidable by the time of its contemporary reconstruction. Moses is further feminized by the obvious link between him and the female figure of Synagogue depicted on the same window (Fig. 5, see above). Both have faces covered, both hold the tablets of the law, and both are opposed to Christian figures (Jesus and Ecclesia, respectively). There is also something vulnerable and disempowering about figures who are covered or being uncovered by veils.[45]

b. *Moses and Synagogue*

The St-Denis window relates the veiled Moses to a more common figure with a covered face: the allegorical figure of Synagogue (Synagoga), usually depicted with a blindfold, a broken staff, and the tablets (often broken or slipping away) of Mosaic law. In *Synagogue and Church in the Middle Ages*, Wolfgang Seiferth surveys the origins and development of an allegorical topos—the feminine personification of Jews or Judaism as Synagoga and Christians or the Church as Ecclesia.[46] He argues that the veil slowly disappears in the history of art, both from Synagogue and from Moses:

> in the window of Suger in the abbey church of St. Denis, Moses stands with veiled head while Christ, beside him, lifts the veil. Claus Sluter shows the veils drawn far back on his enormous bust of Moses. Finally, the Moses of Michelangelo is unveiled: the divine truth can be seen in his face… This was the final and decisive paraphrase of the veil of Synagoga, at a time when she herself had already disappeared from art.[47]

45. For a familiar example, see Michalangelo's Sistine Chapel scene of the covering of Noah by his son Shem, which shows how a veil (in this case the need for it) contributes to the impression of a vulnerable and compromised man.

46. Wolfgang Seiferth, *Synagogue and Church in the Middle Ages* (trans. Lee Chadeayne and Paul Gottwald; New York: Frederick Ungar, 1970).

47. Seiferth, *Synagogue and Church in the Middle Ages*, p. 31.

While I think Seiferth's evolutionary scheme is reductive, I wish briefly to pursue the iconographic link between Moses and Synagoga.

The figures of Synagoga and Ecclesia developed from the New Testament and Christian Fathers,[48] and perhaps also from the idealized and allegorical female figures in Roman art.[49] Synagoga personifies the religious blindness of such biblical texts as Lamentations, Isaiah (6.9-10), and Matthew 23. The first known example comes from the ninth century, the same period as the veiled Moses in the *Vivian Bible*.[50] The image of Synagoga wearing a blindfold first appears in a twelfth-century German allegorical play, *Ludus de Antichristo*.[51] By the time of Suger's anagogical window, she is a familiar figure in Christian art, with her broken or falling tablets, staff, and blindfold.[52] She often appears at Jesus' left beneath the cross, degraded and immoral, while Ecclesia stands triumphantly at his right (Fig. 6):

Figure 6. *Crucifixion Scene with Mary and Ecclesia, Synagoga and John, c. 1200, Trier, in Seiferth,* Synagogue and Church in the Middle Ages, *Plate 25*

Her clear inferiority to Ecclesia in this scene is compounded by a hint of deicide. In the medieval plays, she sometimes personifies the Antichrist. In one case, Elijah (a

48. For example, Paul and Origen (*Homilies on Genesis and Exodus*), and Seiferth, *Synagogue and Church in the Middle Ages*, p. 33.

49. See Donald Strong, *Roman Art* (New York: Penguin Books, 1988), p. 182.

50. Drogo's Sacramentary, Ms. Latinus 9428, Bibliothèque Nationale, cited in Seiferth, *Synagogue and Church in the Middle Ages*, p. 163.

51. Seiferth, *Synagogue and Church in the Middle Ages*, p. 79.

52. See Heinz Schreckenberg, *The Jews in Christian Art* (trans. John Bowden; New York: Continuum, 1996), which includes sixty-six illustrations of Synagoga.

prophet who, like Moses, covers his face—1 Kgs 19) removes the veil of Synagogue to reveal her as the Antichrist.[53]

Synagogue appears with Moses frequently and in various settings. In a window
at Canterbury Cathedral (twelfth–thirteenth century), a nimbed Moses holds a book
on the left while Synagogue, facing him but with face uncovered, holds the two
tablets.[54] In a late thirteenth-century French manuscript (*La Somme le Roy*), Moses
(with horns) receives the tablets from God above while to the right a blindfolded
Synagogue (with broken staff) appears to be dropping the tablets (Fig. 7):

Figure 7. *Moses Receiving the Law and Synagogue,* La Somme le Roy *(popular
compendium of doctrine), c. 1295, Paris, Bibl. de l'Arsenal, 6329, fol. 7vo
(Reproduced with the permission of the Bibliothèque Nationale, France)*

In some cases, and in a further variation of Paul's text, the veil is removed from the
head of Synagogue by the hand of God, while Moses and Aaron stand beside her
(Fig. 8):[55]

53.   Seiferth, *Synagogue and Church in the Middle Ages*, p. 89.

54.   Canterbury Cathedral, Window N., transept N.E. Center, Index of Christian Art, Princeton
University (44.C167.CCiW2.6A).

55.   Fig. 8 comes from the Eton Apocalypse (1260–70): 'In contrast with conventional mid-
century English juxtapositions where Synagogue drops the tablets of the Law or overturns a vessel
to signal her rejection of Christ's blood reverently gathered in a chalice by Ecclesia on the other
side of the cross, the Eton figure raises the tablets toward Moses at the left and hands the upright

Figure 8. *Eton Apocalypse, c. 1260–70, Unveiling Synagogue with Moses and Aaron*—'Synagogue Sees the Truth by Coming to the Faith'
(Reproduced with the permission of the Provost and Fellows of Eton College)

It would be simplistic to suggest that the tradition of veiled Moses transposed into the image of veiled Synagogue, but there are cultural and religious reasons why the former motif would be rare and the latter common. For while Moses does represent the tradition of Judaism and the law so ardently superseded by Pauline thought, he also stands in typological parallel to Paul and Christ. However profoundly his revelation was surpassed by the gospel and New Testament, there is continued respect for Moses in Christian communities from an early time.[56] Moses is a prophet and a patriarch whose status cannot completely be destroyed by his association with Judaism. The interaction of Moses and Synagogue imagery had become so intimate that by the fifteenth-century Moses (with horns) could be seen in her accustomed guise (Fig. 9, next page) and Synagogue could look formidable and almost Mosaic, despite her usual props and phony Hebrew tablets (Fig. 10, next page):[57]

gold vessel presumably to Aaron at the right' (Suzanne Lewis, *Reading Images: Narrative Discourse and Reception in the Thirteenth-Century Illuminated Apocalypse* [Cambridge: Cambridge University Press, 1995], p. 328). The inscription reads: 'Veiled up to now in the obscure figure of the Law, Synagogue sees the truth by coming to the faith' (Lewis, *Reading Images*, p. 328). See also the similar description of a French Missal in Lewis, *Reading Images*, p. 399 n. 293.

56.   See Su-Min (Andreas) Ri, 'Mosesmotive in den Fresken der Katakombe der Via Latina im Lichte der Rabbinischen Tradition', *Kairos* 17 (1975), pp. 57-92.

57.   Konrad Widz wood painting (c. 1430) (Seiferth, *Synagogue and Church in the Middle Ages*, fig 58).

Figure 9. *Moses as Synagogue?* Christ in Majesty, *Missal of Poitiers,*
late fifteenth century, folio 38r
(Reproduced with the permission of Poitiers Cathedral Treasury)

Figure 10. *Synagogue as Moses? Konrad Witz,* Synagogue *(oil on wood),Basel,*
mid-fifteenth century, in Seiferth, Synagogue and Church in the Middle Ages, *Plate 58*

The allegory of Synagogue and Church did not disappear in the modern period. John Singer Sargent's *Triumph of Religion (1895–1919)*, a mural program in the Boston Public Library, depicts the two figures in their conventional guises: Synagogue as a blindfolded woman with a broken staff and a crown falling from her head, and Church as a beautiful woman gazing ahead, surrounded by images of sacraments and the four evangelists. Sargent's main innovation to the conventional imagery was to add an image of Christ crucified on the ground at Church's feet, and to create a strong resemblance between this figure and the female Synagogue.[58] Sargent's program thus linked Synagogue to Christ, though elsewhere in the program he depicted Israel allegorically as a completely veiled figure. As Sally Promey shows in her excellent study of the murals, the proposed imagery of Synagogue led to a fierce controversy over the perceived anti-Jewishness of this imagery.[59] Although Sargent's iconographic program was clearly evolutionary, culminating in the proposed Sermon on the Mount, Promey argues that Sargent's depiction of these figures emphasized 'continuity rather than antithesis'.[60]

c. *Later Images (Fourteenth, Fifteenth, and Twentieth Centuries)*
One of the most striking images of Moses with a veil comes from the fourteenth-century *Queen Mary Psalter* (Fig. 11):

Figure 11. *Moses with Veil in* Queen Mary's Psalter *(fourteenth century), p. 45.*

58. See Salley Promey, *Painting Religion in Public: John Singer Sargent's Triumph of Religion at the Boston Public Library* (Princeton, NJ: Princeton University Press, 2000), figs. 17-18, 26.

59. Promey, *Painting Religion in Public*, pp. 176-202.

60. Promey, *Painting Religion in Public*, pp. 128-29. Sargent's Moses wears no veil, though he is surrounded by prophets who do. Promey observes the dynamics of concealment and revelation in the murals, but she argues that while Sargent was aware of the traditions of allegorical veiling and unveiling from St-Denis and the Sistine Chapel, his use of veils was typical of his own work's preoccupation with public and private selfhood (Promey, *Painting Religion in Public*, pp. 252-53).

At the top of this image, Christ gives Moses the tables while pointing to a city; below, Moses with a veil holds the tablets of the law.[61] In this manuscript, a very large and well-preserved French collection that illustrates most episodes of Genesis through Joshua and hundreds of other biblical and non-biblical scenes (gospels, calendar, saints, bestiary, zodiac, etc.), Moses (with horns) wears the veil (*lunge*, which may be related to *linge*, 'linen') only once.[62]

Unlike the *Farfa Bible*, which showed the face of Moses at two different angles, or the partly removed veil of the St-Denis window, this image simply and effectively allows the viewer to see Moses' face behind the fabric, while the Israelites face Moses from the other side, which is veiled. The artist also seems to have placed the tablets of the law in the line of sight between the Israelites and Moses.

Like the *Farfa Bible*, this illustration is based on Exodus 34 and shows no clear connection to the typology of 2 Corinthians 3. At the same time, it plainly gets the veil wrong, since Moses should only be wearing it when he is *not* acting as spokesman for God, or when he is off-duty. Also like the *Farfa Bible*, Moses holds the tablets while his face is covered. Both images allow the viewer to see the face of Moses while concealing it from the Hebrews, but they do this in very different and ingenious ways. Whether these illustrations mean the veil to indicate a simple barrier between sacred and profane or rather a sign of the Israelites' unworthiness (e.g. *vis-à-vis* the viewer), is open to question.

The same tension between concealment from Israelites and exposure to the viewer appears in the *Berlin Historienbibel* (fifteenth century) (Fig. 12):

Figure 12. *Berlin History Bible, fifteenth century, in S. van der Woude,*
De Keulse Bijbel, *Plate 37*

---

61. Other veils appear in the Moses cycle, including an image of Moses putting tablets into the ark with veiled hands.

62. G. Warner, *Queen Mary's Psalter: Miniatures and Drawings by an English Artist of the 14th Century; Reproduced from Royal Ms. 2 B. VII in the British Museum* (London: British Museum, 1912), Plate 45 (given to Queen Mary in the sixteenth century). His hands are veiled in other images, but this is a more common iconographic image, related to Christian Eucharistic practice, indicating the holiness of what is held.

Moses stands right, holding tablets in his left hand and a veil before his face in the right. There are horns on his head, and the Israelites cower on the left. Like the image of the *Farfa Bible*, Moses is concealed from the Israelites but visible to the viewer. His position between the mountain of revelation and the people down below is iconographically familiar, but the rendering of the veil is not. With his right hand, Moses holds the veil, a long drapery that reaches below his knees, in front of his head. The veil does not conceal the familiar horns on his head, however. In his left hand are the tablets of the law. The five Israelites stand in various poses of astonishment, the one in front actually covering his face in a way similar to Moses.

The most puzzling and complex of all the veiled Moses images comes from a detail of Botticelli's *Rebellion of Korah* in the Sistine Chapel (c. 1481) (Fig. 13):

Figure 13. *Moses with Veil? Botticelli,* Rebellion of Korah,
*detail, fresco, c. 1481. Sistine Chapel, Rome
(Reproduced with the permission of the Central Institute for Cataloguing and
Documentation, Rome)*

Here, in a series of frescoes detailing the life of Moses, the panel on Korah's revolt against Moses includes a scene on the right of Moses surrounded by a mob, three of whom hold stones which they seem ready to throw at Moses. The episode probably comes from Num. 14.1-10, just two chapters before the Korah story.[63] Another man, possibly Joshua,[64] restrains one of the would-be stone throwers. Moses, meanwhile, stands in a defensive posture—his right arm is raised in front of his face, and in his hand is a small piece of fabric that conceals the top of his head from the assailants. His left hand is raised in a gesture that appears to be a papal blessing.

The painted scenes from Moses' life stand in typological relationship to *the Life of Christ* frescoes on the opposite wall of the chapel. The scene of Jesus giving the keys to Peter corresponds to Moses' punishment of Korah and the other rebellious priests. As scholars have observed, the two scenes send a message that justifies papal authority as divinely mandated. Aaron wears the papal garments and joins Moses in the punishment of the illegitimate priests. The Korah rebellion was a common reference in discussions about papal authority. Both the *Gift of the Keys* and the *Korah* panels depict Roman arches, another symbol of papal authority.[65]

This veil is the smallest of all examples shown here (relative to Moses' face), and it is not obviously linked either to Exodus 34 or 2 Corinthians 3. Like other images of Moses in the fresco series, Moses' forehead emits golden rays of light which the veil partly hides from the mob's (but not the viewer's) gaze. While it offers no protection against stoning, the veil separates Moses from the faithless crowd, denying them full visual access to Moses, especially the light beaming from his head. The smallness of the veil may also suggest vulnerability, a Christ-like posture that contrasts the central image of Moses imposing judgment on the Korahites. Unlike the fearful Israelites of Exodus 34, these viewers are violent. But like the Israelites of 2 Corinthians 3, the minds of these rebels seem to be hardened. Taken especially in the context of the typology with Christ, Botticelli's veil may thus be Pauline in a general sense, even though the episode strays far from Exodus 34 and 2 Corinthians 3.

Images of Moses with a veil become much less frequent after the medieval period, and they vanish almost completely after the Botticelli fresco. One exception, and the final case to be presented, comes from a contemporary Jewish children's book, *Moses and the Angels* (Fig. 14).[66] In this illustration by a well-known Jewish artist and illustrator, Moses' face is fully concealed by a prayer-shawl kind of veil. The Jewish tradition of the veil as a *tallit* also appears in the thirteenth-century Kabbalistic work, the Zohar.[67] Podwal's Moses stands apart from all the

63. Though Carol Lewine (*The Sistine Chapel Walls and the Roman Liturgy* [University Park, PA: Pennsylvania State University Press, 1993]) attributes the scene to an extrabiblical Jewish tradition.

64. Lewine, *The Sistine Chapel Walls and the Roman Liturgy*, p. 77.

65. Lewine, *The Sistine Chapel Walls and the Roman Liturgy*, pp. 79-80.

66. Ileene Smith Sobel (introduction by Elie Wiesel), illustrations by Mark Podwal, *Moses and the Angels* (New York: Delacorte Press, 1999).

67. '"They were afraid to come near him" (Exod. 34.30). He wrapped himself in it as in a *tallit*, as it is written: "He wraps Himself in light as in a garment" (Ps. 104.2)', from *Zohar: The Book of Enlightenment* (trans. Daniel C. Matt; New York: Paulist Press: 1983), pp. 51-52. Note that this interpretation, though mystical, also implies Israelite guilt as the reason for the veil. The image of Moses with a *tallit* also appears in a fifteenth-century German Mahzor (Index of Jewish Art 1986/6, fol. 69, card 12), though it does not cover his head.

others in its total concealment of Moses' face as well as the depiction of Moses' veil as a prayer shawl. Interestingly, Podwal conflates the golden calf and breaking of the tablets of Exodus 32 with the veil episode of Exodus 34. Moses appears to look away from this horror in prayerful withdrawal.

Figure 14. *From* Moses and the Angels *by Ileene Smith Sobel, illustrations by Mark Podwal,* © *1999 by Ileene Smith Sobel, illustrations* © *by Mark Podwal, introduction* © *by Elie Wiesel*
(Reproduced with the permission of Random House Children's Books, a division of Random House, Inc.)

d. *Images with the Veil Apparently Pulled Back*
Some images (such as Fig. 15 [next page], a fourteenth-century illustrated Latin Bible) depict Moses with face exposed and a head covering that may or may not refer to the allegory of Jesus raising the veil of Moses in 2 Corinthians 3.[68] Such images of an apparently raised veil may have been influenced by earlier images that illustrate Paul (such as the *Vivian Bible*), but it is not always possible to determine whether such imitations also refer to Paul. As images such as the Eton Apocalypse and Botticelli's fresco show, the veil can appear in contexts beyond Exodus and 2 Corinthians. When the veil is present, it is impossible to determine whether it is merely a convention borrowed from previous works. Is the veil purposeful or

68.   Barberini Latin 613 73r (fourteenth century), dated by Jack Marler at St Louis University at fourteenth century. See also Josephus, *Jewish Antiquities* 12 C. Illum. Man. Oxford Lib., Merton Coll. 317 fol. 19 vo.

vestigial, so to speak? In the absence of clear iconographic cues, the question becomes a matter of artistic intention and audience reception, and therefore difficult to determine. The apparent decline in images of the veiled Moses after the Middle Ages is noteworthy, but this pattern may have more to do with changes in religious art, rather than the kind of evolution suggested by Seiferth.

Figure 15. *Barberini Latin (fourteenth century), 613 73R*
(Reproduced with the permission of the Vatican Library)

The most artistically significant of these is Claus Sluter's Moses (c. 1405) (Fig. 16).[69] Like the Barberini (Fig. 15), Sluter's Moses has stumpy horns and a veil pulled back. Sluter was indebted to imagery from passion plays in which Moses and other prophets legislate the death of Jesus on the precedent of Passover tradition:

> As in the play, *Secundum legem debet mori*, the prophecy inscribed on the scroll displayed by Sluter's Moses is taken from the chapter of Exodus in which the Passover is instituted, and (as specifically stated in the play) the killing of the lamb without blemish is intended to refer to the sacrifice of Christ on the cross.[70]

Despite its strong allegorical context, Sluter's Moses exhibits a courtly style naturalism, with features minutely rendered, including wrinkles on his forehead.[71]

---

69. Moses-fountain, Chartreuse de Champmol, Dijon, cited in Seiferth, *Synagogue and Church in the Middle Ages*, p. 165 (Michelangelo, c. 1513/15).

70. Kathleen Morand, *Claus Sluter: Artist at the Court of Burgundy* (Austin: University of Texas Press, 1991), p. 105.

71. Thanks to my colleague Jane Aiken for this observation. Moses is pictured with tablets in veiled right hand and horns on his head; the imagery may have come from drama: 'A red belted

Whether Moses' head covering alludes to the veil is impossible to tell. Of the six prophets in the Moses fountain, only Moses has such a head covering. Sluter depicted several kinds of head and face coverings in his work, most dramatically the mourners with completely hood-covered faces at the tomb of Philip the Bold.[72] From this we can at least infer that Sluter's use of head coverings was purposeful. It may also have been influential, as the similarly veiled Moses on an eighteenth-century Austrian Haggadah suggests.[73]

Figure 16. *Sluter*, Moses Fountain, *c. 1405, in Morand*, Claus Sluter, *Plate 21*

e. *Analysis of Veiled Moses Images*
Including the contemporary children's book, I have found eight clear examples of Moses with a veil or a mask:
1.   *Vivian Bible*
2.   Eleventh-Century liturgical manuscript
3.   *Farfa Bible*
4.   St-Denis window
5.   *Queen Mary Psalter*
6.   *Berlin History Bible*
7.   Botticelli's fresco
8.   Podwal, contemporary children's book illustration

tunic is worn beneath a voluminous mantle of gold lined with azure. The latter is draped across the figure and over the head to form a cowl' (Morand, *Claus Sluter*, p. 332).
72.   See Morand, *Claus Sluter*, Plate V.
73.   Passover Haggadah, 1752, Index of Jewish Art 1985.1.272, card 92/3.

From the standpoint of iconography studies, this is a disappointing result—only eight images, none of which shows a clear connection to any other. These look like independent and original renderings of the episode, perhaps driven mainly by the task of illustrating that particular scene of the Bible. It would be easier to draw conclusions from dozens or hundreds of renderings of this biblical episode. Nevertheless, the images we have uncannily reflect the dynamics of silence and speech, revelation and concealment, that are so crucial to Exod. 34.29-35.

Why are there so few? Was it a matter of chance that artists and commentators simply did not latch on to this biblical episode? Is it artistically too odd to render an image of concealment? Why are images of Moses with horns so much more common? There is no way to answer these questions decisively, but the images raise some interesting possibilities. In different ways, they all resist the complete concealment of Moses' face, often finding a way to hide him from the Israelites while showing him to the viewer. An advantage of this approach is that viewers have a better chance of 'recognizing' Moses if they can see him. It also makes a distinction between what the Israelites can see and what the (Christian) spectator sees; in the spirit of Paul's reading of Exodus 34, the veil of Moses is not needed by Christians. Thus, though the only images that clearly depict 2 Corinthians 3 are the Vivian Bible of the ninth century and the window at St-Denis, it is possible that the other images also have a Pauline purpose.

But even Abbot Suger's window, Pauline as it is, lacks some of the didactic and rhetorical punch of its textual counterpart: the people of Israel, whose minds are veiled and hardened, do not appear in the image. Torn from its polemical and rhetorical context in 2 Corinthians, the mere image of Jesus removing a veil from Moses' face becomes more open-ended and arresting.

At the same time, the veiled Moses is sometimes juxtaposed and even transposed to the blindfolded Synagogue. Theologically speaking, Moses poses a problem to Christianity: crucial and almost superhuman in his own context, he is nevertheless subordinated to Jesus, quite emphatically so in some cases. Yet how can Moses be judged against a person, an incarnation of God, who was unavailable to him? As a representative of the Jews, Moses remained theologically and artistically ambiguous for Christians. As Ruth Mellinkoff has shown, the horns of Moses are sometimes honorary and sometimes derogatory, and they eventually come to identify figures simply as Jewish.[74] Synagogue offers an alternative—she is symbolic and abstract, perhaps also because she is female. The ascendancy of Synagogue iconography may suggest that Moses splits theologically into the morally corrupt figure of Synagogue and the triumphant Christ/Logos. But this division of Mosaic tradition would erase Moses himself; and the real problem is not Moses but his veil. It was much easier to take Moses by the horns than by the veil, because in that way he can be fixed as a curious but well-defined figure.

It was more common to imagine Jewish blindness as Synagogue than as Moses, in part because of her sex. For a culture in which men define women, there is some

---

74. Mellinkoff, *The Horned Moses in Medieval Art and Thought*.

thing tidy and familiar about the binary choice between Church and Synagogue, good and evil. It was culturally easy to project the simple opposition in female form: Roman art often personified abstractions in idealized female figures, in portraits of goddesses, caryatids, and personifications,[75] and women were seen typically in two-dimensional terms as either venerable or villainous. And while veils and blindfolds are not necessarily feminine in medieval art, covering the eyes and face is certainly disempowering. Moses may be inferior to Christ, but he's a man, and a powerful one at that. The frequency of the female Synagogue and the scarcity of the veiled Moses reflect the Christian feminization (and denigration) of Judaism. It was much easier to represent the spiritual failings of the Jewish people in female form, a stereotype that persisted for centuries.[76]

4. *Beyond the Veil of Moses: Enlightenment Hermeticism and the Unveiling of Nature*

What is the legacy of the veiled Synagogue? Before exploring the possible associations between Synagogue and images of Nature (Artemis) being unveiled, let me review the associations suggested thus far: Moses wears a veil in Exodus 34, a scene that highlights covenant and prophetic communication. Next comes Paul's appropriation of the image in 2 Corinthians 3 in which Christ removes the veil of Moses. Though attested in art history and commentaries, the veiled Moses is a comparatively rare scene. Synagogue emerges as a figure often associated with Moses and more often wearing a veil or blindfold. A veiled woman may be more palatable to Christians because she is an abstraction rather than a biblical person, and allegorical personifications were often female. In addition, Moses is theologically ambiguous, and the figure of Synagogue offers a cultural answer to this ambiguity by assuming the negative associations of the superseded law. In effect, Synagogue allows Moses to divide his negative (Jewish, hidden, and female) side from his redeeming (Christian, present, and male) one.

The act of unveiling itself, as imagined in 2 Corinthians 3, is particularly damaging to Moses' masculinity and integrity. After all, what can we expect this new Moses to be but a mirror image of Christ? And if we identify Moses and Christ too closely, we have dissolved the dichotomy on which Paul's theology depends. But unveiling is also a powerful act of revelation; it carries the suggestion that mysteries will be revealed. From the seventeenth to nineteenth centuries, another iconographic pattern of unveiling was common in European art: the unveiling of Nature in the guise of Artemis. Pierre Hadot analyzes this image in a monograph,[77] and

75. See, for example, the female personifications in Diana Kleiner, *Roman Sculpture* (New Haven: Yale University Press, 1992), pp. 97, 160, and 453. See also Strong, *Roman Art*, p. 182.

76. See Irven M. Resnick, 'Medieval Roots of the Myth of Jewish Male Menses', *HTR* 93 (2000), pp. 241-63 (261-63), and Sander Gilman, 'Salome, Syphilis, Sarah Bernhardt, and the Modern Jewess', in Linda Nochlin and Tamar Garb (eds.), *The Jew in the Text* (London: Thames & Hudson, 1995), pp. 97-120.

77. Pierre Hadot, *Zur Idee der Naturgeheimnisse* (Wiesbaden: Franz Steiner Verlag, 1982).

Jan Assmann links it to modern Egyptology.[78] Neither, however, identifies the biblical substrate of this tradition in the veiled Moses and Synagogue.

Figure 17. Zoology Unveils Nature,
frontispiece to Gerhard Blasius, Anatome Animalium *(1681)*

Hadot traces nineteenth-century images of Nature as a veiled goddess to the mixture of Artemis and Isis traditions. The ancient Artemis of Ephesus appears as a fertile goddess with three rows of breasts, and in the Renaissance she emerges as an allegorical symbol of Nature.[79] But the images Hadot brings under scrutiny show Artemis/Nature with a veil, often being unveiled by another figure (in one case the male personification of Poetry—as Apollo or possibly Orpheus—and in another the female personification of Natural Science, Fig. 17).

The link between Artemis and Isis goes as far back as Plutarch (first century CE), who reports the following temple inscription at a temple in Sais: 'I am all that was, is, and will be, and no mortal has lifted my veil'.[80] Even without its resemblance to the name of God in Exodus 3, this aphorism is pregnant with associations. Edmund Spenser, probably following Plutarch, alluded to the link in *The Faerie Queene*, and the Jesuit Athanasius Kircher identifies the veiled Isis as the secret workings of nature in his 1652 *Oedipus Aegyptiacus*. By the eighteenth century, the veiled image of Isis/Artemis had become well-established, appearing for example in Boudard's 1759 *Iconology*.[81]

78.   Jan Assmann, *Moses the Egyptian*, pp. 111-43.
79.   Hadot, *Zur Idee der Naturgehimnisse*, p. 4.
80.   Hadot, *Zur Idee der Naturgehimnisse*, p. 7.
81.   Hadot, *Zur Idee der Naturgehimnisse*, p. 8.

Although Hadot's account of the veiled Isis/Artemis is erudite, it overlooks the iconographic tradition of a veiled Moses or Synagogue. The connection is admittedly tenuous, even though it becomes more suggestive with the analogy between the Sais inscription and Exodus 3. In *Moses the Egyptian*, Jan Assmann locates the identification of YHWH with Isis in Karl Reinhold's masonic treatise, *Die Hebräische Mysterien oder die älteste religiöse Freymaurerey* (1788).[82] Reinhold's ideas were popularized in Friedrich Schiller's 1790 lectures, *Die Sendung Moses*, a work that identified Moses and the Hebrew tradition with Egyptian religion. Also like Reinhold, Schiller suggests that Moses received the highest revelations of philosophical truth along with the religious teachings preserved in the Bible. For Schiller, Moses was a kind of proto-philosopher of the eighteenth century variety, and the full truth of his revelations—the unity and impenetrability of God and nature—only comes to light in the modern period. Assmann documents how this YHWH-as-Isis doctrine of an Egyptian Moses influenced Kant,[83] Beethoven, Goethe, and others. At the same time, even when the topic is Moses, Assmann neglects to associate the veiled Isis with a veiled Moses or Synagogue!

What are the implications of the association between the veiled Isis and the veiled Moses and Synagogue? First, the veiled figure of Nature (Isis/Artemis) is further evidence of the pattern of female allegorical figures with veils.[84] More to the point, the analogy between Moses and Nature as figures to be uncovered suggests the cultural tradition linking the revelation of the Book of Scripture to the Book of Nature.[85] It is not surprising that the empiricism of the natural sciences would depict itself as unveiling the secrets of a feminine nature, just as Christianity sees itself as unveiling a feminized Moses and a female Synagogue. What *is* remarkable, though, is that the missing link between the veiled Moses and the veiled Nature—if the link is real at all—seems to have been a Western image of ancient Egypt.

Orientalist and therefore feminizing, the modern fascination with ancient Egypt led to the identification of YHWH with Isis/Artemis and Nature.[86] In the eyes of Schiller and others, the projects of idealism, Egyptian mystery religion, hermeticism, the natural sciences, and Mosaic religion all shared the common concern for the 'sublime' and 'supreme cause of all things'.[87] If Synagogue was a negative

82. Assmann, *Moses the Egyptian*, p. 120.
83. Kant writes, 'The veiled goddess before whom we of both parties bend our knees is the moral law in us, in its inviolable majesty' (Immanuel Kant, 'On a Newly Arisen Superior Tone in Philosophy', in Peter Fenves [ed.], *Raising the Tone of Philosophy: Late Essays by Immanuel Kant, Transformative Critique by Jacques Derrida* [Baltimore: The Johns Hopkins University Press, 1993], pp. 51-81 [71]).
84. See also Cesara Ripa, *Baroque and Rococo Pictorial Imagery* (ed. Edward Maser; New York: Dover, 1971), which first appeared in 1593. A number of veiled female figures appear here, especially Anima Rationalis (p. 5) and Stips [Alms] (p. 138). My thanks to Jane Aiken for suggesting this reference.
85. Assmann, *Moses the Egyptian*, p. 103.
86. For the link between Orientalism and women, see Alev Lytle Croutier, *Harem: The World Behind the Veil* (New York: Abbeville Press, 1989), pp. 173-206.
87. Assmann, *Moses the Egyptian*, p. 128.

feminine version of the veiled Moses, then Nature/Isis was a more positive but still disempowered transposition of Moses. By unveiling Moses, Paul's Christ boldly uncovers the glory and mysteries of Hebrew Scripture. By unveiling Nature, Schiller and other idealists repeat the gesture on a grander scale. The veil of Moses was nearly forgotten or repressed by the eighteenth century, but by the circuitous route of popular Egyptology and hermeticism, it had re-entered Western tradition.[88]

5. Conclusion

The avoidance of Moses' veil in written and pictorial traditions is unsurprising, especially since it competes against the stunning image of Moses with a glowing face or horns of light. For a prophet to be concealed and silent, if only at certain times, seems contrary to what prophets by definition do, though there are many biblical episodes that highlight prophetic silence and concealment.[89] In order to choose the veil as a subject, a commentator must explain it in terms of some moral failing or risk a definition of prophecy that includes silence and concealment at its very core. It is this second path that has been so rarely chosen by Jewish and Christian interpreters. At the same time, as Margaret Miles shows in *Image as Insight*, art can be more ambiguous than a written text, which can 'direct its own interpretation' and 'present a detachable conclusion'.[90] Basic to the life of many communities, art can serve a 'corrective' function in a tradition; Miles argues such a role for artistic images of women in fourteenth-century Italian art. Images of Moses' veil, I suggest, have an uncanny ability to evoke Exodus even when they illustrate Paul.[91] Each of these images shows the veil or mask without completely covering Moses' face, making the tension between revelation and concealment visible and compelling. And despite their negative associations, the feminizing qualities of the veil images (including Synagogue and the veil of Nature) expand their range of meaning. The vulnerability and feminization of the veiled Moses also evoke the mystery and fragility of revelation.[92]

But I suspect that the avoidance and transformations of Moses' veil reflect a somewhat narrow definition of prophecy and revelation—one based on a metaphysics of presence rather than absence, speech and writing rather than silence. It

---

88. This preoccupation with ancient Egypt continued to shape images of Moses in modern literature; see Chapter 2.

89. See my 'Prophetic Concealment in a Biblical Type Scene'.

90. Margaret Miles, *Image as Insight* (Boston: Beacon Press, 1985), p. 34. See also David Morgan, *Visual Piety* (Berkeley: University of California Press, 1998).

91. The idea of revelation that includes the veil would be more typical of contemporary thought: death of God theology, Levinas, postmodern theology. Emphatic reference is made to the veil in two recent books on Moses: Jonathan Kirsch, *Moses: A Life* (New York: Ballantine, 1988), and Nohrnberg, *Like Unto Moses*. Dynamics of revelation and concealment also inhere in Chinese fiction; see Anthony C. Yu, *Rereading the Stone: Desire and the Making of Fiction in Dream of the Red Chamber* (Princeton, NJ: Princeton University Press, 1997), p. 16.

92. The ability of art or language to evoke the very thing it seeks to suppress underlies a number of contemporary views of language and cultural expression, including, for example, works by Jacques Derrida, James Scott, and Judith Butler.

may be simplistic to say that the horns of light are masculine and the veil is feminine, but I would say that the avoidance of the veil reflects a patriarchal definition
of revelation as presence in speech and writing. This metaphysics is certainly
familiar enough in the post-biblical period, but whether it underlies the notion of
revelation in the Hebrew Bible is something I dispute. In fact, the veil in Exodus
figures centrally in a complex episode in which speech and writing are central. The
conspicuous concealment by the veil in Exodus 34 makes silence and absence part
of the process of revelation. Yet in Jewish and Christian tradition, the veil of Moses
usually comes to stand for sin, weakness, and absence.

As a metaphor for a negative moment in the process of revelation, the veil of
Moses has analogues in religious traditions of silence, mysticism, the *via negativa*,
and negative theology.[93] But these traditions developed in the post-biblical period
and make few references to such biblical motifs as the veil of Moses. The silence
about the veil of Moses is not simply inadvertent but also a kind of anxiety. Anxiety, according to Kierkegaard, is a 'dizziness of freedom, which emerges when the
spirit wants to posit the synthesis and freedom looks down into its own possibility,
laying hold of finiteness to support itself'.[94] This freedom is the freedom to
encounter the veil of Moses or to reject it. The anxiety before the veil corresponds
to an anxiety before the text, for as the tradition of rereading Moses' veil shows,
how Moses is read can determine nothing less than how the Bible is read, and the
status of Moses is tied directly to the status of the Torah. To accept a version of
Moses who is disempowered, and hence feminized, by a veil, was almost always
too costly a bargain for Jewish and Christian interpreters. But to encounter the veil
episode of Exodus is to accept ambiguity, silence, and an endlessly paradoxical
idea of revelation.

---

93.   The cases of Jacob of Serugh and Pseudo-Dionysius approach this description. There are
also clear affinities between negative and apophatic theology and post-structuralism. See Jacques
Derrida, 'Sauf le nom (Post-Scriptum)', in his *On the Name* (ed. Thomas Dutoit; trans. John P.
Leavey, Jr; Stanford: Stanford University Press, 1995), pp. 35-85.
94.   Kierkegaard, *The Concept of Anxiety*, p. 61. See Mordechai Agmon, 'The Idea of the
Radiant Skin of Moses' Face and the Veil', *Beth Miqra* 104 (1985), pp. 186-88. I wish to thank the
following for their helpful comments on this chapter: Jane Aiken, Andrew Becker, David Burr,
Anne-Marie Knoblauch, Jack C. Marler, Terry Papillon, and Fabrice Teulon.

Part II

UNCANNY BIBLICAL TEXTS

Chapter 5

MOSES' HEAVY MOUTH:
DISCOURSE AND REVELATION IN EXODUS 4.10-17

The commission of Moses in Exodus 3–4 resembles other biblical commission scenes, but it places special emphasis on whether and how Moses will communicate. Like the other episodes under examination in this book, it bears directly on the issue of revelation: how divine speech becomes human speech in Moses. Contrary to post-biblical traditions of biography, I argue that revelation, not the person of Moses, is a primary concern of the text. Moses' claim to be 'heavy of mouth and heavy of tongue' (Exod. 4.10) leads YHWH and Moses to talk about talking. While YHWH issues directives on the substantive issues of what Moses shall say and do, Moses initiates a dialogue about procedural matters. When YHWH commissions Moses to bring Israel out of Egypt, Moses responds, 'Who am I that I should go to Pharaoh?' and 'What shall I say to them?' The subsequent profession of ineloquence is the ultimate objection: if Moses cannot speak, how can he lead on YHWH's behalf? But what is the significance of this ineloquence? This chapter analyzes Exod. 4.10-17 with attention to what is said and how it is said. I suggest that the episode's elaborate focus on problems of speech forms a kind of writing concerned with the problem of revelation.

Like the episode of the veil in Exodus 34, Moses' final objection rarely appears in post-biblical tradition. It has little to offer commentators concerned with the biographical veneration and moral teachings of Moses. Those who do mention the episode, Philo and Josephus for instance, typically present it as a case of Moses' humility in the face of divine majesty. Philo glosses it as follows:

> But though he believed, he tried to refuse the mission, declaring that he was not eloquent, but feeble of voice and slow of tongue, especially ever since he heard God speaking to him; for he considered that human eloquence compared with God's was dumbness, and also, cautious as he was by nature, he shrank from things sublime and judged that matters of such magnitude were not for him.[1]

Insofar as it suggests that Moses is somehow flawed, the biblical scene undermines Philo's purpose of defending Moses against anti-Jewish attackers. Moses is not

---

1. Philo, *Moses*, p. 319. See also the shorter version in Josephus, *Jewish Antiquities*, IV, p. 283. In the modern period, the novelist Sholem Asch offers a modified version of the humility interpretation: 'an invincible humility made him doubt his fitness for the mission: how should he, with his stammering tongue, his proneness to excitement, be the spokesman of Israel before Pharaoh?' (*Moses*, pp. 110-11).

really impaired as a speaker; he only demurs because all human speech falls short of the divine. Despite his hagiographic focus, Philo nevertheless identifies an issue central to my analysis of the biblical text: the limitations of spoken revelation.

The passage reads as follows:

> But Moses said to the LORD, 'Oh, my Lord, I have never been eloquent, neither in the past nor even now that you have spoken to your servant; but I am slow of speech and of tongue'. Then the LORD said to him, 'Who gives speech to mortals? Who makes them mute or deaf, seeing or blind? Is it not I, the LORD? Now go, and I will be with your mouth and teach you what you are to speak.' But he said, 'Oh, my Lord, please send someone else'. Then the anger of the LORD was kindled against Moses and he said, 'What of your brother Aaron, the Levite? I know that he can speak fluently; even now he is coming out to meet you, and when he sees you his heart will be glad. You shall speak to him and put the words in his mouth; and I will be with your mouth and with his mouth, and will teach you what you shall do. He indeed shall speak for you to the people; he shall serve as a mouth for you, and you shall serve as God for him. Take in your hand this staff, with which you shall perform the signs.' (Exod. 4.10-17 NRSV)

1. *Moses' Objection*

YHWH seems to have a stake in preserving this tense, tenuous dialogue. Unlike other prophets who object only once, Moses thinks of as many objections as he can, and YHWH answers them all. Even when Moses ignites (חרה) YHWH's anger in 4.13, YHWH still continues the negotiation process. While the Exodus call narrative parallels other prophetic commissions (e.g. those of Jeremiah and Ezekiel), this encounter differs from the others in at least two important ways: first, unlike other prophets, Moses seems to reject YHWH's promise to be with his mouth in v. 13 (cf. Jer. 1.9); and second, YHWH capitulates to Moses' arguments, introducing a third, mediating party who will act as Moses' mouth (4.16) or prophet (7.1). Unlike other prophets, whom YHWH compensates for inarticulateness,[2] I suggest that Moses' speaking disability goes uncorrected because it paradoxically *enhances* his role, drawing attention to his writing and elevating him above the status of ordinary prophet.[3]

---

2.   For example, by touching Jeremiah's mouth (Jer. 1.9) or providing Ezekiel with the scroll to eat (Ezek. 3.1-2).

3.   In the second commission episode (from P, set off by the genealogies of Moses and Aaron), Moses complains that Israel didn't listen to him, implying that he, not Aaron, did the talking; he then calls himself a man 'of uncircumcised lips' (6.12, 30). God responds in 7.1 that with respect to their second task, Moses is to be God to Pharaoh and Aaron will be his prophet. Compared with 4.16, which orders Moses to act *as* (–ל) God to Aaron and Aaron *as* mouth to Israel, the second commission, by replacing simile with metaphor, seems stronger: as far as Pharaoh is concerned, Moses is God and Aaron is his prophet. The strength of the second case, in which Moses *is* God to Pharaoh, may stem from the fact that the opponent here is a man-god, Pharaoh. For the people, Moses can only act *as* God, but for the purposes of opposing Pharaoh (perhaps on his own terms), Moses will be God. Aaron is not included in this later discussion; with very few exceptions (most notably in v. 27), he hears YHWH's word only from the mouth of Moses. It is not until ch. 28 that he finally takes on a clear priestly role.

The heavy mouth of Moses is a case of the general element of 'objection' in Norman Habel's taxonomy of prophetic call narratives.[4] The elements include (1) divine confrontation; (2) introductory word; (3) commission; (4) objection; (5) reassurance; and (6) sign. What makes Exod. 4.10-17 so striking is that Moses extends the objections and reassurances beyond their usual length (see, e.g., Isa. 6; Jer. 1; Ezek. 3). Recognizable as a formal feature of prophetic narratives, the dialogue between Moses and YHWH in Exod. 4.10-17 constitutes (for the reader familiar with biblical tradition) a variation on the theme of prophets' stories. How it resembles and differs from other stories of prophetic commission, therefore, lends it much of its force and meaning.[5]

Moses' specific objection of ineloquence probably involves some kind of physical speech impediment.[6] Thus, like Jeremiah's complaint that he is too young (1.6), the objection is neither fictional nor unjustified: to be 'heavy of mouth and heavy of tongue' (4.10) is not the modesty, false or genuine, of a great orator. Nevertheless, Moses' plea has an unmistakable poetic eloquence, making effective use of repetition, alliteration, and formal address. Translated literally, it reads: 'Please (בי), my lord, not a man of words (דברים) am I (אנכי), neither (גם) yesterday nor (גם) the day before nor (גם) since you spoke (דברך) to your servant, for (כי) heavy (כבד) of mouth and heavy of tongue am I (אנכי)'.[7]

YHWH's reply (4.11) significantly appropriates two key terms used by Moses: פה ('mouth') and אנכי ('I'). The implication is that Moses doesn't need to tell YHWH

4. Norman Habel, 'The Form and Significance of the Call Narratives', *ZAW* 77 (1965), pp. 298-301.

5. See my 'Prophetic Concealment in a Biblical Type Scene'.

6. See Jeffrey H. Tigay, '"Heavy of Mouth" and "Heavy of Tongue": On Moses' Speech Difficulty', *BASOR* 231 (1978), pp. 57-67. Several ancient sources shared the view that Moses had a speech impediment; see Kugel, *The Bible as it Was*, pp. 296-97.

7. Two literary tropes—*inclusio* and parallelism—appear in the speech. First, Moses forms his remark into a small *inclusio* with statements that place the first person pronoun in predicate position: 'not a man of words am I', and 'heavy of mouth and heavy of tongue am I'. The first statement is negative and introduced by בי, and the second is positive and introduced by כי. Among the many parallelisms are the repeated use of גם, the forms of דבר, and the double use of כבד with the semantic parallels 'mouth' and 'tongue'. YHWH replies in a similarly poetic vein: 'Who has given (שם) a mouth to man, or (או) who makes him (ישום) dumb or (או) deaf (or possibly "dumb") or (או) open-eyed or (או) blind? Is it not I (אנכי), YHWH?' Parallelism runs through this disputational reply of YHWH. The repetition of או echoes Moses' גם, and the two forms of שם ('put' or 'make') apply directly to Moses' double use of דבר ('word', 'speak'): YHWH puts and Moses speaks. In addition, חרש can mean dumb as well as deaf, and פקח, meaning 'open-eyed', may represent a disease of the eyes. This suggestion and many other helpful comments come from Terence E. Fretheim. Thus, contrary to most interpretations, YHWH's statement may present two pairs of semantic parallels indicating disabilities: two terms for dumbness and two for blindness. This reading yields a more balanced parallelism and supports the view that Moses' disability is real and that YHWH knows this very well. My understanding of parallelism comes mainly from the following three sources: Dennis Pardee, *Ugaritic and Hebrew Poetic Parallelism: A Trial Cut* (VTSup, 39; Leiden: E.J. Brill, 1988); James Kugel, *The Idea of Biblical Poetry* (New Haven: Yale University Press, 1981); and Adele Berlin, *The Dynamics of Biblical Parallelism* (Bloomington: Indiana University Press, 1985).

about his mouth because he put it there, and even though Moses uses polite language, YHWH doesn't miss his emphatic double use of the pronoun. By imitating Moses' parallelistic form and repeating parts of his speech, YHWH implies that Moses' attempt to sound unworthy and humble is in fact an arrogant affront to YHWH's knowledge and power. In the disputational question-and-answer style of wisdom literature (with parallels in Ps. 94 and Job 38), YHWH accuses Moses of faithlessness and an excessive pride that for some commentators evokes *hubris*, the flaw of Greek tragic protagonists.[8]

The dialogue in vv. 10-11 may be seen as a miniature debate initiated by Moses and won by YHWH. Moses first poses a new and understandable challenge to YHWH's plan, and YHWH replies with a rhetorical question-and-answer that mirrors and undercuts Moses' objection. As victor, YHWH then shifts the discourse from dialogue back to directive: 'Go now, for I will be with your mouth (פֶּה) and teach you what to say' (4.12).

As a response to Moses' concern, this statement is as much a promise as an order. The scolding of 4.11 is followed by a more consoling tone, first in a brief order (וְעַתָּה לֵךְ), a common phrase in the prophetic call formula, cf., e.g., Isa. 6.8) and then in an expression of promise and support that reiterates the two key terms פֶּה and אָנֹכִי, along with the verb 'I will be' (אֶהְיֶה), reminiscent of the disclosure of the divine name in 3.14. YHWH's statement is gentle but firm; after winning the debate, there is a clear attempt to return to the discourse of directive.

Another shift—from the general to the particular—takes place in vv. 11-12. In the disputational response to Moses, YHWH points out that he puts the mouth in man (אָדָם) universally and then promises to be with Moses' mouth in particular. The first point defeats Moses on his own terms, and the second redirects the discourse to YHWH's specific agenda for action. By twice quoting Moses' use of פֶּה and אָנֹכִי, YHWH shows a true mastery of dialogue and persuasion. The ability to borrow terms from a conversation partner shows that YHWH is flexible and listens well; the artful use of these terms for a new purpose (the referent of אָנֹכִי, for example, changes) shows a rhetorical ability to direct and control the dialogue.

But in v. 13 Moses arouses YHWH's anger with a cryptic, poetic request. The plea, which translates literally as 'Please, my Lord, send, I pray, by the hand [of the one whom] you will send', appears in Childs' commentary as 'Please, O Lord, send anybody else'.[9] According to Gesenius, Moses' statement is an elliptical and poetic way of saying, '"send, I pray thee, by the hand of him whom thou wilt send", i.e., by the hand of some one else'.[10] The medieval commentators Rashi, Ibn Ezra, and Abarbanel, on the other hand, interpret the phrase as a request to send Aaron

---

8.   Brevard Childs, *The Book of Exodus: A Critical, Theological Commentary* (Philadelphia: Westminster Press, 1974), p. 78. For the idea of Moses as tragic hero, see Hillel Barzel, 'Moses: Tragedy and Sublimity', in K. Gros Louis, S. Ackerman and T.S. Warshaw (eds.), *Literary Interpretations of Biblical Narratives* (Nashville: Abingdon Press, 1974), pp. 120-40. I also thank Jon Levenson for his comments on this subject.

9.   Childs, *Exodus*, p. 49.

10.   GKC, p. 488. 'By the hand' (בְּיַד) forms a construct with the independent relative clause formed by the verb תִּשְׁלָח, with the demonstrative pronoun הוּ and the relative אֲשֶׁר suppressed.

instead of Moses: 'By the hand of him, whom Thou usest to send, and this is Aaron'.[11] But why does this imply someone else? Why is Moses' hand excluded from the possibilities? What is the plain sense of this passage? How can YHWH send by the hand of the one he will send? How can YHWH choose by means of the one he has chosen? A closer look at this utterance may provide some clues.

Moses' statement is an *idem per idem* construction. According to Jack Lundbom, *idem per idem* is a type of tautology often used by God in the Hebrew Bible to terminate debate.[12] Modern examples include 'But rules are rules', and 'Que sera sera'.[13] Lundbom shows how God uses the *idem per idem* to discontinue dialogues with Moses, most notably in the disclosure of the divine name in Exod. 3.14.[14] What is interesting here is that Moses, not God, uses *idem per idem*. The question is: For what purpose? If YHWH has already discontinued the dialogue, then why would Moses need to do so here? How are we to interpret Moses' imperative to send whomever YHWH wishes? Is it respectful, as many commentators have suggested, or impertinent, as William Propp speculates?[15]

The three interpretations of v. 13 given so far—a plea to send anyone else, a plea to send Aaron specifically, and a tautology intended to end the dialogue—all seem incomplete to me. On the one hand, if Moses is asking for YHWH to send anyone else or Aaron, then why isn't this stated more directly (instead of ביד תשלח, perhaps איש אחר or את אהרן)? This interpretation ignores Moses' request to send by the hand of the one YHWH sends. On the other hand, the statement must be more than a dismissive stoppage of dialogue, contrary to Lundbom's view. In order for that to be the case, the dialogue would have to be still in progress, but as I have shown, YHWH has already closed it with a command and promise. In fact, Moses attempts here to reopen the dialogue with his remark, at least long enough to make a servile request of YHWH.

Noting the manner of Moses' request is essential to understanding it. Gesenius and Childs rightly observe that Moses asks YHWH to send someone else, but they say little about how the request is made; neither addresses the fact that Moses doesn't exclude himself or the problem of the already-chosen hand ('send by the hand of him whom you have chosen'). According to Rashi, Moses asks specifically for Aaron as a substitute rather than an assistant; but the text is not that explicit. Finally, Lundbom's interpretation of *idem per idem* as a termination of dialogue, while it applies to God's use of the trope, fails to describe its use in 4.13; instead of cutting God off, Moses seems to be reopening the dialogue, albeit ambiguously.

Umberto Cassuto recognizes that Moses does not exclude himself from the statement, but he interprets Moses' unenthusiastic words in 4.13 as an implicit

11. M. Kalisch, *A Historical and Critical Commentary on the Old Testament—Exodus* (London: Longman, Brown, Green & Longman, 1855), p. 72.

12. Jack R. Lundbom, 'God's Use of the *Idem Per Idem* to Terminate Debate', *HTR* 71 (1978), pp. 193-201. The two main examples adduced by Lundbom are Exod. 3.14 and 33.19.

13. Lundbom, 'God's Use of the *Idem Per Idem*', p. 196.

14. Lundbom, 'God's Use of the *Idem Per Idem*', p. 197.

15. See William Propp, *Exodus 1–18* (AB, 2; Garden City, NY: Doubleday, 1999), p. 213.

unwillingness to serve: 'by the hand of whomever Thou dost wish to send, except me'.[16] He explains:

> This restriction, 'except me', he does not dare to utter explicitly, and his words are so phrased as to be construed even as an expression of assent: by the hand of whom Thou wishest, and if it is Thy wish to send by my hand, I shall obey. But the Lord, looking in his heart, understands that he is still hesitant and full of misgivings and that if he will agree, he will do so without enthusiasm.

Cassuto offers two opposing interpretations—one of the text and the other of sub-text—and because of God's angry response, he favors the subtext. But in order to find this interpretation convincing, one must share Cassuto's view that God's anger reacts against something outside the text: Moses' heart. Such extratextual evidence, especially about something as unknown as God's thoughts and Moses' psychology (equally but more famously elusive in 4.24-26), weakens the interpretation. Although Moses' statement in 4.13 seems polysemic, I suggest the following new interpretation: Moses is in fact asking for what God provides—to send by the hand of him whom he has sent, that is, by Moses' hand.[17] Using an indirect, poetic, and respectful expression, Moses may be asking YHWH to consider sending someone *in addition to*, not instead of, himself. Another use of שלח in the imperative appears in the call of Isaiah (6.8): הנני שלחני. Here, as in Exodus 4, there is a dialogue between YHWH and the prophet in which the commission is negotiated—and agreed upon—with the prophet's use of this verbal form.[18] Since this person would be sent by Moses' hand, a natural choice would be his brother, Aaron. 'Even now', says YHWH, Aaron is on his way to meet Moses, 'and when he sees you his heart will be glad' (v. 14).

Aaron, introduced here for the first time, is presented as Moses' brother, the Levite, and as the one who, God claims emphatically, *can* speak.[19] All three terms identify Aaron in relation to Moses: brother, Levite (which also means 'joined to'), and speaker. As if conjured out of divine and narrative necessity, Aaron conveniently emerges from his brother's shadow with no independent identity in order to solve the problem of the heavy mouth.[20] Just as YHWH puts the mouth into the

---

16. Umberto Cassuto, *A Commentary on the Book of Exodus* (trans. Israel Abrams; Jerusalem: Magnes Press, 1967), p. 49.

17. The interpretation of ביד as referring to Moses' hand goes at least as far back as *Exodus Rabbah*, where Moses' request is characterized as an incredulous question why God would send by Moses' hand to save the people when God usually saves them by the hands of angels.

18. Another related feature of these texts is the common occurrence of phonetic parallelism, often achieved by repeating verbal forms. Cf. Isa. 6.9; Obad. 1.1; Jer. 1.7; Hos. 1.2.

19. Both the use of the infinitive construct דבר with the imperfect ידבר and the inclusion of the pronoun הו make this statement emphatic. See Cassuto, *Exodus*, p. 50.

20. In addition to reading הלוי as 'joined to', it is hard to resist the visual and aural resemblance between Aaron's name (אהרן) and the word אחרון (which appears nearby in v. 8), meaning 'other' or 'latter'. Such a connection would suggest a definition of Aaron as 'the other guy'. To carry this speculation a bit further, v. 8 can perhaps serve as a gloss on the Moses/Aaron relationship: if the people don't believe the first sign (i.e. Moses), then maybe they'll believe the latter (אחרון) sign. In other words, YHWH will take two different approaches and see which one works

generic person (אָדָם), Moses, as Aaron's 'God', puts words into the mouth of Aaron, the generic assistant. Yet not until ch. 28, when he receives his priestly office, does Aaron take on a consistent and truly distinctive role; and it is not until the golden calf episode in ch. 32 that he acts independently. It remains a question open to interpretation why Aaron does not in fact fulfill the spokesman role. It could be that Aaron's mere presence gives Moses the confidence to overcome his speech difficulty, or that his role is only a convenient way to introduce an important priestly figure into the story. Nevertheless, the text unequivocally asserts the oratorical role and reiterates it in ch. 7.

Still, Moses' request remains vague and elusive. Without naming Aaron, Moses asserts the need for a second, a mediator for the mediator, to be sent by the hand of the one sent. Without explicitly accepting God's commission, he suggests that the hand by which God sends will be his own, thus reopening the negotiation with a bid for an assistant. This interpretation accounts for God's twofold response of anger and the commission of Aaron. After YHWH has answered Moses' objections and closed the dialogue, Moses reopens it by telling God what to do; anger is an understandable response. The choice of Aaron may thus be construed both as a punishment—for Moses must now share his power with one who will abuse it (Exod. 32)[21]—and as a compromise, since God fulfills Moses' request to choose an additional person.

Reading v. 13 in this way means that both parties gain and give up something: Moses increases his stature by adding an assistant in the hierarchy of revelation, but he must also concede that his leadership is temporary and will be replaced by the institution of Aaron's levitical party. (The appearance of Jethro in vv. 18-20, who, like Aaron, offers Moses an institutional framework to routinize the religion later in ch. 18, is an interesting parallel.) YHWH, on the other hand, angrily grants Aaron as a concession to Moses but successfully appoints Moses in the end. From this standpoint, the attempt to kill Moses in 4.24-26 may indicate that the divine wrath remains unabated.[22]

Still, the agreement represents a triumph for divine–human dialogue (cf. Exod. 32 and Num. 11–12). In response to Moses' request, YHWH reasserts directive over dialogue (vv. 14-17), but the speech, which begins with a question ('Isn't there Aaron your brother?'), remains interactive. Without using the customary imperative verbal form, YHWH tells Moses what he and his brother will do, shifting from

best. This trial-and-error account could explain the change in plan from the appointment of Aaron as speaker to his relative silence in carrying out the tasks of organizing the Hebrews and persuading Pharaoh to release them.

21.   As Cassuto, *Exodus*, p. 50, points out.

22.   The 'bridegroom of blood' episode resembles Gen. 32–33, where Jacob combats a mysterious representative of God while awaiting a meeting with his brother Esau. Fraternal rivalry and friendship coincide in both texts as metaphors for the divine–human relationship, an unstable arrangement that leads to mysterious violence and the re-establishment of divine sovereignty. In Exod. 4, the divine attempt to kill Moses dramatizes the ambivalence of YHWH and Moses toward the compromise they have just arranged. See Pamela Tamarkin Reis, 'The Bridegroom of Blood: A New Reading', *Judaism* 40 (1991), pp. 324-31 (325).

procedural to substantive concerns: he is coming to meet you, you will put words in his mouth, he will speak for you, you will take in your hand the rod with which you will do the signs. The repeated promise to be with Moses' mouth and to instruct the two brothers on what to do opens the possibility for continued dialogue in the future. In thus blending the dialogical and directive forms of discourse (as well as procedural and substantive concerns), YHWH and Moses seem to have come to a tentative meeting of the minds.

2. *Moses and Aaron*

Despite the necessity of Aaron's commission and his superior eloquence, Moses clearly stands above him in the chain of command. Moses will talk to Aaron, who is already on the way to meet Moses (has God commissioned him already?), and, echoing God's language in v. 11, put words in his mouth (ושמת את־הדברים בפיו). At the same time, YHWH, repeating key words אנכי and פה from 3.14, 4.10 and 4.11, will be with their mouths (ואנכי אהיה עם־פיך ועם־פיהו). Aaron will do the talking, he will act 'as' (the force of the ־ל is unclear) a mouth to Moses, and Moses will be (as) God (לאלהים, not יהוה) to Aaron.

But since this plan is not consistently carried out in Exodus or elsewhere in the Pentateuch, since Moses usually does the talking, then what is the role of Aaron? In the plague narratives for example, it is Moses (or 'Moses and Aaron') who speak(s), while Aaron often mutely performs the signs. Is he Moses' alter ego, an articulate Cyrano for the bashful Moses, a political front man for a powerful holy man, or the priestly inheritor of the cult established by Moses? Why does Moses need a helper when other prophets work alone?[23] Historians would undoubtedly reply that Aaron's traditional priestly role explains his appearance, but this sheds no light on his spokesman role here.

Because the text is so emphatic about Moses' ineloquence despite his effective speaking elsewhere, it seems to me that any interpretation of this passage must understand Moses' inability not as a regrettable circumstance to be overlooked but rather as an *inherent* and *positive* feature of Moses' role as prophet and leader. For if Aaron is the more capable speaker, then why doesn't YHWH simply abandon Moses and replace him with Aaron? Even though the selection of Aaron arises out of contingency, YHWH's decision to keep Moses despite his protests suggests that Moses and his handicap are necessary to the process of revelation and salvation.

---

23.   According to Frank Moore Cross, the coleadership of Moses and Aaron reflects an underlying historical rivalry between the Mushite and Aaronid priestly schools (Frank Cross, *Canaanite Myth and Hebrew Epic* [Cambridge, MA: Harvard University Press, 1973], pp. 196-97). Cross argues that the northern Elohistic source (E) contained a polemic against the Aaronid school and that other sources in the ancient tradition militated against the Mushite priestly line. Our final version of the text (probably edited by P) suppressed and perhaps sought to resolve this controversy, which was a dead issue at the time of redaction. While the historical circumstance may help explain why Moses shares power with Aaron, it does not explain the specific nature of their relationship any more than a speech impediment does.

3. *Discourse and Revelation*

To return to my initial question: What is the significance of ineloquence in Exod. 4.10-17? I argue that Moses' heaviness of mouth is real, that YHWH does not correct it, and that it serves as an *asset* to his leadership rather than a liability. Even though the selection of Aaron arises out of contingent circumstance, YHWH reacts to these events by elevating inarticulate Moses to the status of prophet, leader, and lawgiver. Moses fits into a category by himself, as one who acts *as* God to Israel and *is* God (metaphorically) to Pharaoh (the statement in 7.1 has no –ל prefix).[24] Aaron, who is defined by and 'joined to' Moses, represents the more conventional human leadership role of spokesman and performer of signs. While Moses achieves an unparalleled intimacy with YHWH, his charismatic leadership is only temporary, and it is Aaron who must later institutionalize in a priestly cult what Moses has begun.

The main parts of the so-called prophetic call formula—confrontation, introductory word, commission, objection, and sign—all appear in Exodus 3–4, but the four objections in the Moses story give it a highly protracted form.[25] In addition, YHWH gives Moses something more than just a sign of reassurance in 4.14-16; he offers a concession (though without correcting the heavy mouth). In the call narratives of Jeremiah, Ezekiel, and Isaiah 6 and 40, there is no such concession; YHWH merely offers reassurance. Only with Moses is there a prolonged negotiation and compromise.

YHWH's preference for an ineloquent person of action (cf. Exod. 2.11-15) and willingness to grant him a spokesman sets Moses apart from other prophets, who work primarily through the spoken word. In fact, the commission in Exod. 7.1-2, a close parallel to Exod. 4.16 likely from the priestly tradition, names Aaron as the prophet and Moses as God to Pharaoh. I believe that Moses' closeness to God and inarticulateness suggest something about the nature of revelation in Exodus. Martin Buber comments:

> Sent as bearer of the word, intermediary between heaven and earth through the word, Moses possesses no mastery over freely coursing speech. He has been created thus and has been chosen thus. By this a barrier is raised between him and the human world. He who has to establish the covenant between the people and YHVH is, so to speak, not accepted fully into the covenant of his tribe... And in this way the tragedy of Moses becomes the tragedy inherent in Revelation. It is laid upon the stammering to bring the voice of Heaven to Earth.[26]

Moses is elevated *because of*, not despite, his speaking difficulty. But how? If speaking well is unimportant to his work and Aaron is supposed to relieve Moses of that handicap but does not, then in what does Moses' commission consist? The

24. See Terence E. Fretheim, *The Suffering of God* (Philadelphia: Fortress Press, 1984), pp. 50-51.

25. Habel, 'Form and Significance', pp. 297-323. See also Michael Fishbane, *Text and Texture* (New York: Schocken Books, 1979), pp. 68-69.

26. Buber, *Moses*, p. 59.

most common pious response to the question is that Moses' speech impediment shows that God can do all things. Calvin, for instance, declares: 'It seems a mockery, then, to give a commission of speaking to a stammerer; but in this way (as I have said), He causes His glory to shine forth more brightly, proving that He can do all things without extrinsic aid'.[27] But how, exactly, can this be? If the speech defect has in fact not been corrected, then how is Moses' speech glorious rather than simply difficult to understand?

There are at least two other traditional explanations for Moses' heavy mouth: one is to make it a kind of punishment, following Propp's suggestion that the impediment would be removed if Moses were to agree to the commission.[28] Moses' speech impediment, in other words, is somehow his own fault. A more elaborate explanation of the impediment is the ancient story that Moses received it from a burning coal. Perhaps with the burning coal of Isaiah's commission as background, the story goes that the young child Moses, who had just thrown Pharaoh's crown to the ground, was tested to see if he was capable of rational choice:

> If he puts his hand out for the burning coal, then he has no sense and he ought not to be condemned to death; but if he puts his hand forth to the gold, then he does have sense and you should kill him. At once they brought before him a piece of gold and a burning coal, and Moses put forth his hand to take the gold. But the angel Gabriel came and pushed his hand aside and his hand seized the coal and he put it to his mouth with the coal still in it and his tongue was injured, and from this he became 'heavy of speech and heavy of tongue'. (Exod. 4.10)[29]

This story brilliantly merges two motifs: Moses the heroic victim of persecution (an extension of the danger associated with his birth in Exod. 1–2), and Moses the prophet like Isaiah, whose mouth is touched by burning coal. For Isaiah, the coal purifies 'unclean lips' (Isa. 6.5, טמא־שפתים; cf. Exod. 6.30, ערל שפתים), while for Moses it saves the life of the savior, leaving a permanent injury.

I propose another possibility: that the diminution of speech in Moses' commission implies the magnification of Moses' other means of communication—writing. Although the dialogue between Moses and YHWH concerns speech rather than writing, I suggest that the speech impediment leads to the issue of writing nevertheless. Let me describe three concepts of writing: first, writing as a subject of concern in the Bible; second, writing as a canonical concern of the Bible; and third, writing as a category of discourse that applies not only to inscriptions but also to the capacity of discourse to be cited, iterated, and interpreted.

Writing is an explicit part of Moses' activity. At several key points in Exodus (17.14; 24.4; 34.27), Moses writes the words of YHWH as memorial, law, and covenant. These acts of writing, along with the writing of the law and the song at the conclusion of his life (and of the Pentateuch) in Deuteronomy 31, are among the most important actions performed by Moses, since they are connected with the

27.   John Calvin, *Calvin's Commentaries* (trans. Charles Bingham; Grand Rapids: Baker Book House, 1989), I, p. 92.

28.   Propp, *Exodus 1–18*, p. 212.

29.   *Exod. R.* 1.26, cited in Kugel, *The Bible as it Was*, p. 298.

preservation and codification of the events related in the Pentateuch. Likewise, the paradox that Moses, the charismatic prophet, was also an inarticulate scribe while Aaron, the forbear of the priestly caste of which scribes were members, was said to be his spokesman, blurs the lines between speech and text, past and present.

The shift in emphasis from speech to writing can also be marked by comparing Exodus 4 and the writing of the tablets and golden calf episode in Exodus 32–34. As I argue in Chapter 4 and elsewhere,[30] the episode of Moses' shining face and veil in Exodus 34 represents a recommissioning of Moses as a prophet. Exodus 4 and 32–34 thus represent two commissioning narratives, the first concentrating on speech and presenting Aaron as a partner, and the second emphasizing writing (not only of the two sets of tablets, but also of the divine 'book' in 32.33) and the failure of Aaron as a partner. The original, speech-based plan laid out in Exodus 4 (and 7.1, in which Aaron is Moses' prophet) fails by the time of the golden calf episode, a crisis so serious that it causes Moses to contemplate his own death. The extraordinary theophany of ch. 33 leads to the inscription of a second set of tablets, a covenant ceremony, and the frightful transformation of Moses' face.

The concern with writing takes on a larger dimension in the context of the biblical canon. In Deuteronomy 31, Moses writes a Torah (31.9, 24) that may be interpreted to include Deuteronomy, including the provision that God will raise up a prophet for the people and put words into his mouth (18.18; see also Isa. 51.16). If Moses is such a prophet, as Exod. 4.12-15 and Deut. 34.10 suggest, then Moses the *writer* encompasses Moses the *prophet*: Moses is a speaking character in a story written by himself. The reflexivity of Moses as a writer of the story and a figure in it express the paradox of what Derrida calls 'the writing being' and 'the being written'.[31] From a canonical perspective, Moses is both, and his speech impediment, by minimizing speech, maximizes writing.

The metaphor of writing is explicit in the call narrative of Ezekiel, in which he eats a sweet-tasting scroll inscribed with lamentations: 'Eat this scroll, and go, speak to the house of Israel' (Ezek. 3.1). The spoken message of Ezekiel comes from a written text; writing thus takes priority over speech as the more authoritative form of communication. The metaphor implies that the prophet's words are the authoritative expression of God and not the spontaneous utterances of the prophet. Even though Exodus 4 makes no reference to writing, the analogy to Ezekiel is telling: YHWH will teach Moses what to say, despite his speech impediment (4.12). The oracles of the prophet are a kind of text from which he reads; Moses' uncorrected speech impediment underscores the divine source of his oracles.

According to Paul Ricoeur, 'Writing is the full manifestation of discourse', a 'fixed' form of discourse.[32] Unlike speech, which tends to be spontaneous and limited to only one utterance, writing has the capacity to transcend the moment of utterance and the voice of the speaker. Of course, by saying this, Ricoeur

---

30. Britt, 'Prophetic Concealment in a Biblical Type-Scene'.

31. Derrida, *Of Grammatology*, p. 18.

32. Paul Ricoeur, *Interpretation Theory* (Fort Worth: Texas Christian University Press, 1976), pp. 25-26.

immediately opens himself to post-structuralist critics such as Derrida who challenge the traditional distinction between speech and writing. In light of this, I would extend Ricoeur's definition of writing to include utterances that can, in Derrida's words, be 'cited'; writing in this sense is a statement that is 'iterable'— we can hold it up to scrutiny, we can analyze it, we can make sense of it through interpretation.[33] In this way, statements—written or spoken—can be described in terms of their 'citability' or 'iterability'. Iterability depends on the ability to repeat an utterance. Inscription is one source of iterability, but so are formalized types of discourse, such as decrees, divinely given oracles, prophetic call narratives, and elaborate literary structures and discourses such as the dialogue in Exod. 4.10-17.

Like Ezekiel, Moses speaks the words of YHWH, which constitute a kind of writing insofar as they are fixed and iterable. Exodus 4 itself constitutes a kind of writing, not simply because it has been inscribed, but because its poetic shape and rhetorical structure carry the marks of fixed, iterable discourse. Yet there is a paradox in the dialogue: this highly wrought literary text remains a lively, even surprising record of speech. The dialogue suggests an astonishing balance of power between Moses and YHWH as each of them vies for advantage. Moses does become the prophet of YHWH, and his speech defect does imply that his words will follow YHWH's script rather than his own initiative. At the same time, the provision of Aaron as a kind of mouthpiece and assistant to Moses foreshadows a number of events in which Moses shares more of YHWH's glory than other prophets do. Like the blurring of human identity between Moses and Aaron, there is a blurring of divine authority in Moses and YHWH; both are authors and scribes of the Exodus event. The writing of the law has a dual causality in the figures of Moses and YHWH. On Sinai, after YHWH's continuous presentation of law in chs. 20–23, we are told (in 24.4) that Moses wrote it all down. But later in v. 12, YHWH tells Moses to come up and receive the tablets he (YHWH) has written. Earlier, in the first reference to Moses' writing in 17.14, after the defeat of Amalek, YHWH tells Moses to write it in 'the book' (what book?) as a memorial (זכרון). But in clear antonymic parallelism to the *act* of writing, the *message* of the writing is to be that YHWH will *completely erase* (מחה אמחה) the memory (זכר) of Amalek. Moses writes about God's un-writing of the enemy; writing records the memory of the removal of an enemy from memory.

Moses brings the law—given by God and written by Moses and God—down from Sinai to the people in a written form. Just as importantly, the biblical narrative, in which Moses lives, leads, and dies, must be received in written form. 'Writing' here means not only the inscription of characters on stone or parchment, but also a way of understanding events. Such an understanding construes events as capable of being rendered but not captured in language; writing constitutes, recalls,

---

33. 'Could a performative statement succeed if its formulation did not repeat a "coded" or iterable statement, in other words if the expressions I use to open a meeting, launch a ship or a marriage were not identifiable as *conforming* to an iterable model, and therefore if they were not identifiable in a way as "citation"?' (Jacques Derrida, 'Signature Event Context', in *idem, Margins of Philosophy* [trans. Alan Bass; Chicago: University of Chicago Press, 1982], pp. 324-26).

and canonizes events. Buber observes: 'By means of...[writing] one can embody in the stone what has been revealed to one... What Moses says may be clumsy, but not what he writes; that is suitable for his time and for the later times in which the stone will testify.'[34] The tradition attributing the authorship of the Pentateuch to Moses, still alive in many religious communities today, affirms that writing is a category implicit in the biblical notion of revelation. Despite its doubtful historicity, this tradition understands writing to be primary to language, rather than secondary to speech.[35]

Far from being a derivative supplement to other forms of language, writing lies at the foundations of language, the vehicle of biblical revelation and memory through the ages. In Exodus, the problem of revelation appears first and most fully in the call of Moses, in which the speech of God confronts the speech impediment of Moses.[36] Revelation, which Ricoeur says 'takes place between the secret and the revealed'[37] and for Benjamin represents the 'highest mental region of religion',[38] depends in this case upon the stability and interpretive possibilities of a written text. In Exod. 4.10-17, where Moses and YHWH speak about speaking, an abundance of poetic and eloquent language calls attention to the fact that this exchange appears in written form. Moses may not be a man of words, but the skillfully written language of his discourse with YHWH bears careful reading and rereading. Alternating modes of discourse and surprising uses of repetition, *inclusio*, parallelism, and *idem per*

34. Buber, *Moses*, p. 140. Buber's point finds support in recent historical work on the role of writing in ancient Israelite society and religion. Pointing to archaeological evidence and such texts as Josh. 8.32 and Deut. 27.2-4, Aaron Demsky has suggested that monarchic Israel was a literate society and that the scribal arts of writing and reading were central to the priesthood and Israelite religion in general ('Writing in Ancient Israel and Early Judaism: Part One, The Biblical Period', in Martin Jan Mulder and Harry Sysling [eds.], *Mikra* [Philadelphia: Fortress Press, 1988], pp. 1-20 [15-19]). For instance, Demsky observes the significance of a priestly blessing written on an amulet, claiming it 'would indicate the wider application afforded by writing by freeing the power of the oral blessing from the limitations of time and place of the cultic setting and making it the personal and constant possession of the owner of the amulet' (p. 17). Tracing the importance of writing even earlier to the biblical period, Demsky writes, 'in the view of the biblical authors the nascency of the people of Israel and of the established forms of its religion as going back to the Exodus and Sinai is inherently connected with writing' (p. 18).

35. Another contemporary thinker in the Jewish tradition, Jacques Derrida (see Susan Handelman, *The Slayers of Moses* [Albany: State University of New York Press, 1982]), writes: 'By a hardly perceptible necessity, it seems as though the concept of writing—no longer indicating a particular, derivative, auxiliary form of language in general...is beginning to go beyond the extension of language. In all senses of the word, writing thus *comprehends* language... Either writing was never a simple "supplement", or it is urgently necessary to construct a new logic of the "supplement"' (Derrida, *Of Grammatology*, pp. 6-7).

36. For a discussion of the prophetic call motif in terms of the 'psychology of the sublime', see Herbert Marks, 'On Prophetic Stammering', in Regina Schwartz (ed.), *The Book and the Text* (Oxford: Basil Blackwell), pp. 60-80.

37. Paul Ricoeur, 'Toward a Hermeneutic of the Idea of Revelation', in *idem*, *Essays on Biblical Interpretation* (Philadelphia: Fortress Press, 1985), pp. 73-118 (94).

38. Benjamin, 'On Language as Such and on the Language of Man', in *idem*, *Reflections*, pp. 314-32.

idem display the complexity and reciprocity of the divine–human relationship. The discourse of the spoken word, with its highly stylized and complex rhetoric, its polyvalent meaning, its reflexivity, and the uneasy oscillation between dialogue and directive, substance and procedure, can only come to life through writing. By de-emphasizing speech, the episode calls attention to the power of writing through the dual agency of YHWH and Moses: both are speakers *within* the story, but they are also writers *of* the story—Exodus can be called the Word of God or the Book of Moses.

The implied priority of writing over speaking offers insight into what Buber calls the tragedy of Moses and the tragedy of revelation. In Moses and in writing, this tragedy lies in the concept of mediation. Whether the mediator is called allegorist, prophet, or translator, his or her work is always linguistic. Like translation, media-tion is both necessary and impossible: something always gets lost along the way. For both Moses and YHWH, Exodus is a long process of mediation that entails enormous sacrifice; YHWH risks the mediation of the Word in written form, and Moses risks his life in the dangerous position of mediator between God and people. While Moses' heavy mouth helps to transcend the spoken word, it also hampers his own career as a prophet among humans: he could never be an Aaron. The tragedy of Moses, then, stems not from the tragic flaw of *hubris* but from what Aristotle calls *hamartia* (imperfection).[39] The symbol of Moses' *hamartia*, I would suggest, is his heaviness of mouth. The mediation of language thus determines what is tragic both for Moses (who is ineloquent) and for God (in the category of revelation). And it is only through writing that the speech of God and Moses can be reread, reinterpreted, and remembered.

39.   Aristotle, *The Poetics* (Cambridge, MA: Harvard University Press, 1982), p. 46.

Chapter 6

THE TORAH OF MOSES:
DEUTERONOMY 31–32 AS A TEXTUAL MEMORIAL

Deuteronomy 31–34 is a pivotal text: it signifies conclusion and transition, the death of Moses and the establishment of written tradition. If Deuteronomy presents the 'farewell speech of Moses',[1] then these final chapters are the peroration. In terms of its main points—the death of Moses, the centrality of Torah (תורה), and commissioning of Joshua—the text is clear. But with respect to chronology, action, structure, and the meaning of some terms, Deuteronomy 31–34 is far from clear or univocal.

This chapter analyzes the narrative structure and content of Deuteronomy 31–32 in the context of Deuteronomy 31–34. I propose that two narrative strands alternate in Deuteronomy 31–32: one on the death of Moses and commission of Joshua, and another on the recording and promulgation of texts. These two strands appear to harmonize in Deut. 32.44-47. While my methods are literary, I avoid modern standards of coherence and single authorship. This approach suggests that the redactor(s) chose a principle of inclusiveness (of a certain kind) over unity or precision, partly because of the text's importance, rather than despite it.

I also suggest, heuristically, that the text's self-reference as 'witness' (עד) and the concept of memorial reflect the overall function of the narrative in Deuteronomy 31–32.[2] Like a stone monument, the text ascribes itself didactic and memorial purposes for a community and its generations to come. As a textual memorial, the text appears to draw together distinct elements and synthesize them in one passage (32.44-47) in a way that puts emphasis on the subject of writing and reciting, hence canonizing, Torah.[3]

---

1. Gerhard von Rad, *Deuteronomy: A Commentary* (trans. Dorothea Barton; Philadelphia: Westminster Press, 1966), p. 22. This chapter first appeared in *BibInt* 8 (2000), pp. 358-74.

2. The metaphorical and heuristic idea of Deut. 31–32 as a textual memorial reflects a postmodern approach to biblical studies, one that 'accepts indeterminacy, polyvalence and subjectivity as necessary elements in the study of a reality that is incapable of ultimate definition' (Terence J. Keegan, 'Biblical Criticism and the Challenge of Postmodernism', *BibInt* 3 [1995], pp. 1-14 (2).

3. One of the chief difficulties of 32.44 is that the LXX refers not to the Song but to the תורה. See Norbert Lohfink, 'Zur Fabel in Dtn 31–32', in R. Bartelmus, T. Krueger, and H. Utzschneider (eds.), *Konsequente Traditionsgeschichte* (Göttingen: Universitätsverlag, 1993), pp. 255-80 (261). Although the focus of this study is the narrative sections of Deut. 31–32, its scope extends to Deut. 31–34 as a whole. There is little discussion of the structure and contents of the Song of Moses,

1. *The Question of Narrative Chronology*

As Jeffrey Tigay observes, Deuteronomy 31, with its abrupt transitions and multiple sources, differs strikingly from the more seamless redaction of Deuteronomy 1–30, but its structure is more design than accident.[4] The narrative sections of Deuteronomy 31 and 32 frame the poetic texts Moses recites (the Song of 32.1-43 and the Blessing in 33.2b-29), just as they form part of the overall frame of Deuteronomy.[5] The poetic texts interrupt the narrative, deferring the presentation of what happens next. The narrative itself alternates between episodes about the death of Moses, the commission of Joshua, and the promulgation of written law.

The documentary strands of Deuteronomy 31–32 (J, E, D, P, and independent material) account for its general complexity but not for its particular structure.[6] Conversely, literary context may account for its general structure (the alternation between stories about texts and about Moses and Joshua) but not for its complexity. Why did the redactor(s) assemble so composite a text? Answers to this question fall into two main groups: those that treat the text as a confusing puzzle to be re-assembled, and those that see it as an elusive but deliberate composition.[7] Both approaches,

---

the Blessing of Moses, and the narrative of Moses' death in ch. 34. For these texts, the governing assumption is their integrity and discreteness; as such, they comprise part of Deut. 31–34. The narrative designates and frames the Song and Blessing, a fact that justifies their 'bracketing' for present purposes. In the case of ch. 34, as I indicate, uncharacteristic language and contents set the death, burial, and appraisal of Moses off from the rest of the text.

4. Jeffrey H. Tigay, *The JPS Torah Commentary: Deuteronomy* (Philadelphia: Jewish Publication Society of America, 1996), pp. 505-506.

5. For a review of literature on the textual history and structure of Deut. 31–34, see Steven Weitzman, *Song and Story in Biblical Narrative* (Bloomington: Indiana University Press, 1997), pp. 37-58 and especially p. 160 n. 13. See also Tigay, *Deuteronomy*, pp. 288-340.

6. S.R. Driver, for instance, divides Deut. 31 into JE, D, and D2 as follows: (1) vv. 1-13—D; (2) vv. 14-15—JE; (3) vv. 16-22—JE/D2; (4) v. 23—JE/D; and (5) vv. 24-30—D/D2 (*A Critical and Exegetical Commentary on Deuteronomy* [ICC; New York: Charles Scribner's Sons, 1906], p. lxxvii). Richard E. Friedman's more recent analysis is not significantly different: *Who Wrote the Bible?* (New York: Harper & Row, 1987), p. 255. For his part, Tigay argues that the complexity of Deut. 31 is more a matter of design than accident and cannot be explained solely on the basis of documentary layers, Tigay, *Deuteronomy*, pp. 505-506.

7. The most interesting case for textual confusion as a mistake is the speculation made by Alexander Rofé, who suggests that the confusion of song and teaching (תורה) stems from a copyist's error ('The Question of the Composition of Deuteronomy 31 in Light of a Conjecture about a Confusion in the Columns of the Biblical Text', *Shnaton* 3 [1978–79], pp. 49-76). But Rofé's explanation overlooks clear patterns within the text and fails to account for other irregularities in ch. 31; see Tigay, *Deuteronomy*, p. 505. Michael Fishbane ('Varia Deuteronomica', *ZAW* 84 [1972], pp. 349-52) suggests that תורה and Song are coextensive in Deut. 31 and that vv. 25-29 are inserted between the repeated phrase עד תמם, an example of 'repetitive resumption' (*Wiederaufname*). A more typical approach, in the tradition of Driver, Noth, and von Rad, is to concentrate on the text as a collection of historically distinct documentary layers. See, for example, Jon Levenson, 'Who Inserted the Book of the Torah?', *HTR* 68 (1975), pp. 203-33. On the other hand, Tigay considers the text to be skillfully crafted (*Deuteronomy*, p. 505). Norbert Lohfink and his student, Jean-Pierre Sonnet, also see the text as an elaborate composition, but they seek also to rearrange it into a coherent narrative: Lohfink, 'Der Bundesschluss im Land Moab-Redaktionsgeschichtliches

however, tend to look far beneath the text's surface, for scribal error or insertions, to reconstruct it as a continuous narrative. By contrast, this study stays close to the surface of the text and attempts to describe it in its own terms.

Two main story lines intertwine in the text: the imminent death of Moses (which includes choosing Joshua as successor) and the production and preservation of texts.

Table 1. *Narrative Strands in Deuteronomy 31–32*

Death and Joshua	Torah and Song	Harmonization
31.1-8		
	31.9-13	
31.14-15		
	31.16-22	
31.23		
	31.24-30a	
	(32.45-47)*	32.44-47
32.48-52		

[* Although I classify this passage as a harmonization of the two narrative strands, the predominant subject is Torah and Song.]

First, Moses announces his impending death and commissions Joshua as his successor (31.1-8). He then writes down this Torah (תורה), giving it to the Levites with instructions for its ritual recitation (vv. 9-13). In vv. 14-23, YHWH tells Moses to present himself with Joshua in the tent of meeting; then, after appearing to them in a pillar of cloud, YHWH commands Moses to write down and teach the Israelites a Song that will act as a witness against them after they become unfaithful. Moses obeys, and YHWH commissions Joshua directly.

The text then returns to the scene of Moses writing the תורה, followed by a speech of Moses, echoing that of YHWH in vv. 16-21, admonishing the Israelites to use the written תורה as a witness against their future infidelity (vv. 24-29). The instructions here differ from those in vv. 9-13, and it is unclear whether the antecedent of תורה coincides with that of the earlier passage or with that of the Song mentioned just before. The first uninterrupted narrative concludes (in v. 30) with Moses reciting 'this Song' to the Israelites. As this brief synopsis makes clear, the narrative of Deuteronomy 31 raises questions about the reference of תורה and Song (שירה) and about the chronology of the passage itself. Moses writes the תורה, then YHWH tells him to write the Song (which he does), then Moses finishes writing the תורה, whereupon he recites the Song. Do the two texts and two sets of instructions overlap or follow one another?

After the narrative of ch. 31, there are two distinct, shorter narratives in Deuteronomy. The first is in 32.44–33.2a, and the second is the conclusion in ch. 34. Following the poetic text of Moses' Song, the narrative reports that after Moses *and*

zu Deut. 28,68–32,47', *BZ* 6 (1962), pp. 32-55; and 'Zur Fabel des Deuteronomiums', in G. Braulik (ed.), *Bundesdokument und Gesetz: Studien zum Deuteronomium* (Herders Biblische Studien, 4; Freiburg: Herder, 1995), pp. 65-78; Jean-Pierre Sonnet, *The Book Within the Book: Writing in Deuteronomy* (Leiden: E.J. Brill, 1997), pp. 118-82.

Joshua (only Moses was mentioned before) finish reciting the Song, Moses tells the people to put the words he has spoken into their hearts so that they and their children will follow the תורה and live long in their newly acquired land (vv. 44-47). YHWH then commands Moses to ascend Mt Nebo in order to see the land across the Jordan and then to die because of his unfaithfulness at Meribath-kadesh (vv. 48-52). Then, abruptly and without any response from Moses, the narrative introduces the second poetic text, the Blessing of Moses, 'with which he blessed the children of Israel before his death' (33.1-2a).

The main questions raised by Deut. 32.44–33.2a concern its relation to earlier and later events. First, why does the text claim that Moses *and* Joshua recite the Song, when in 31.30 only Moses is reported to do so? Second, what is the relationship between this Song and the words of the תורה referred to in 32.45? Third, what is the chronological relationship between YHWH's order to Moses to ascend Nebo and die and the introduction and recitation of the Blessing in ch. 33? If the Blessing immediately follows the command, why is there no reply or immediate action taken by Moses? It seems impossible that the Blessing could occur after he ascends the mountain, since Moses appears to be alone there, and the action between his ascent and death is uninterrupted according to ch. 34.

These questions of chronology can be understood not simply as textual problems but rather as central components of the text's meaning. The patterned alternation between the two story lines takes the following form:

Table 2. *Alternating Narrative Strands in Deuteronomy 31–32*

	Passage	Narrative Strands
1.	31.1-13	Death and Joshua → Torah and Song
2.	31.14-22	Death and Joshua → Torah and Song
3.	31.23-30a	*Song*
4.	32.44-47	*Harmonization* (Death and Joshua + Torah and Song)
5.	32.45-52	Torah and Song → Death and Joshua

There are other ways of dividing the elements of the narrative, either by documentary source (see nn. 5 and 6) or by other literary structures. For instance, Tigay proposes a chiasmus in 31.9-27 with the following structure: A, Teaching (vv. 9-13)–B, Joshua (vv. 14-15)–C, Poem (vv. 16-22)–B', Joshua (v. 23)—A', Teaching (vv. 24-27).[8] Norbert Lohfink and Jean-Pierre Sonnet analyze the chapter according to speeches, with the theophany in 31.14 as a central, pivotal moment.[9] While the evidence for central turning-points in 31.14 or 31.16-22 may be persuasive, I suggest that the elements fit into a larger structure of alternating narrative strands, as Table 2 illustrates.

In 'The Presentation of Synchroneity and Simultaneity in Biblical Narrative', Shemaryahu Talmon identifies 'resumptive repetition', along with the *yqtl–qtl*

8. Tigay, *Deuteronomy*, p. 505.
9. Lohfink, 'Zur Fabel in Dtn 31–32', pp. 261-63, and Sonnet, *The Book Within the Book*, pp. 126, 147-48.

structure and specific temporal language, as a narrative technique to indicate simultaneity in the Bible.[10] Burke Long carries this analysis further to show how resumptive repetition may also mark off other forms of 'asynchronous' narration, including retrospective narration and commentarial excursus.[11] Long's study also explores the 'imaginative and fictive dimensions' of this technique, such as contrast, characterization, commentary, and ambiguation.[12]

Whereas Talmon and Long concentrate on single interruptions of narrative flow, set off by resumptive repetition, the pattern in Deuteronomy 31–32 appears to be the alternation between two distinct narrative lines (see Table 3, below). There are repetitions within Deuteronomy 31–32, but they do not appear in every narrative transition. The Deuteronomic admonition of Moses to Joshua in 31.7 recurs (with YHWH as speaker) in 31.23: חזק ואמץ כי אתה תביא את־בני ישראל אל־הארץ אשר־נשבעתי. Moses writes in 31.9, 22, and 24. And finally, Moses writes and recites 'to the very end' (עד תמם) in 31.24 and 30.[13] These repetitions do lie at or near transitions between episodes in Deuteronomy 31–32 and may constitute resumptive repetition. But they do not account for all the transitions in the narrative; the phrases 'be strong' and 'the land you pass over to possess it' may be understood rather as stock Deuteronomic phrases.[14] Like the analyses of Tigay and Lohfink, the phenomenon of resumptive repetition provides only a partial description of the narrative structure of Deuteronomy 31–32. It is not always clear, in fact, how to distinguish resumptive repetition from the related structures of *inclusio*, chiasmus, and ordinary repetition.[15] The difficulty of applying these descriptions to Deuteronomy 31–32 is that none of them explains the apparent alternation between narrative strands in the text.

Although resumptive repetition does not mark off all transitions in Deuteronomy 31–32, Talmon and Long's studies provide useful suggestion for this analysis. Since Deuteronomy 31–32 does not read as a continuous narrative, two questions follow: What kind of asynchrony is it, and what effects does it have?

The most significant effect of asynchronic narration in Deuteronomy 31–32 is to ambiguate the chronology without losing emphasis on the central issues of textual transmission and leadership.[16] The reader of the text may come away puzzled about chronology, but the commission of Joshua and the importance of the Torah and Song is beyond doubt. By its references to the Torah and Song, the text is also self-referential, or in Long's term, 'metalinguistic'.[17] This is clearly a text about texts,

10. Shemaryahu Talmon, 'The Presentation of Synchroneity and Simultaneity in Biblical Narrative', in *Literary Studies in the Hebrew Bible* (Jerusalem: Magnes Press, 1993), pp. 112-133.

11. Burke O. Long, 'Framing Repetitions in Biblical Historiography', *JBL* 106 (1987), pp. 385-99.

12. Long, 'Framing Repetitions', pp. 390-97.

13. Thus Fishbane, 'Varia Deuteronomica'; see n. 7, above.

14. Moshe Weinfeld, *Deuteronomy and the Deuteronomic School* (Oxford: Oxford University Press, 1972), pp. 342-43.

15. See Long, 'Framing Repetitions', p. 390 n. 19, as well as Michael Fishbane, *Biblical Interpretation in Ancient Israel* (Oxford: Oxford University Press, 1985), pp. 85-87. See n. 33, below.

16. Long, 'Framing Repetitions', p. 394.

17. Long, 'Framing Repetitions', p. 388.

even more than it is a text about human leaders (see below). Finally, instead of creating a sense that the flow of narration has been interrupted, the sustained asynchrony in Deuteronomy 31–32 instills a general sense of atemporality, as if time is suspended rather than interrupted.[18] Like the Song itself, which poetically summarizes the covenantal relationship, Deuteronomy 31–32 seems to suspend the flow of time.

After shifting three times from the subject of Moses' death to the Torah (תורה), the two narrative strands combine and harmonize in the pivotal passage in 32.44-47. At the same time, the emphasis on תורה and Song in vv. 45-47 places it also in the 'Torah and Song' narrative strand. After this harmonization, the text shifts focus back to the death of Moses (vv. 45-52), and this remains the narrative focus of chs. 33–34.

These progressions suggest that the two strands are not only simultaneous but linked in other ways as well. For example, the abrupt transition from 31.8 to 31.9 could suggest that Joshua and the text both substitute for the authority of Moses. The alternation between the strands also suggests Joshua and תורה to be *competing* forms of authority.

According to the structuralist theory of Algirdas Greimas, most narratives can be analyzed in terms of one or more hidden antitheses.[19] In Deuteronomy 31–32, unlike the more seamless narratives of modern literature, the antithesis between Joshua and תורה (as responses to the loss of Moses) appears to lie on the surface. If this is so, then in 32.47 the תורה clearly prevails over Joshua: 'This is no trifling matter for you, but rather your very life; through it you may live long in the land that you are crossing over the Jordan to possess'. In fact, the priority of תורה over Joshua as an authority resurfaces in Josh. 1.5-9, where the injunction to obey the תורה is inserted into a formulaic military exhortation.[20]

The tandem story lines of Deuteronomy 31–32, then, ultimately give precedence to תורה, although ch. 32 concludes with a transition to the book's *dénoument*: the Blessing and death of Moses. The final two chapters of Deuteronomy—the Blessing in ch. 33 and the story of Moses' death (ch. 34)—thus form a kind of double appendix beyond the scope of narrative in Deuteronomy 31–32. Still, a number of comments are in order. First, the Blessing's link to Genesis 49, along with its double mention of תורה in vv. 4 and 10, places it squarely in the hermeneutical tradition of chs. 31–32. Chapter 34 opens with the fulfillment of YHWH's command in 32.49-52 that Moses climb Mt Nebo, and it proceeds with Moses' viewing of the land and YHWH's prohibition on Moses' going there. Then follows Moses' death and burial by YHWH in an unknown place, the narrator's description of Moses' good health at death, and the Israelite's thirty-day mourning period. Finally, after reinforcing the legitimacy of Joshua's leadership, the narrative concludes with a tribute to Moses' unique greatness.

18. Long, 'Framing Repetitions', p. 396.
19. Algirdas Greimas, *On Meaning: Selected Writings in Semiotic Theory* (trans. Paul J. Perron and Frank H. Collins; Minneapolis: University of Minnesota Press, 1987), pp. 64-76.
20. Fishbane, *Biblical Interpretation in Ancient Israel*, p. 384.

Although there are few chronological or textual difficulties in ch. 34, what is striking is its uncharacteristically evaluative quality. In addition, the narrative steps briefly outside its typical timeframe with the statement that there has not arisen *since* in Israel a prophet like Moses (ולא קם נביא עוד). The temporal term 'since' (עוד), which links the time of the story to the time of its telling, is an etymological cousin of עד ('witness'), an important term in Deuteronomy 31–32 that I propose to take as a genre designator. Chapters 33–34 thus echo the priority of תורה in Deuteronomy 31–32, even though their focus is the last words and death of Moses.

2. *The Question of Reference: Torah and Song*

Table 3. *Torah and Song in Deuteronomy 31–34**

Torah	Song	Combination ('All these Words')
[27.3]		
31.9-13		
	31.19-22	
31.24-29		
	31.30	
	32.44	
		32.45
32.46-47		

[* See also the references to תורה in the Blessing: 33.4, 10.]

Both episodes that mention תורה (31.9 and 31.24) follow passages that make no mention of the תורה, raising the question: At what point does the תורה end and the story resume? In the face of this ambiguity, it seems unlikely that the reference of תורה in Deuteronomy 31 is restricted to one or two specific texts. Rather, I propose that the texts in the chapter are presented in a self-consciously generalized light. In the context of several layers of redaction, these ambiguities expand the reference of תורה. According to this reading, the text's ambiguities of temporality, agency, and communication all serve to focus attention on Moses' acts of writing and the directions for how to treat these writings (see Tables 2 and 3).

The final episode in ch. 31 (vv. 24-30) recalls and overlaps vv. 9-13: Moses finishes writing the תורה, gives it to the Levites to place in the ark of the covenant, and begins to recite the Song. It is possible that תורה refers always to the Song, a reading that avoids the chronological confusion of shifting from legal text to Song in vv. 29-30.[21] On the other hand, תורה may refer primarily to the legal code and secondarily to the Song.[22] The repetition of עד from v. 19 links תורה with the Song, but the treatment of the text suggests it is law. According to von Rad, there was an effort by a later editor to legitimate the Song by linking it to the law: 'All that can be said is that whoever wanted to establish the Song of Moses securely as part of this block of traditions adapted for his purpose a form of words which treated

---

21. Fishbane, 'Varia Deuteronomica', p. 50.
22. See Driver, *Deuteronomy*, p. 343; von Rad, *Deuteronomy*, p. 190.

originally of writing down the law'.[23] If this is so, what we have is a self-conscious text that is self-consciously assembled. While תורה probably refers to some part of the legal code in vv. 9-13, here it wavers between the primary meaning of law and the secondary reference of Song. The ambiguity of the term is never resolved as such, but in 32.46 תורה appears to refer both to the law and the Song. In other words, ambiguity is replaced by a broadened reference. In a passage (32.44-47) that appears to harmonize the two narrative strands, תורה means both law and Song. Two problems of continuity—narrative chronology and reference—thus seem to dissolve in Deut. 32.44-47.

3. *Redactional Harmonization in 32.44-47?*

Any reconstruction of biblical redaction is speculative, but textual evidence has led to suggestive hypotheses on the process. On the one hand, redaction differs radically from modern-day editing: seamlessness and continuity are not the guiding principles they are in editing. On the other hand, there is sufficient clarity and structure in biblical texts to deny the contention that redaction is mere cutting and pasting of existing materials. One example of this artful linking of different materials is the repetition of a phrase before and after an interpolation, the so-called repetitive resumption (*Wiederaufnahme*) found in such texts as Ezek. 20.32-35, Hag. 1.5-7, and Isa. 2.11-17.[24]

The seams between different documentary sources may be connected in a number of ways: an *inclusio* formed by a passage at the beginning and end of a pericope, a *Leitwort* that appears in both documentary sources, the weaving together of two traditions (often yielding doublets), and a brief harmonizing passage or gloss.[25] Deuteronomy 32.44-46 appears to represent the latter, harmonizing tendency. In Deut. 32.44-45, the two main narrative strands—the deployment of תורה and Joshua before Moses' death—are combined. If the combination reflects the work of the redactor, then it may provide an idea of how a text makes sense and even what constitutes a text:

> And Moses came and spoke all the words of this song in the people's hearing—he and Joshua son of Nun. And then Moses began to speak all these words to all Israel. And he said to them: 'Take to heart all the words that I witness to you today, that you may command your children to keep them and to do all the words of this torah'.

Unlike all other sections of Deuteronomy 31–34, which address the commission of Joshua and the writing and recitation of תורה separately, this brief text combines the two strands. In addition, the passage juxtaposes the two distinct elements of the

23. Von Rad, *Deuteronomy*, p. 190.

24. Curt Kuhl, 'Die "Wiederaufnahme"—ein literarkritisches Prinzip?', *ZAW* 64 (1952), pp. 1-11. See also Bernard Levinson's review of *Wiederaufnahme* and other redactional activity in Deuteronomy in *Deuteronomy and the Hermeneutics of Legal Innovation* (New York: Oxford University Press, 1997), especially pp. 18-20.

25. Fishbane, *Biblical Interpretation in Ancient Israel*, pp. 221-28.

תורה and the Song. Deuteronomy 32.44-46 thus appears to reach for a harmonization of the main elements of Deuteronomy's conclusion.[26] Whether written later than the rest of the text or not, the passage refers emphatically to texts and speech outside itself, including the Song and תורה. The passage is thus written with the other elements of Deuteronomy 31–34 in mind and seems motivated by the impulse to combine them.

Four additional observations on Deut. 31.44-46 are warranted. First, the word 'all' appears four times, a fact that illustrates the emphasis on comprehensiveness. (The term also appears in 31.1, 11, 12, 18, 28, and 30.) If the passage comes from a later phase of editing or redaction, it takes pains to include all the elements that it combines. Second, the reference to Joshua at the end of the clause appears to modify the statement that Moses spoke alone. This apparent modification has the effect of leaving Moses in the position of pre-eminence and of suggesting that Joshua was added later as an editorial afterthought. By displaying a modification of the subject of the sentence, then, the authors or editors display the process of editing itself.

Third, a number of phrases and terms in vv. 44-47 appear earlier in ch. 31 (especially vv. 16-30); even though many of these are Deuteronomic formulas, their high incidence here is noteworthy: 'The land that you are crossing over the Jordan to possess' (31.13); the teaching of a text as a witness (31.19 and 21); recitation of words (vv. 28 and 30). In this way, the harmonizing text of vv. 44-47 can be seen loosely as a kind of *inclusio* with the תורה/Song story line of ch. 31, thus affirming the emphasis on the תורה over against Joshua's commission. Finally, the term 'witness' has links to at least one biblical idea of text (see below). The combination of elements in Deut. 32.44-46 makes sense not as continuous narrative but as a redaction and harmonization of different sources.

4. *The Question of Genre*

What is the genre of Deuteronomy 31–32, and how does it explain the text's structure? Steven Weitzman suggests that the Song of Moses (Deut. 32) and its context share several characteristics with the ancient text *Words of Ahiqar*:

> the imputation of the teaching to a dying sage; the characterization of the teaching's recipients as ungrateful, even treacherous; the sage's disowning of the teaching's recipients, who deny responsibility for past misdeeds; and the transmission of the final teaching in both oral and written forms.[27]

If Deuteronomy 31–32 follows a familiar literary pattern, then the ingenuity of the redactor, in concluding Deuteronomy fittingly with diverse sources *and* meeting the external criteria of a dying sage genre, is truly extraordinary. This possibility also helps explain the apparent novelty of the text: if the writing and recitation of texts are expected elements, then the editorial seams linking the two story lines pose less

---

26. See Sonnet, *The Book Within the Book*, pp. 178-80.
27. Steven Weitzman, 'Lessons from the Dying: The Role of Deuteronomy 32 in its Narrative Setting', *HTR* 87.4 (1994), pp. 377-93 (383).

difficulty. The problems of chronology and reference would remain as part of this text's layered history, but they would not threaten to make the text incoherent. Even within the tradition of texts like *Ahiqar*, however, Deuteronomy 31–32 appears unusually hybrid. I suggest the heuristic model of memorial, based on the term ascribed to the Song in 31.19: 'witness' (עד).[28] A brief philological survey of this term will demonstrate the point.

The term עד appears seven times (in different forms) in the narrative of Deuteronomy 31–32: three times as a noun (31.19, 21, and 26), twice adverbially (31.2, 27), and twice as verbal constructions (31.28 and 32.46). Jeffrey Tigay notes that 'witness' must originally have denoted the Song alone in the JE source (31.19) and that the D source must later have applied it to the תורה (31.26).[29] To suggest that עד accurately describes the genre of Deuteronomy 31–32 does not purport to demonstrate a full-blown ancient literary category. The idea that the entire text— Song and תורה—constitutes a 'witness' or 'memorial' simply suggests a model for understanding the text other than as a mere compilation or scribal error.

In its verbal form, עוד can mean 'to repeat', 'surround', 'restore', or 'witness'. The related adverbial form, עוד, notably appearing in 31.2, 27 and 34.10, denotes temporal continuation. BDB (p. 729) suggests that the connotation 'witness' comes from '*reiterating*, hence *emphatically affirming*'. In other words, repetition over time leads to witness; a characterization that fits perfectly with the characterization of the Song as a memorized text known to the people and their offspring.

The nominal form of עד, when it means 'witness' or 'testimony', often has a concrete physical quality, like the stones set up by Jacob and Laban in Gen. 31.41- 54, the witness altar in Josh. 22.28, and the placement of a stone in the divine sanctuary as a witness to the book of the תורה of God in Josh. 24.22-27; in that text, both the people and the stone are designated witnesses against future transgressions. A related term, עדה, can refer in Priestly sources to Israelite leaders (e.g. Lev. 8.3-4; Num. 16.19). Probably the most significant term in this set appears in Exod. 31.18 in reference to the 'two tablets of העדות, tablets of stone written with the finger of God'. There are also several nominal uses of עדות in Deuteronomy (4.45; 6.17, 20), always coupled with חוק (literally, 'something engraved', hence 'a decree') and משפט ('judgment', 'ordinance'), that refer to the תורה and מצות given by YHWH and Moses to the people. Even within Deuteronomy, then, עד may denote repetition or witness, stone artifact or written text.

---

28. The link between עדות and memorials is made by James E. Young in *Writing and Rewriting the Holocaust*: 'Like *edut*, the literary testimony of the Holocaust thus seems to accrue an ontologically privileged status, similar to that of earlier "testament"' (p. 21). Later, Young considers the function of Holocaust memorials in what could be a description of biblical tradition: 'Like the lives of other memorials, that of the Warsaw Ghetto Monument consists in three parts: its literal conceiving and construction; its finished form as public memorial; and its life in the mind of its community and people over time. For meaning and memory here depend not just on the forms and figures in the monument itself, but on the viewers' responses to the monument, how it is used politically and religiously in the community, who sees it under what circumstances, how its figures are used and recast in new places, in foreign contexts' (p. 181).

29. Tigay, *Deuteronomy*, p. 506.

The Song, which lives in the mouths and memory of the people and their descendants (31.21) and describes YHWH as a rock forgotten by the people (32.4, 18), resonates with all the semantic valences of עֵד: repetition, witness, artifact, and covenantal text all describe the Song of Moses. Other uses of the term in the Bible bear interesting parallels to Deuteronomy 31. In Gen. 31.44-49 and Josh. 22.26-29, as well as in Deut. 6.17 and 2 Kgs 23.3, עֵד is linked intimately to covenant language and formulas. In Isa. 30.8-14, a poetic oracle is characterized as a linguistic memorial, a traditional, liturgical, and hermeneutical site at which different textual layers appear crowded together.[30]

The notion of Deuteronomy 31–32 as a textual witness or memorial helps resolve the paradox that the general meaning of the narrative is clear but that the details of narration, chronology, and focus are confusing. By selecting this term to refer both to the Song and the תורה in Deuteronomy 31, the final redactor created (purposefully or not) a set of associations rich with meaning: (1) the Song and Torah (תורה) will be both long-lived and enduring; (2) both texts have the capacity to survive in human memory and experience even when their messages are disregarded; (3) both texts have a concreteness akin to stones; (4) both texts have a covenantal function; and finally, (5) a textual memorial may be composite—like the tablets of the law in Exodus which were written once by God and once by Moses (Exod. 31–32), a textual memorial may come from more than one hand, and like the term תורה in Deuteronomy 31–32, a textual memorial may take on broader and broader reference as a textual tradition develops. The redaction of Deuteronomy takes עֵד beyond the original sense of 'witness' and comes to mean, like the texts it describes, much more. Like a monument built up over generations, the textual memorial of Deuteronomy 31–32 is layered, as the complexities of chronology, agency, and reference demonstrate. In other words, textual 'witness' or 'memorial' describes the continuity and complexity of inner-biblical exegesis.

5. *Literary Concerns*

Deuteronomy 31–32 displays its own poetics in explicit and implicit terms: תורה, Song (itself a combination of genres),[31] speech, narrative, biography.[32] In fact, one

---

30. Weitzman, *Song and Story in Biblical Narrative*, p. 51. Consider other memorials, for example, Vietnam and the Kotel in Jerusalem, at which tradition and innovation, openness and closure, appear side by side. Other suggestive possibilities include ancient burial sites and the whole range of memorial practices in classical Judaism; see Yosef Yerushalmi, *Zakhor: Jewish History and Jewish Memory* (Seattle: University of Washington Press, 1982). See also the analogous discussion of sacred text as an 'archive of pure language' in my *Walter Benjamin and the Bible*, pp. 24-31, 43-47.

31. See Otto Eissfeldt, *Das Lied Moses Deuteronomium 32.1-34 und das Lehrgedicht Asaphs Psalm 78 Samt Einer Analyse der Umgebung des Mose-Liedes* (Berlin: Akademie-Verlag, 1958), and G.E. Wright, 'The Lawsuit of God: A Form-Critical Study of Deuteronomy 32', in B.W. Anderson and W. Harrelson (eds.), *Israel's Prophetic Heritage* (New York: Harper, 1962), pp. 26-67.

32. This is the problem of whether literary patterns are in the eye of the beholder. See the fine discussion of how to distinguish genuine biblical parallelism from modern interpretive creation in

could say that the most impressive feature of the text's poetics *is* its hermeneutics—how it visibly combines disparate traditions that parallel other biblical texts. This inner-biblical exegesis is constitutive of the text and prompts my heuristic suggestion that Deuteronomy 31–32 is a textual memorial (עד). Some textual parallels help illustrate this hermeneutical process.

In Exodus 17, YHWH commands Moses to record the defeat—and erasure—of Amalek in a book. As Joseph Blenkinsopp observes, this act accompanies the building of an altar and the recital of poetry. Adducing the similar textual examples of Num. 21.14, Josh. 10.13, 1 Samuel 14, and 2 Sam. 1.17-27, he speculates on the nature of these collected narratives of divinely activated victory:

> We may infer from what we *do* know that they would have been incorporated into the historico-theological context of sacred history, would go back to recital at the religious festivals of the shrines, and betray their presence beneath the prose redaction of a later day.[33]

The hermeneutical processes within the Bible also intersect with canon formation. The depiction of biblical figures writing and promulgating texts not only legitimates these texts; it also provides clues about criteria and practices for their production and transmission. In addition to the example of Moses' writing in Exodus and Deuteronomy, Jeremiah and his scribe Baruch are also depicted as writers of divine speech (Jer. 32.2 and ch. 36). The clearest example of this inner-biblical exegesis and canon formation is Ezra's public reading of the תורה in the fifth century BCE (Neh. 8).

Although questions of structure and chronology belong to the domain of literary studies, literary critics often reflect contemporary views of textual coherence. Discovering verbal, thematic, and structural patterns in biblical narrative, some literary criticism invokes contemporary notions of artistic unity (and the assumption of a single authorship).[34] This approach arises partly from a polemical response to historical-critical studies of the Bible, which tend to dismantle the text into its

---

Adele Berlin, *The Dynamics of Biblical Parallelism*, as well as her article, 'Literary Exegesis of Biblical Narrative: Between Poetics and Hermeneutics', in Jason Rosenblatt and Joseph Sitterson, Jr (eds.), '*Not in Heaven': Coherence and Complexity in Biblical Narrative* (Bloomington: Indiana University Press, 1991), pp. 120-28.

33. Joseph Blenkinsopp, 'Jonathan's Sacrilege', *CBQ* 26 (1964), pp. 423-49 (443).

34. See, for example, Meir Sternberg, *The Poetics of Biblical Narrative* (Bloomington: Indiana University Press, 1985), and Gabriel Josipovici, *The Book of God* (New Haven: Yale University Press, 1988). The emphasis on coherence and a single authorship reached its peak in Harold Bloom's commentary in *The Book of J* (New York: Grove, 1990). Aesthetic criteria such as irony, tragedy, wordplay, and intertextuality also bear the stamp of modern literary criticism, and they often describe the Bible convincingly. Reading the Bible as literature thus implies the modern, 'secular' discipline of literary criticism to the exclusion of reading the Bible as historical document or divine revelation. In fact, one could portray current debates among literary and historical critics of the Bible as the latest installment in an ancient Western struggle (dating at least back to Plato) over the value of human literary imagination. But by celebrating biblical texts as coherent works of human creativity, some literary approaches overlook the complexity of the Bible.

component documentary parts.[35] Other literary scholars of the Bible, notably Robert Polzin, Danna Nolan Fewell, Adele Berlin, Burke Long, and David M. Gunn, concentrate on the narrative complexity of the Bible.[36] By drawing attention to a text as composite as Deuteronomy 31–32, this chapter suggests a model of coherence—textual witness and memorial—dramatically different from modern standards of unity. While the importance and message of תורה are clear in Deuteronomy 31–32, the text's structure invites dialogue with contemporary theorists, like Mikhail Bakhtin and Walter Benjamin, who highlight polyphony and fragmentation in modern literature.[37]

6. *Conclusion*

The preceding interpretation of Deuteronomy 31–32 as a textual memorial offers an alternative to predominant literary approaches to the Bible. Recognizing the radical difference between Western texts by a single author (often stressing originality) and ancient texts written by a series of (often hidden) hands, the model of textual witness or memorial comes from the implicit poetics of the text itself. Instead of explaining away difficulties of chronology and reference, this analysis has sought to show how they reveal a layered composition and a hermeneutical process in which תורה and Song, Moses and text, myth and ritual, intertwine in artful and ultimately (as in Deut. 32.44-47) coherent ways. By a harmonization of elements that gives predominance to matters of producing and reciting (hence, canonizing) the תורה, Deuteronomy 31–32 models a textual hermeneutic of unity within diversity. As part of Moses' last words, the narrative of Deuteronomy 31–32 places great emphasis on matters of writing and תורה. The poetic texts of the Song and Blessing (in Deut. 32–33), to which I now turn, are not part of the story of Moses at all, but they interrupt the narrative as complex and reflexive texts that strengthen the connections between the death of Moses and written tradition.

35. See Robert Polzin, *Samuel and the Deuteronomist* (Bloomington: Indiana University Press, 1989), pp. 10-17, and Robert Alter's introduction to the Hebrew Bible in Robert Alter and Frank Kermode (eds.), *The Literary Guide to the Bible* (Cambridge, MA: Harvard University Press, 1987), pp. 11-35 (24-29).

36. Robert Polzin, 'Deuteronomy', in Alter and Commode (ed.), *The Literary Guide to the Bible*, pp. 92-101, and *idem, Moses and the Deuteronomist* (New York: Seabury, 1980); Dana Nolan Fewell and David M. Gunn, 'Tipping the Balance: Sternberg's Reader and the Rape of Dinah', *JBL* 110 (1991), pp. 193-211; Long, 'Framing Repetitions'; and Adele Berlin, *Poetics and Interpretation of Biblical Narrative* (Bible and Literature Series, 9; Sheffield: Almond Press, 1983).

37. Sternberg's contention that the text is a 'foolproof composition' remains tenable, I suggest, despite the complexities of the text (*The Poetics of Biblical Narrative*, pp. 50-56). See my 'The Book of Life: The Hebrew Bible as a Sacred Text in Deut. 31–34 and in the Philosophy of Walter Benjamin' (PhD dissertation, University of Chicago, 1992), and *Walter Benjamin and the Bible*, pp. 13-32.

Chapter 7

THE SONG AND THE BLESSING: POETIC DISCOURSE
IN DEUTERONOMY 32–33

Moses recites two poetic texts in Deuteronomy 32–33, a didactic Song about God and Israel, and a Blessing upon the tribes of Israel (an obvious parallel to Gen. 49). These poetic texts antedate the surrounding narrative and thus involve a kind of intratextual canonization. But unlike the more univocal biblical poems linked to Moses (e.g. Isa. 63 or Pss. 105 and 106), these texts are complex and ambiguous, and their place in Deuteronomy is problematic. What are their origins? How do they contribute to the end of Deuteronomy, which marks the end of Moses' life *and* the Torah? This chapter focuses on the second question, emphasizing the relationship between the poems and the narrative of Moses' last actions and death. The Song and Blessing summarize the divine–human relationship while making reference to themselves as texts. Through analysis of the two texts in context, I explore how the Song and Blessing enhance and complicate Moses' role as a source of biblical tradition.

To call the Song and Blessing poetry marks them as different from their surrounding narrative. The boundaries between poetry and narrative in Deuteronomy 31–34 are imposed by the text itself (as I show in Chapter 6), by their formal qualities, and by their introductory and concluding statements. What are the formal characteristics of the Song and Blessing? What literary and social expectations attach to each? Setting aside questions of date and specific stages of transmission, what functions do these texts perform in the narrative context? The following analysis claims that the Song and Blessing self-consciously combine diverse textual strata into a sacred text that is at once a fixed document, a *traditum*, and the manifestation of an interpretive process, or *traditio*.[1] The attribution of these texts to Moses lends them authority, but for readers who see their obvious complexities, it also complicates 'Moses'.

My analysis reflects the kind of approach taken by the rabbis of traditional midrash, for whom the question of how to read the final chapters of the Torah was

---

1. See Fishbane, *Biblical Interpretation in Ancient Israel*, p. 83. It is important to delineate the limitations of my analysis of the poetic texts. First, there is no attempt to fix an exact date for either text, although I rely on the scholarly consensus that both antedate the composition of the Deuteronomic narrative. Both the Song and the Blessing lack specific historical clues, leaving their original sources, meanings, and dates in the background of their position in the canonical text. Contemporary literary and canonical interpretation begins with evidence in the text itself and its position in relation to the entire narrative.

always tied to questions of how this scripture was given by God to Israel through Moses. The early (Tannaitic) *Sifre* on Deuteronomy, for instance, dedicates fifty sections (*pisqa'ot*) to the Song and Blessing, many of them dealing with the question of Moses and the Torah.[2] My approach also builds on a number of recent studies of the Song and Blessing that link internal structure to canonical context. Jos Luyten contrasts the Song to other historical psalms (Pss. 78; 105; 106; 114; 135; 136; Exod. 15) by arguing that the Song's primeval and eschatological elements 'break through the historical schemes' of historical psalms and the narrative frame of Deuteronomy, opening up broader dimensions of temporality in the text.[3] In *Song and Story in Biblical Narrative*, Steven Weitzman argues that the Song of Moses represents a literary convention of including poetic texts in ancient farewell speeches. Through analysis of a wide range of ancient texts, Weitzman shows how the Song of Moses resembles this ancient literary pattern while also contributing to what he calls 'scripturalizing revision', the process of revising the narrative as Israel develops its sacred scripture.[4] Casper Labuschagne has argued that the Song lies at the structural and thematic center of Deuteronomy 31–34.[5] Stefan Beyerle's study offers similar insights into the Blessing in its canonical setting.[6]

My study of the Song and Blessing is not a line-by-line analysis but focuses rather on problems already identified in the narrative, namely: canonical context, literary structure, Moses' (and YHWH's) agency, temporality, and implicit notions of scripture and revelation. Poetic style, structure, and convention are as important as meaning to this approach. Thus, if the Song of Moses propagates traditional covenant theology, the question becomes how this theology is expressed. Or, in the case of the Blessing, the issue is how the tribes are exalted poetically. What kinds of poetic imagery, parallelism, and language appear, and with what intensity? The rationale for such an approach is partly that while the messages of the poetic texts may not be unique, these particular literary expressions are.

The analysis of Deuteronomy 31–32 as a textual memorial (Chapter 6) concluded that Deuteronomy emphasizes Torah as a dynamic tradition of unsurpassed importance to the children of Israel. The poetic Song and Blessing add layers and complexity to this tradition. Following explicit instructions from God to Moses in Deut. 31.19, Moses recites a Song that characterizes the covenant relationship between God and Israel, but the narrative ambiguates the Song: Is it spoken only or also written? Is it Torah as well as Song? Does Moses only recite it or does he compose it as well?

2. *Sifre: A Tannaitic Commentary on the Book of Deuteronomy* (trans. Reuven Hammer; New Haven: Yale University Press, 1986), pp. 306-56, 297-378.

3. Jos Luyten, 'Primeval and Eschatological Overtones in the Song of Moses (DT 32, 1-43)', in Norbert Lohfink (ed.), *Das Deuteronomium: Entstehung, Gestalt und Botschaft* (Leuven: Leuven University Press, 1985), pp. 46-47.

4. Weitzman, *Song and Story in Biblical Narrative*, pp. 13, 37.

5. Casper Labuschagne, 'The Setting of the Song of Moses in Deuteronomy', in M. Vervenne and J. Lust (eds.), *Deuteronomy and Deuteronomic Literature* (Leuven: Leuven University Press, 1997), pp. 111-29 (113).

6. Stefan Beyerle, *Der Mosesegen im Deuteronomium* (Berlin: W. de Gruyter, 1997), especially pp. 289-94.

The Blessing of Moses arrives unannounced in Deuteronomy 33. Although it is not mentioned before or after, the mention of תורה in vv. 4 and 10 (even if these are later glosses) binds it explicitly to the context of Deuteronomy 31–34. Mountains appear in 32.49-50 and also early in the Blessing (33.2). Another *Leitwort* is the root for 'holy' (קדש), which appears in 32.51 and 33.2 and 3. The root 'gather' (אסף) in 33.5 echoes its double use in 32.50. References to the Exodus and wanderings also evoke the canonical context. The Song and Blessing thus lend continuity to an overtly composite text. As poetic texts about the past and future, the Song and Blessing interrupt the narrative flow of Moses' last actions and death to expand the text's frame of reference. Though spoken by Moses, the Song and Blessing are also unmistakably 'written'. They form part of the canonical Torah and the תורה written by Moses (31.19, 24), and their complexity and intertextuality fit the definition of 'writing' as a formalized manifestation of discourse (see Chapter 5).

1. *Parallelism and Biblical Poetry*

Parallelism is the primary formal principle of Hebrew poetry.[7] For present purposes, parallelism may be defined as some salient relationship—similarity, identity, opposition, or membership in a set—among linguistic elements within a poem. Parallelism usually comes in paired units, and it may be repetitive, semantic, grammatical, or phonetic. The word 'salient' is key to this definition, and it points to the context of the poem: in some poems a given relationship will stand out, and in others it will not. In phonetic parallelism, for example, similarity of one consonant or vowel between two words is usually not salient, but it may be, especially if the two words are parallel in some other way.

In a similar vein, Adele Berlin recognizes that parallelism must be 'perceptible' in order to 'serve the poetic function' and identifies four principles of this perceptibility: proximity, similar surface structure, frequency of equivalences, and expectation of parallelism.[8] Berlin does not attempt to define parallelism, however; rather, she aims to 'show the enormous linguistic complexity of parallelism', and her list is merely a tentative set of guidelines.[9] At the same time, she argues, these guidelines are 'often violated: exact repetition and identical surface structure are avoided in favor of a variety of equivalent forms of expression'.[10] This combination of similarity and contrast in parallelism supports the poetic function, which according to Roman Jakobson occurs 'when the word is felt as a word and not a mere representation of the object being named…when words and their composition, their

7. Dennis Pardee, 'Ugaritic and Hebrew Metrics', in Gordon D. Young (ed.), *Ugarit in Retrospect: Fifty Years of Ugarit and Ugaritic* (Winona Lake, IN: Eisenbrauns, 1981), pp. 113-30 (128). See also Roman Jakobson, 'Grammatical Parallelism and its Russian Facet', in Krystyna Pomorska and Stephen Rudy (eds.), *Language in Literature* (Cambridge, MA: Harvard University Press, 1987), pp. 145-79.
8. Berlin, *The Dynamics of Biblical Parallelism*, pp. 130-39.
9. Berlin, *The Dynamics of Biblical Parallelism*, p. 129.
10. Berlin, *The Dynamics of Biblical Parallelism*, p. 135.

meaning, their external and inner form, acquire a weight and value of their own instead of referring indifferently to reality'.[11]

Some critics express reservations about viewing parallelism as a poetic element. According to James Kugel, the regularity perceivable in some parts of the Bible ought not automatically to be identified as poetic:

> For in using this term, biblical critics have unconsciously assumed something about the Bible...that, on inspection, will simply not hold true. There is in the Bible no regularizing of a consistency comparable to those familiar to us from Western poetics. Parallelism...is a frequent, but not infallibly present (or absent) form of heightening adaptable to a wide variety of genres. The equation parallelism = poetry has led critics both to overlook parallelism in 'unpoetic' places—in laws, cultic procedures...and, on the other hand, to attribute to biblical parallelism a consistency it lacks.[12]

While reductionistic and anachronistic assumptions about Hebrew poetry are certainly to be avoided, it isn't obvious that the term 'poetry' necessitates them. Calling parallelism a poetic element does not require a crude division of biblical literature into prose and poetry or an exaggeration of the consistency of parallelism. On the contrary, it refers to a textual element that, with varying degrees of consistency, gives 'words and their composition...a weight and value of their own'.

In Hebrew poetry, parallelism characteristically appears between or within line segments (also called cola), and this is where analysis of parallelism is usually concentrated. I refer to the basic unit of analysis, which can either be a bicolon or tricolon, as a line. Since verses overlap with the lines here, I use the term 'line' as well. This is the type of parallelism James Kugel refers to in his well-known formulation, 'A is so, and *what's more*, B is so'.[13]

Parallelism may also occur between adjacent or even distant lines, but such cases can easily blur the distinction between poetic craft and coincidence. For example, two parallel elements separated by twenty lines may be a coincidence; this alone is not a salient relationship. For this reason, analysis of distant parallelism is best employed along with near and internal parallelism.[14] Indeed, this close fit between smaller and larger parallel structures is one of the defining characteristics of biblical poetry.

Parallelism, then, must be seen as a poetic element that occurs in many different genres in various forms with various effects. As Jakobson suggests, parallelism often transcends mere repetition or echoing to penetrate all levels of a poetic text: 'Pervasive parallelism inevitably activates all the levels of language: the distinctive features, inherent and prosodic, the morphologic and syntactic categories and forms, the lexical units and their semantic classes in both their convergences and

11. Roman Jakobson, 'What is Poetry?', in Pomorska and Ruby (eds.), *Language in Literature*, pp. 368-78 (378).

12. James Kugel, *The Idea of Biblical Poetry* (New Haven: Yale University Press, 1981), p. 70.

13. Kugel, *The Idea of Biblical Poetry*, p. 8.

14. See Ziony Zevit, 'Roman Jakobson, Psycholinguistics, and Biblical Poetry', *JBL* 109 (1990), pp. 385-401.

divergences acquire an autonomous poetic value'.[15] In short, parallelism becomes the organizing principle from which most of the text's poetic elements (Kugel calls them 'heightening effects') emerge.[16]

The main difficulty with the analysis of biblical poetry is the absence in the Hebrew Bible of a complete, indigenous poetics. Thus, while it is possible to identify many formal characteristics of biblical poetry, it is much more difficult to understand their functions and effects. What were the criteria for poetry, let alone good poetry, in the Hebrew Bible? How did the meaning and function of poetic texts change through the history of their transmission? Jakobson's notion of poetic function as giving words a weight and value of their own has limited explanatory power, offering little more than the designation of poetry as being somehow special. Certainly the language of biblical poetry calls attention to itself, but as Kugel points out, it does so in many ways and for many different reasons.

One advantage of the two poetic texts in Deuteronomy 31–34 is that the narrative *does* specify just how these texts are special. In that sense, we already have a kind of rudimentary poetics of the Song and the Blessing. Of course, the terms refer primarily to the function and content of the poetic text rather than to abstract formal characteristics, and it is also unclear when terms such as שׁירה (or שׁיר, 'song') were applied to poetic texts in the Bible. Nevertheless, there are clear formal links between the Song of Moses and other biblical songs, for example, the Song of Deborah in Judges 5, while the Blessing of Moses closely parallels Jacob's Blessing in Genesis 49. In the context of a text about sacred texts (Deut. 31–34), the Song and the Blessing contribute to a complex biblical notion of sacred text.

2. *Deuteronomy 32: The Song of Moses*

The Song of Moses is a poem of vast scope about the relationship between YHWH and Israel. In terms of genre, the poem has didactic, lyrical, and narrative components. In biblical terms, we may ask whether to view it more properly as a שׁירה, as the text indicates, or as a משׁכיל (didactic poem), the term applied to its close parallel, Psalm 78.[17] It may also be described as a character portrait of YHWH or as a meditation on divine justice in history. Most of all, the poem represents a multifaceted statement of the covenantal relationship between YHWH and Israel.

The scope of the poem covers nothing less than the history of Israel from the covenant to the struggles against the nations. As the narrative indicates, the Song points toward Israel's future after the death of Moses, and in this sense it is prophetic. But the Song is also retrospective, reminding the listener of the parceling

---

15. Jakobson, 'Grammatical Parallelism and Its Russian Facet', p. 173.
16. Kugel, *The Idea of Biblical Poetry*, p. 94.
17. See Eissfeldt, *Das Lied Moses Deuteronomium 32.1-34*. Although Eissfeldt dates Ps. 78 later than the Song of Moses and the label משׁכיל may significantly postdate both texts, the heavy use of wisdom vocabulary, including the verb שׂכל in v. 29, along with the parallels to Ps. 78, suggests it is possible to view Deut. 32 as either a שׁיר or משׁכיל. Another genre consideration is the Song's striking link to formulaic wisdom vocabulary: see James Boston, 'The Wisdom Influence Upon the Song of Moses', *JBL* 87 (1968), pp. 198-202.

out of land to the sons of Jacob. The Song relates the history of Israel roughly from Exodus to the author's present time, but it lacks historical specificity. Rather, it presents Israel and YHWH in a more synchronic light, highlighting development and structural dynamics, as I show below. As such, the Song constitutes a *mise en abyme*, 'a microstructure that contains a summary of the overall fabula in which it functions'.[18] The fabula in this case extends beyond the immediate narrative to the broader biblical context; thus, the Song of Moses is a canonical *mise en abyme*.

The poem is linked to several literary traditions, including the lawsuit of the suzerain against a disobedient vassal, the רִיב (cf. Isa. 1; Jer. 2; Mic. 6; Ps. 50).[19] But this tradition is remote from the text itself. For instance, the poem begins with a didactic introduction and has lexical links throughout to the wisdom tradition.[20] In all, the poem demonstrates a considerable literary originality that draws from its many sources and makes it difficult to date.[21] It is possible to identify several semantic fields in the poem associated with these genres: legal language, wisdom language, pastoral and fertility language, and prophetic language about the nations. Any interpretation of the Song must account for the interaction of all of the genres and semantic fields represented in the poem.

Structurally, the poem combines narrative continuity with regular parallelism and well-developed poetic imagery. It is a highly polished and finished work with a clear beginning, middle, and end; the first six verses introduce the speaker and state the theme of the poem. Next follows a lengthy narrative of YHWH's faithfulness (vv. 7-14), Israel's unfaithfulness (vv. 15-18), YHWH's punishment and subsequent restraint (vv. 19-33), and a resolution that reasserts YHWH's dominion and admonishes the nations to praise YHWH (vv. 34-43). The narrative is thus framed by a speaker's introduction and closing admonition to the nations. YHWH is the key agent of action in the poem, but the speaker of the poem (Moses in the canonical context) also performs the action of presenting it in a self-conscious way. By contrast, Israel's only actions in the poem are faithless rejections of YHWH. What relation exists between the speaker of the poem and YHWH?

The text divides more specifically into the following parts.

> Parenetic introduction (vv. 1-3)
> Condensed contrast (vv. 4-6)
> YHWH's faithfulness (vv. 7-14)
> Israel's transgression (vv. 15-18)
> Punishment (vv. 19-25)
> Restraint, nations (vv. 26-33)
> Reconciliation; YHWH reasserts dominion (vv. 34-42)
> Hymn-like conclusion (v. 43)[22]

18. Mieke Bal, *Lethal Love: Feminist Literary Readings of Biblical Love Stories* (Bloomington: Indiana University Press, 1987), p. 75.
19. G.E. Wright, 'The Lawsuit of God', pp. 26-67.
20. Boston, 'The Wisdom Influence', pp. 198-202.
21. A.D.H. Mayes, *Deuteronomy* (Grand Rapids: Eerdmans, 1981), pp. 380-82.
22. Von Rad's analysis differs slightly; see *Deuteronomy*, p. 196. These divisions are designed primarily for the heuristic purposes of literary analysis rather than historical-critical study.

Temporally, the parenetic/liturgical frame of the poem represents both a narrative past (Moses recites the poem at the time of the story) and a liturgical present, in which the speaker recites the poem and the people respond; the narrative precedes the liturgical frame, but the Song progresses from past to present and prophetic future. Driver hypothesizes that the Song dates from the early eighth century and that it was later attributed to Moses and incorporated into the text by the Deuteronomic editors.[23] He comments, 'The original aim of the poem was to point a moral from the past; but naturally, when it came to be regarded as a work of the Mosaic age, it was understood differently, as a warning for the future'.[24] In other words, when the poem was attributed to Moses, it shifted from historical narrative to prophecy, from past to future by way of the more distant past. Other commentators suggest an even earlier date for the poem,[25] but in any case, the temporal structure of the poem is complex and, as is usually the case with biblical poetry, ambiguous.

The narrative part of the poem consists of three main parts: a statement of divine–human harmony (vv. 7-14), a conflict stemming from human transgression (vv. 15-25), and a kind of resolution based on YHWH's restraint (vv. 26-42). The two turning points in the poem are thus v. 15, where Israel transgresses, and v. 26, where YHWH decides not to destroy Israel; these transitions require close analysis.

Formally, the poem is composed of highly regular bicolonic lines and exhibits semantic, repetitive, phonetic, grammatical, and syntactic parallelism. In the first verse, which translates, 'Give ear, heavens, and I will speak; let the earth hear the speech of my mouth', the two pairs of three words each mirror each other semantically and syntactically. The common pair 'heavens and earth' forms a merismus indicating the entire cosmos.[26] Grammatically, the pattern of imperative–noun–first person verb in the first colon becomes jussive-noun-object in the second. The important phonetic parallelisms are the definite article ה, which appears three times, and the sound *shema* that appears both in השמים and ותשמע.

The second two verses of the poem continue the connection between the speaker's speech and natural phenomena: 'May my teaching drip like rain, my speech trickle like the dew; like raindrops upon the spring shoots, and like copious showers upon the herb. For the name of YHWH I will proclaim; ascribe greatness to our God!' Grammatical, semantic, and repetition parallelism are pronounced in v. 2, beginning with the pattern of jussive–כ–noun–noun with pronominal suffix, followed by a כ–noun–עלי–noun combination in the second bicolon. In v. 3 a chiastic structure appears: noun–divine name–verb; verb–noun–divine name. By varying the established pattern of symmetrical parallelism, the exhortation forms a kind of cadence, just as it also shifts in focus from the speaker's speech to a request that the audience should speak.

---

23. Driver, *Deuteronomy*, p. 345.
24. Driver, *Deuteronomy*, p. 349.
25. Eissfeldt, for example, dates it to the eleventh century; see *Das Lied Moses Deuteronomium 32.1-43*, p. 42.
26. Wilfred G.E. Watson, *Classical Hebrew Poetry: A Guide to Its Techniques* (JSOTSup, 26; Sheffield: JSOT Press, 1984), p. 321.

The speaker of the poem addresses the heavens and earth, compares his didactic speech to water upon plants, establishes a motif (the name of YHWH), and admonishes the audience, which includes only natural objects, to recognize YHWH's greatness. In fact, a close parallel to this command appears in Ps. 29.1-2, where it is the sons of gods (בני אלם), not the sons of Israel, who are exhorted to ascribe glory and strength to YHWH.[27] In both cases there is a grand scope surpassing the human level. The Song of Moses begins by connecting the speaker to nature, not Israel. In a style characteristic of prophetic and wisdom literature, with the formulaic invocation of heaven and earth (cf. Isa. 1.2; Ps. 50.4) and the appeal to teaching (לקחי, cf. Prov. 1.5; 4.2), the introduction stretches past the people to the heaven and earth, not so much to make it a witness against Israel, as Deut. 31.28 suggests, but rather to elevate the praise of YHWH to a cosmic scale.[28]

The other exhortation to worship comes at the Song's close: 'Give a ringing cry for his people, nations, for he avenges the blood of his servants; he brings back vengeance to his adversaries and propitiates the land of his people' (v. 43). Here the semantic and repetitive parallelism goes beyond the simple bicolonic pattern of 'A is so, and what's more, B is so' to tie the two bicola together in an A–B–B'–A' chiastic structure, so that the second half of the first bicolon parallels the first half of the second, especially by repeating the root נקם ('avenge'), while the first and last cola are linked by the repetition of אמו ('his people'). The parallelism of the last verse varies the usual bicolonic pattern, effectively doubling the length of the standard poetic unit.

Instead of heaven and earth, the audience here is the nations who must be convinced that YHWH takes vengeance for his people and triumphs above other nations and their gods. Israel appears not as the righteous author of its history but as a faithless and powerless servant; the adulation of YHWH as a rock comes not through Israel's achievements but because of its rebellion. If different functions are allotted to the Song and the law in ch. 31, it may have to do with the Song's explicit audience: heaven and earth, and the nations. With Israel thus removed from Israel rhetorically as well as temporally, the interpretation of the Song as a witness against Israel becomes clearer.

The Song's second section (vv. 4-6), a condensed statement of the entire poem, introduces the central metaphor of the text: YHWH as a rock (cf. vv. 1, 15, 18, 30, 31, and in related uses, vv. 13, 22, 37, and 41). Quite simply, the two bicola in v. 5 assert the justice and perfection of YHWH, and the following verse contrasts it with Israel's imperfection. Though weak, the metaphor of structural soundness appears in both descriptions, with YHWH as the well-formed rock and the defective people who are a twisted generation (דור עקש). The conceit on physical soundness and construction persists even in the rhetorical questions of v. 6: 'Is this how you repay YHWH, people of foolishness and no wisdom? Isn't he your father who acquired (or created, קנך) you? (Didn't) he make you and firmly establish you?' It is YHWH the

---

27. Cf. also Ps. 68.34.
28. Driver, *Deuteronomy*, p. 349.

rock who purchased, formed, and constructed the people. The metaphor of the rock
appears often in the Hebrew Bible (more often than its literal use), and it has analogues in other ancient Semitic texts. As Michael Knowles points out, the Song
applies this well-known cultural metaphor to the context of Israelite covenant:
'The image of the Rock thus becomes an instrument of religious polemic, a means
whereby to demonstrate conceptual continuity while at the same time ideological
supremacy, even exclusivity'.[29]

In response to the rhetorical questions, the speaker exhorts the audience, this
time Israel,[30] to remember the days of old and to ask their fathers to tell them about
those times. Here terms of remembering and speech are critical: the root זכר
('remember') and בין ('discern') each appear; and three words for speech also occur
(שאל, נגד, and אמר). Then, with a two-verse *inclusio* using the root נחל ('inherit',
'possess'), the speaker specifies what Israel should remember, namely, the time
when YHWH allotted the nations their respective inheritances because, conversely,
YHWH's portion is his people. Israel and YHWH mutually inherit each other.

In the more lyrical passages that follow v. 9, other images include YHWH as an
eagle protecting Israel, YHWH's anger taking the form of arrows, swords, and pestilence, and sacrificial flesh and wine. The poetic qualities of vv. 10-12 create the
dramatic power of a boldly progressing form, with the chain-like structure that links
the couplets and the image of the eagle. Semantic boundaries are jumped until the
surge is stopped abruptly by v. 12. The result is impressionistic; the message of
divine protection is not a reasoned proof from tradition as transmitted by the elders,
but an appeal to the emotions.[31]

Stephen Geller shows how the poetic structures and language at this point in the
poem create the effect of mounting tension in vv. 10-14 that leads to the dramatic
transition in v. 15.[32] Another poetic feature of this passage is the gender-matched
parallelism in v. 14. The phrase חמאת בקר וחלב צאן ('curds of the herd and milk of
the flock') forms a chiasmus of gender (f.–m.–m.–f.), a device that not only height-
ens semantic and grammatical parallelism but also, one scholar suggests, expresses
a certain kind of surprise.[33] In any case, the central crisis of the poem emerges not
in specific historical or covenantal terms but rather in a highly poetic presentation
of physical imagery.

It is also worthwhile to trace the various appearances of 'rock' (צור) in these
passages. In addition to the references to YHWH as a rock mentioned above, the verbal form of the word appears in v. 10 with the meaning 'to keep or confine': 'he
surrounded him, he was attentive to him, he kept him as the middle of his eye'. As

29. Michael Knowles, '"The Rock, His Work is Perfect": Unusual Imagery for God in
Deuteronomy xxxii', *VT* 39 (1989), pp. 307-22 (322).

30. Though the LXX suggests original term was not 'sons of Israel' but 'sons of God ('El or
'Elim)'. See Fishbane, *Biblical Interpretation in Ancient Israel*, p. 69.

31. Stephen Geller, 'The Dynamics of Parallel Verse: A Poetic Analysis of Deut. 32.6-12',
HTR 75 (1982), pp. 35-56.

32. Geller, 'The Dynamics of Parallel Verse'.

33. Watson, *Classical Hebrew Poetry*, p. 126.

rock, YHWH shuts in his people; like the verb סבב to which it stands parallel, צור can mean to enclose in either a benevolent or warlike way, perhaps implying that protection has its price. In a more literal sense, צור and its synonymic parallel סלע represent rocky sources of honey and oil which Israel is given to suck (cf. 8.15). The image is at once nurturing and harsh; ינק characteristically describes a nursing mother, and honey and oil are desirable foods, but to make rock the source of this nourishment creates poetic contrast and surprise, even if there is a naturalistic explanation, such as the rocky soil in which olive trees and honey are found.[34] The image, which recalls two tellings of the story of water from the rock at Meribah (Exod. 17.1-7; Num. 20.2-13), suggests a deep ambivalence toward the covenant, as well perhaps to the gender of YHWH.[35] Literally and metaphorically, YHWH the rock is also the motherly source of nourishment for Israel.

But the fertility and plenty of vv. 13-14 become obesity and decadence in v. 15, the turning point at which Israel rebels against YHWH. The word for the oil that Israel sucked out of the rock, שמן, reappears twice here, along with two semantic parallels (עבה and כשה), all describing Israel as fat: 'But Jeshurun [Israel] grew fat and kicked; you grew fat, thick, and gorged'. If ordinary parallelism follows the form 'A is so, and what's more, B is so', then this passage would translate, 'A and B are so, and what's more, A, A1, and A2 are so'; the message could hardly be more emphatic. The original metaphorical use of צור as YHWH also returns in v. 15: 'And he forsook God who made him and treated with contempt the rock of his salvation'. Here the parallelism is much more symmetrical, with two very condensed phrases expressing Israel's abandonment of the righteous YHWH. The restated metaphor of YHWH as צור represents the end of the preceding idyllic imagery, including the oxymoron of the rocks flowing with honey and oil.

The transition from the idyllic language of vv. 13-14 to the obesity and rebellion of v. 15 calls into question the value of divine plenty. If divine favor and wealth lead to decadence, as the transition suggests, then is the rebellion and chastisement of Israel a necessary consequence? If not, then what other factors account for the reversal? If so, then desire for wealth and agricultural wellbeing is called into question.

The narrative shift of Israel's rebellion is also a poetic shift from lyrical imagery to covenantal language of jealousy, other gods, burning anger, arrows and pestilence, and death. Details of Israel's provocation and forgetfulness of YHWH lead to YHWH's anger and punishments. In reciprocal manner, YHWH's response matches Israel's actions even in even the same language. YHWH sees (וירא) and spurns them for the provocation, declares he will hide his face from them and that he will see (אראה) their end. Vision becomes YHWH's means of perception and sanctions against Israel. The terms for jealously (קנא) and provocation (כעס), which applied to Israel's effect on YHWH, are repeated to describe YHWH's punishment of Israel: 'They have made me jealous with no god; they have provoked me with their idols.

34. Driver, *Deuteronomy*, p. 359.
35. See Ilana Pardes, *The Biography of Ancient Israel* (Berkeley: University of California Press, 2000), especially pp. 45-60.

So I will make them jealous with no people; I will provoke them with a foolish nation.' (Cf. the chiastic and parallelistic use of בעם in vv. 16, 19, 21, 27.) Symmetrical and parallelistic thinking underlie the punishment: Israel makes YHWH jealous with no god (בלא־אל), so YHWH makes Israel jealous with no people (בלא־עם). They provoked YHWH's anger with idols (בהבליהם, 'vain winds'), so YHWH will provoke theirs with a foolish (נבל) nation. Replacing god for God justifies replacing people for people.

As YHWH's diatribe continues (vv. 23-25), the language of punishment becomes more graphic and natural in emphasis, ranging from arrows and swords to famine and murderous beasts. Such images parallel the nature imagery in vv. 10-14, whereas the preceding verses center more on the divine–human relationship. The return to naturalistic imagery suggests the following chiastic structure for the narrative of the poem: A (vv. 10-14)–B (vv. 15-18)–B' (vv. 19-21 or v. 22)–A' (v. 22 or vv. 23-25). More will be said about the poem's overall structure below.

A new tone and direction emerge in v. 26, where YHWH seems to reconsider the punishment of Israel because of its likely effect on the nations. Using the perfect instead of the characteristic imperfect, as well as many qualifying conjunctions (e.g. פ, לולי, כי), YHWH indicates the past possibility that he would do these things (with something like the equivalent of the Latin pluperfect subjunctive).[36] 'I would have said, "I will cleave them, I will make their memory cease among men", if I did not dread the vexation of the enemy, lest their adversaries misconstrue it, lest they say, "Our hand is on high, YHWH has not done all this".'

YHWH faces a dilemma: if he punishes the people severely, the nations might mistake this for a failure of YHWH himself. Presumably the shift appears in v. 26 at the pinnacle of an accelerating list of possible punishments. What makes this last sanction pivotal? Answering the question is difficult, since the verb אפאיהם is either a *hapax legomenon* or a textual error that could be corrected as אי פה הם ('where are they?') or אפיצם ('I will scatter them'; cf. LXX). In any case, the following threat to remove their memory among men would equally threaten to remove the memory of YHWH as well. With his particularly loyal and even jealous attachment to Israel, YHWH's legacy remains tied to that of Israel, so wiping them out would also risk wiping himself out in the eyes of the nations.[37]

All of this, of course, appears in a text whose declared purpose is to serve as a witness against Israel, unforgotten in the mouths of their offspring, after they have become fat and broken their covenant with YHWH. There too the earlier narrative provides a gloss on the Song of Moses, highlighting the function of the Song as a reminder of Israel's actions. Memory and textuality are important to the connections between the Song and its narrative context: the Song is written and remembered as a witness against the people (31.19-22). But why does Israel remember the Song but forget its covenant? Is the Song irresistibly memorable despite its

---

36. GCK, p. 313.

37. Cf. Num. 14.13-25, where Moses makes a similar point to YHWH with respect to the Egyptians. An interesting variant of this tradition appears in Ezek. 20; see Fishbane, *Biblical Interpretation in Ancient Israel*, pp. 365-67.

damning content? If so, has this to do with its poetic or aesthetic qualities? Does its persistence depend on oral or written transmission? Israel's attachment to the Song suggests an analogy: despite its incriminating content, Israel can't forget the Song, just as YHWH can't forget the children of Israel despite their obvious shortcomings.[38]

As mentioned before, v. 26 marks a transition in the Song to an argument for restraint from punishing Israel on account of the nations (vv. 26-33). If YHWH were to have terminated the memory of Israel, their enemies might misconstrue this to be the result of their own or their gods' action. The passage strings together several conditional clauses to characterize the hypothetical outcomes of this action.

There is some disagreement among commentators on the reference of גוי in v. 28: is it Israel or one of the enemies mentioned just before?[39] For reasons of continuity with the preceding and following passages, I believe the term refers to one of the enemy nations; the shift in v. 26 clearly raises the new issue of the nations, and this theme persists to the end of the poem. At the same time, and as is usually the case with oracles against the nations, through ambiguity and implication, Israel too is indirectly implied; for if it were not for the faithlessness of Israel, the issue of the nations' misunderstanding would not arise. Indeed, many of the statements about Israel earlier in the poem have counterparts in this section (e.g. with the repetition of covenantal language and such imagery as צור and ענב).

Since it is the enemies who exult over Israel in the preceding hypothetical clauses, v. 28 functions as an explanation:

> For they are a nation perishing of counsels,
> and there is no understanding in them.
> If they were wise, they would consider this,
> they would understand their final end.
> How could one give chase to a thousand,
> or two cause ten thousand to flee,
> unless their rock had sold them
> and YHWH had shut them up?
> For their rock is not like our rock...

The enemies would misconstrue YHWH's punishment of Israel because (כי) they have no understanding of their past losses to an outmanned Israel or of the inferiority of their own rock. The lack of wisdom (עצה, חכם, בין) describes the nation(s),

---

38. Since these issues concern the canonical interrelationship between narrative and Song, they receive more analysis in Chapters 6 and 8. The remainder of the Song, however, may also shed light on these problems.

39. Mayes argues that continuity with the following verses justifies seeing the term as a reference to one of the enemy nations (*Deuteronomy*, pp. 389-90). Others (e.g. Driver and Craigie) see it as a passage about Israel, based on the language and context; see Driver, *Deuteronomy*, p. 371, and Peter C. Craigie, *The Book of Deuteronomy* (Grand Rapids: Eerdmans, 1976), p. 386. Among medieval commentators, Rashi and Ramban think the nation is not Israel but one of the enemies (Rashi, *The Pentateuch and Rashi's Commentary: Deuteronomy* [eds. Rabbi Abraham Ben Isaiah and Rabbi Benjamin Sharfman; Brooklyn: S.S. & R., 1950], p. 302; Ramban, *Commentary on the Torah: Deuteronomy* [trans. Rabbi Charles B. Chavel; New York: Shilo, 1976], p. 365).

but the judgment applies likewise to Israel, as parallels within the poem suggest (vv. 6, 20). Further, while the poem here discusses and addresses the nations, it rhetorically contrasts Israel against the nations, just as the introduction of the poem appears to address not Israel but heaven and earth. In this way, the Song of Moses goes first over the heads of Israel (to heaven and earth), so to speak, and then beneath them (to the nations), in a poem primarily about and still addressed to Israel.

The motif of the rock and wisdom language serve to promote YHWH and tie the Song together. The message remains fairly consistent even as it shifts through the phases of addressing the heavens and earth, narrating Israel's faithlessness, and considering the problem of the nations. As a term signifying literal mountains as well as rival deities, the צור motif points for William F. Albright to an ancient time of 'virile monotheism' (despite the image of YHWH as nursing mother in v. 13!) when 'Yahwism was fighting for its life against both external and internal foes—in brief, to the period when Samuel rallied Israel against its hereditary enemy [the Philistines] as well as against the paganism rampant in its midst'.[40] The wisdom influence on the Song, meanwhile, maintains an emphasis on teaching and understanding. The juxtaposition of these two elements, together with the play of temporality and audience (nature, Israel, the nations) gives the Song a combined mythic and didactic character.

Language of agriculture and sacrifice continues the comparison of Israel and the nations in vv. 32-38, creating a parallel with the earlier pastoral language. Their vines, grapes, and wine are poisonous, and YHWH claims vengeance (נקם) against them, asking rhetorically and sardonically, 'Where are their gods, the rock in which they seek refuge, who ate the fat (חלב, v. 14) of their sacrifices, who drank the wine of their libations? Let them rise up and help you, let him/them be a shelter for you' (vv. 37-38).

The poem then asserts in its strongest terms yet the central monotheistic message, with five instances of the first person pronoun in the seven cola of vv. 39-40. YHWH is the agent *par excellence*, carrying out actions of war and natural force alike. To put it differently, YHWH reaches a point in the poem at which the assertion of identity becomes possible and necessary—possible because of the decisive defeat of the rival divinities before Israel and the nations, and necessary because of the doubt and vexation (כעם) inflicted upon YHWH by Israel.

The textual reconstruction of the final verse of the Song has been the subject of much scholarly debate because of the LXX and Qumran variants. Albright emends and translates as follows:

> Rejoice with Him, O heavens,
>   and bow before him, O sons of God!
> Rejoice with His people, O nations,
>   and work hard for it, O angels of God!

---

40. William F. Albright, 'Some Remarks on the Song of Moses in Deuteronomy XXXII', *VT* 9 (1959), pp. 339-46.

Truly He will avenge the blood of his sons,
    and He will visit retribution on His foes...
    and He will cleanse the land of His people![41]

Without weighing the relative merits of various reconstructions of the verse, it is important to note the strong evidence that the closing verse exhorts not only the nations but also the heavens and sons of God to rejoice. In effect, the conclusion of the poem connects with the beginning, which also addresses the heavens. It also links the cosmic and political levels of creation in the joint recognition of YHWH's activity. Given this connection, the omission of Israel from the equation of praise becomes conspicuous.

The Song of Moses summarizes the relationship of YHWH and Israel not historically but rather from developmental perspectives. In developmental terms, we can say that Israel and YHWH separate, individuate, and then try to re-establish their relationship.[42] But the Song addresses the YHWH–Israel relationship in terms that include other parties in an interdependent system, specifically the nations and the heavens and earth.[43] The first important transition in the poem, vv. 14-15, presents Israel's rebellion against YHWH in terms of a child's rebellion against a parent. YHWH, who had provided Israel with food to be sucked out of the rock, is faced by an unfaithful child who kicks and makes YHWH jealous and angry. It becomes a developmental task for Israel and YHWH to recover from this break, individuate (so to speak), and develop a 'healthy' covenant relationship. Israel, who nurses at the rock in v. 13, must be weaned from this immature condition, while YHWH must rediscover his identity apart from reaffirmation by Israel. Toward this goal, the poet takes a broader, systemic perspective, addressing the interrelationships of YHWH, the heavens and earth, Israel, and the nations. The poem finally reaffirms YHWH's identity by witnessing to dominion over the nations and natural creation, after holding back from the threat of obliterating his people (v. 26). The threat of violence against Israel is replaced by the image of revenge against her enemies (vv. 41-43).

Israel, meanwhile, emerges in a more complicated situation that can only be understood from the Song's canonical context. Because it functions as a witness against future transgressions, the task of individuation from YHWH in the Song must be provisional, part of an ongoing cycle of separation and return, transgression and reconciliation. Although the Song refers to past events, Moses appropriates it as a prophecy for the future, a witness against the people who remember it without, interestingly, heeding its lessons.

The developmental perspective clarifies the issue: if the Song tells the story of YHWH and Israel as a complex interpersonal relationship, then its function for the people becomes not simply a chastisement for future wrongdoings but also a con-

---

41. Albright, 'Some Remarks on the Song of Moses', p. 341.

42. For a discussion of these stages in developmental psychology, see Erik Erikson, *Childhood and Society* (New York: Norton, 1950), *Identity: Youth and Crisis* (New York: Norton, 1968), and *The Life Cycle Completed* (New York: Norton, 1982).

43. For a survey of structuralist approaches to the social sciences and humanities, see Jean Piaget, *Structuralism* (New York: Basic Books, 1970).

structive, perpetual, and explanatory account of these transgressions. Perhaps the idyllic harmony described in vv. 9-14 represents an unhealthy or immature intimacy between YHWH and Israel that inevitably must give way to separation and individuation. According to the canonical context of the Song, this moment coincides with the death of Moses and the crossing of the Jordan. Among non-Yahwistic nations in a new environment and without Moses, Israel rebels but also faces new opportunities.[44]

Memory and witness are touchstones of the Song's wisdom perspective. The Song is a witness remembered by Israel against itself; it calls the cosmos and nations as witnesses in its lawsuit (ריב) against Israel; it exhorts Israel to remember the Song (v. 7) and entertains the possibility of removing Israel from all human memory (v. 26). Something similar appears in the first biblical reference to Moses' writing, the paradoxical erasure and writing, memory and forgetting, of Amalek in Exodus 17 (see Chapter 5). In a sophisticated way, the Hebrew Bible associates texts with the promotion and control of human memory.

The hybrid genre of the Song of Moses—lawsuit (ריב), song (שיר), and didactic poem (משכיל), and their respective semantic fields—is accompanied by a correspondingly complex set of interpretive issues. Within its canonical context it represents a canonical *mise en abyme*, or a condensed statement of the covenantal relationship between YHWH and Israel rendered, as I have argued, not historically but rather in developmental and structural terms. Uttered from the mouth of Moses, the Song will function as a witness against Israel after his impending death. The people will remember a Song in which YHWH contemplates removing Israel from memory, but they will fail to heed its message. Yet the Song does not necessarily fail as a didactic poem, for as a witness against the people and compensation for the loss of Moses, it describes Israel's relationship to YHWH on a grand scale. In this sense, the teaching of the Song, which is addressed to the heavens and earth, the nations, *and* Israel, focuses not so much on Israel's rebellion as on how it arises and the opportunities it presents for the divine–human relationship. In its narrative context, the closed canonical text of the Song displays an ongoing process of memory, development, and interpretation.

3. *Deuteronomy 33: The Blessing of Moses*

The Blessing of Moses appears abruptly; only a brief prose introduction links it to the rest of the narrative, whereas the Song is mentioned four times in ch. 31. At the same time, the Blessing has a clearer canonical parallel in the Blessing of Jacob (Gen. 49) than the Song has in the Hebrew Bible. To the reader familiar with Genesis, Deuteronomy 33 represents an unmistakable link to that text.

---

44. In another poetic conflation of temporal language, the impending revenge against the enemies in 32.35 (קרוב יום) parallels the impending death of Moses (קרבו ימיך, 31.14), implying another linkage between the past event of the narrative and the present and future events of the Song.

Noting the major differences between the Blessing of Moses and the Blessing of Jacob, such as the addition in Deuteronomy 33 of exordium and conclusion, the theocratic and eulogistic character of the blessings, and the narrative introductions to each blessing, Driver observes,

> the Blessing of Moses may be said to be pitched in a higher key; the tone is more buoyant; the affluence, or other distinctive character, of the tranquility, and contentment are the predominant characteristics of the age. The most salient features are the isolation and depression of Judah...the honour and respect with which Levi is viewed...the strength and splendour of the double tribe of Joseph, v. 13-17, and the burst of grateful enthusiasm with which the poet celebrates the fortune of his nation, settled and secure, with the aid of its God, in its Palestinian home (v. 26-29).[45]

Von Rad notes the relative stability and optimism expressed in the blessings and their placement within the frame of an 'informative psalm of praise': 'It is from this point of view, that is to say, as a prediction of the dying Moses, that according to the present text the sayings about the tribes are intended to be understood'.[46]

Poetically, the poem subdivides into twelve parts: the exordium, the ten blessings, and conclusion.[47] Because prose narrative introductions separate the parts, the Blessing appears more as a collection of twelve short poems than as a single poetic unit, with great variation in the kinds and degrees of parallelism.

In the blessing on Benjamin, for example, three sets of three-word units or 'cola' with high levels of repetition, semantic, and grammatical parallelism, follow a two-word epithet, יְדִיד יְהוָה ('beloved of YHWH', v. 12). The blessing on Joseph, which follows Benjamin, is the longest and perhaps most poetically regular passage. It begins with one tricolon and follows with seven bicola, with all but one of the cola consisting of three words, all but four cola beginning with a –וֹ ('and') and/or a –מִ ('from') prefix. In litany-like fashion, the blessing begins five of the cola with the word מִמֶּגֶד ('from the finest') and three with the pronoun הֵם ('they'). At the other poetic extreme is the blessing on Gad (vv. 20-21), which doesn't divide easily into any clear pattern, although it exhibits considerable semantic, repetitive, and phonetic parallelism (e.g. קָדְקֹד, רֵאשִׁית, and רֹאשׁ and the use of the consonants ה, ק, and שׁ). Each of the parts thus has a discrete subject and position in the text. The Blessing raises many historical and geographical questions about ancient Israelite religion and the tribal confederation (amphictyony), but the focus of this analysis is semantic and poetic, with special attention to the exordium (vv. 2-5), Levi (vv. 8-11), and the conclusion (vv. 26-29).

The introduction to the Blessing combines imagery of YHWH as a cultic king divinity with the Exodus narrative of the giving of the תּוֹרָה on Sinai; historical,

---

45. Driver, *Deuteronomy*, p. 386.

46. Von Rad, *Deuteronomy*, p. 205. These sayings about the tribes take on a prayer-like function in the text, according to von Rad (p. 208).

47. There are only ten blessings because Simeon is not mentioned, and the blessings on Zebulun and Issachar are combined (vv. 18-19).

human event merges with idealized theophany. Frank Moore Cross dates the poem to the eleventh or tenth centuries: 'In these poems one finds the language of the theophany of the Divine Warrior utilizing mythical elements from the theophany of the stormgod as warrior. The theophanic language of the prose sources of the Sinai revelation is secondary, derived from the hymns of the Wars of YHWH, where the (Exodus-) Conquest motif is naturally and primitively linked with theophany.'[48]

In the first set of images, YHWH descends Sinai, shines forth from two holy mountains of Edom, and becomes king to Jeshurun.[49] Although the original significance of these images is unclear, here they introduce and invoke the Sinai theophany that culminates in Moses commanding the תורה in v. 4. The poem continues, 'And he was a king in Jeshurun, when he gathered the heads of the people to himself, together the tribes of Israel'. The immediate antecedent to the indefinite 'he' here is Moses, although most interpreters argue (for theological reasons) that YHWH is the subject of the action. Still, from a strictly grammatical point of view, 'he' could be either Moses or YHWH, an ambiguity that parallels the blurred and dual agency of the narrative. It seems appropriate to the Blessing, a blend of formulaic generalities and tribal specificity, that its exordium should juxtapose divine and human agency, historical narrative and cultic praise.

Levi's blessing recalls the leadership of Moses and Aaron and reinforces the priestly function of the tribe. A high degree of grammatical and semantic parallelism characterizes the poem's nine bicola at the same time as it presents narrative, descriptive, and hortatory elements. The Thummim and Urim, a kind of oracular lots, underline the priestly authority of the Levites.[50] The strong link to the wilderness stories continues with the place names Massah and Meribah, derived from the verbs נסה ('to test') and ריב ('to strive', also the name of the lawsuit genre).[51] Levi is remembered, especially in the person of Moses, as the tribe that tests YHWH; in Exodus 17 the people test God and Moses strikes the rock out of which water springs, but in the other main version of the story, Numbers 20, Moses and Aaron participate in the rebellion of the people by striking the rock one time too many. It is this action that justifies Aaron's death in Num. 20.24, and at the end of Deuteronomy it is Moses' turn to die (cf. the close parallel to Numbers in Deut. 32.50-52).

Levi is identified with rebellion either through Moses and Aaron or the tribe in general, depending on which version of the story the poet has in mind.[52] In any case, it is interesting that this episode becomes a defining characteristic of Levi in a blessing that reinforces the priestly role of the tribe. Perhaps it is not too far-fetched to see a link between the deaths of Aaron and Moses and the subsequent role of the Levites as offerers of cultic sacrifice (Aaron) and teachers of the תורה (Moses)

48.   Cross, *Canaanite Myth and Hebrew Epic*, p. 86. For the argument on the date, see Frank Moore Cross and David Noel Freedman, 'The Blessing of Moses', *JBL* 67 (1978), pp. 191-210 (192).

49.   Citing its use in Deut. 32.15, Driver suggests the name Jeshurun 'shows that Israel is here contemplated under its *ideal* character'(*Deuteronomy*, p. 394).

50.   Von Rad, *Deuteronomy*, p. 206. Cf. also Exod. 28.30 and 1 Sam. 14.41.

51.   Cf. Exod. 17.7.

52.   Driver, *Deuteronomy*, p. 400.

(v. 10). For as Moses says in Deut. 31.27-29, the Levitical function of the תורה compensates for the loss of Moses as a leader.

Taking תורה in a sense that is admittedly broader than the text originally indicated, it may be suggested that the death of Moses and Aaron is part of the תורה and at the same time necessitates its importance in replacing the dead leaders in the religious community. Indeed, the incident at Meribah itself belongs to the תורה, at least in the mind of the Deuteronomic redactor of the text, so it may be a kind of divine irony that the Levites are here identified by the rebellion of Moses and Aaron, because it is precisely this that led through their deaths to the need for teaching the תורה. The Blessing exploits the wordplay of place names to make rebellion central to Levi's identity (v. 8); and regardless of its original meaning, the Meribah episode here is linked directly to the death of Moses and the compensatory function of תורה. The Levites inherit their function from the transgression of their ancestors. This possibility gains strength from the ambiguity of the term תורה in both the narrative and poetic passages of Deuteronomy 31–34, as I have argued.

Commentators have found v. 9 difficult to interpret. Rashi, for example, relates it to the Levites' execution of the idolatrous Israelites in Exod. 32.26-29, arguing that אחיו cannot be literal in either passage.[53] Driver, following *Targum Onkelos*, maintains that 'The intention of the poet is to describe the disinterested spirit in which the ideal Levite discharged his priestly office'.[54] In either case, most commentators connect the refusal or failure to recognize family members with the golden calf episode in Exodus 32 where the Levites distinguish themselves by killing idolatrous kinsmen and receive a commission for divine service (cf. Exod. 32.29). Like the story of Massah/Meribah, the slaughter after the golden calf episode casts the Levites in an ambiguous moral light; Childs remarks, 'At the cost of son and brother the Levites have won their position as the blessed of the Lord', even as the story implicitly condemns Aaron, the Levite instigator of the idolatry.[55] The Levites inherit their priestly duties of teaching תורה and offering sacrifice only through the loss of Moses, Aaron, and many kinsmen.

The conclusion of the Blessing (vv. 26-29) appears to be a continuation of the poem's introduction, the 'informative Song of praise' to YHWH. Following the simple introductory statement, 'There is none like El, Jeshurun', the passage lists divine attributes and actions in a highly ordered set of bicola exhibiting high levels of semantic, grammatical, chiastic (cf. v. 26b-c), repetitive (ישראל, אשר, גאוה, עזר), and even gender-matched[56] parallelism. Interestingly, the text begins by stating that El is beyond compare and near the end states that Israel is thereby also beyond compare (vv. 26, 29). Like the Song, the Blessing here stresses the mutuality of

---

53. Rashi, *The Pentateuch and Rashi's Commentary*, p. 323. See also Beyerle, *Der Mosesegen im Deuteronomium*, pp. 131-33.

54. Driver, *Deuteronomy*, p. 401.

55. Childs, *Exodus*, p. 571. Also cf. the negative tone of the blessing on Levi and Simeon in Gen. 49.5-7.

56. In the matched pairs מגן עזרך (m.) and חרב גאותך (f.). See Watson, *Classical Hebrew Poetry*, p. 124.

YHWH and Israel, although the tone in the Blessing is lighter; as Driver says, 'It breathes the bright and happy spirit of the earlier narratives of Kings'.[57]

Frank Cross identifies the beginning and end of the Blessing with the march of conquest from the south tradition, along with Judg. 5.4-5, Ps. 68.8-9, and Hab. 3.3-7.[58] In this tradition the divine warrior returns from battle and proceeds northward to enthronement or a new temple: 'Primary is his manifestation as Victor and King in the storm'.[59] If this is the case, then the Blessing of Moses appears to be framed by a hymn to YHWH rooted in much earlier traditions. The legacy of territorial conquest by the amphictyony gains legitimacy from the cosmogonic conquest of YHWH.

As a whole, the Blessing, like the Song, concerns the problems of temporality, agency, and sacred text. Even though the Blessing appears suddenly, it comes from the mouth of Moses, man of God (33.1), and it draws upon many layers of past tradition to make a prophetic statement about the future. Moses parallels Jacob in granting the Blessing, appropriating and expanding from the parent–child context to a prophet–nation benediction. The explicit references to events related in Exodus and Numbers situate the text in a larger narrative context. The past of narrative discourse also gives way to the future time of prophetic blessing, a future that is partly fulfilled for its post-Mosaic audience, who have already crossed the Jordan and established territorial claims.

The Blessing juxtaposes Moses' commandment of a Torah (תורה) (v. 4) with a poem of YHWH as divine warrior, suggesting the interdependence and dual agency of YHWH and Moses, and that YHWH's glory requires human linguistic expression. Scholars have shown that the statement is a late addition to the original Song. 'the scribal addition in Deut. 33.4 is a theological *tour de force*—a forceful theological intrusion—which contemporizes the neutral topographic imagery of v. 2 in the light of developing (but independent) covenantal-nomistic traditions.'[60] תורה and the semantically related terms צוה, ברית, and משפט add a covenantal dimension to the poem's celebration of YHWH's conquest and Israel's amphictyonic success. Whether it is the law or the Song mentioned in Deuteronomy 31, תורה is also the text written and recited by Moses for the people. Like the legal texts, the narrative, and the Song, the Blessing of Moses is a sacred text that is in part *about* sacred texts, openly displaying its multiple layers.

4. *Conclusion*

The two poetic texts at the end of Deuteronomy appear for important but different canonical reasons. The narrative in ch. 31 characterizes the Song of Moses as a witness against the people for their future unfaithfulness. Moses is told by YHWH to write down the Song and teach it to the people, not to prevent their wrongdoing but

57. Driver, *Deuteronomy*, p. 387.
58. Cross, *Canaanite Myth and Hebrew Epic*, p. 86.
59. Cross, *Canaanite Myth and Hebrew Epic*, p. 156.
60. Fishbane, *Biblical Interpretation in Ancient Israel*, p. 76.

simply to confront them with their iniquity. Thus the Song which relates Israel's future unfaithfulness enters an oral and written canon that serves to reiterate and counteract it.

The Blessing has an even more obvious canonical function, with its close literary echoing of Jacob's Blessing in Genesis 49. Its main effect is to create a parallel between Moses and Jacob/Israel as two great patriarchs whose last actions are words that anticipate the twelve tribes' history. Jacob's Blessing refers directly to his sons and indirectly to the tribes, while Moses' Blessing refers metonymically to the sons as forebears of the tribes. A nation emerges from family in Jacob's Blessing, while Moses' atavistically reinforces the familial dimension of nation. Both texts are metonymic, but in opposite ways: in Genesis 49, the parts (sons of Jacob) anticipate the whole (the amphictyony), while in Deuteronomy 32 the whole points back to its foundational parts.

Unlike straightforward narrative, the poetic texts occupy no particular temporal position. Moses recites the Song and Blessing in the story, but their future orientation and poetic structure involve the reader directly, almost as if to dissolve the boundary between reader and the listeners at Horeb. Indeed, by recording the poetic texts here in a much later narrative context, the final editors of Deuteronomy have performed an analogous operation. In a loose way, the Song and Blessing echo the liturgical pattern of the curse and blessing, respectively, in chs. 27–30. Also like the earlier chapters, both poetic texts likely have a liturgical or cultic origin.[61] Linking narrative and liturgical elements, the two poetic texts bring together past, present, and future.[62] With the hybrid genre of the Song and the Blessing's hymnic frame, both poems successfully combine diverse literary and theological traditions through parallelism. It is chiefly parallelism that achieves the poetic function of heightening and intensifying the language of the Song and Blessing, one result of which I am arguing is an attempt to link the story's historical past with the reader's present.

The Song and Blessing both represent the entire trajectory of Israel's destiny, though in different and complementary ways. In the Song, the YHWH/Israel relationship is described in developmental and structural terms with an emphasis on the emerging identities of YHWH and Israel. By summarizing the Pentateuch without mentioning many historical details, the Song functions as a *mise en abyme* in the text. The Blessing, on the other hand, rests on more specific traditions, some of which undoubtedly do not survive in the Hebrew Bible,[63] and it reaches forward into Israel's future after settling in the land across the Jordan. If the Song emphasizes Israel's development away from YHWH, the Blessing paints a more harmonious picture of the relationship within the contexts of the conquest hymn tradition and the amphictyony. Both poetic texts interrupt the flow of the narrative to make sweeping liturgical statements of the divine–human relationship and thus make the

---

61. See, e.g., Craigie, *Deuteronomy*, pp. 370, 391.

62. There are also parallels between the two texts, such as the theme of the greatness of YHWH as צוּר in the Song and as divine warrior in the Blessing, and terms such as טל ('dew', 32.2 and 33.28).

63. Von Rad, *Deuteronomy*, p. 208.

final text seem relevant and contemporary. Deuteronomy's sophisticated and self-conscious notions of temporality,[64] agency, and textuality account for its successful combination of diverse strata into a sacred text that is at once *traditum* and a manifestation of an interpretive *traditio*. Placed in the divinely favored mouth of Moses (Exod. 4), the Song and Blessing lend him their dynamic complexity and timelessness. Just as they blur the boundaries of time and tradition, the Song and Blessing show Moses as both a 'writing being' and a 'being written'.

64.   For a complete discussion of conceptions of time in Deuteronomy, see Wilch, *Time and Event* (Leiden: E.J. Brill, 1969), pp. 64-76.

Chapter 8

THE BIRTH, DEATH, AND WRITING OF MOSES

The birth and death narratives of Moses (Exod. 1–2; Deut. 31–34) make an unlikely pair for comparison, since they deal with such different subjects and probably come from different documentary sources.[1] Yet on their own these episodes suggest that the biblical Moses is the biography of Moses. Both scenes resemble the legends of other ancient heroes: Hugo Gressmann compared Moses' nativity story to legends of Cyrus, Sargon, and several others. Steven Weitzman has established parallels between Moses' death and the 'famous last words' of other ancient teachers.[2] The closing verses of Deuteronomy (34.7-12) venerate Moses in such emphatic terms that one might assume the entire books of Exodus through Deuteronomy to be hagiography.

But Moses remains an elusive character, even in the birth and death stories. This chapter attempts to show that the birth and death of Moses call attention to the process of forming a written tradition centered on covenant and people rather than the legend or biography of a hero. In each case, the text deflects attention from Moses to the people and traditions of Israel. Brief and ambiguous at their core, the birth and death scenes leave significant gaps, as if to signal that Moses is not their only focus. But as Auerbach implies in *Mimesis*, gaps are in the eye of the beholder; the expectation of a seamless, linear narrative about a hero's life comes from the Hellenistic tradition of Philo and Josephus. Though his virtue and greatness are part of their message, Exodus and Deuteronomy never sustain their focus on Moses as Philo and Josephus do. Like the narrative of Deuteronomy 31–32 (Chapter 6), biographical concerns are secondary to texts and traditions of Israel in the birth and death stories. Even in these most biographical scenes, Moses appears within the fabric of written tradition rather than above it.

Most biblical scholars view the birth and death episodes as rather late additions to the Pentateuch. Gressmann noted that the motifs of infanticide or Moses' survival in the ark do not appear in other biblical versions of the Exodus story. And while the incident at Meribah (Exod. 17 and Num. 20) anticipates the death story, the panegyric on Moses in Deut. 34.7-12 is usually attributed to later redactional

---

1.   For the source analysis of the birth story, see Propp, *Exodus*, pp. 145-46. Friedman's analysis of Deut. 34 does not differ markedly from Driver's; see Friedman, *Who Wrote the Bible?*, p. 255.
2.   Weitzman, *Song and Story in Biblical Narrative*.

layers. Since Chapters 6 and 7 have dealt with Deuteronomy 31–33, the present discussion concentrates only on Deuteronomy 34.

I begin with exposition of Exodus 1–2 and Deuteronomy 34 in turn, and follow with a comparative analysis of the birth and death traditions. The analysis focuses on the biblical text, but it makes selective use of post-biblical traditions, including religious art.[3] My argument is that the birth and death episodes, which focus more on the person of Moses than any other texts in the Pentateuch, are nevertheless ambiguous sites of tradition formation and competing interpretations. Moses is a 'being written' and a 'writing being',[4] a body and a text, at the same time. When Moses' body changes hands in both episodes, the question of who has the body of Moses becomes inseparable from the question of who has the text of Moses.

1. *Language, Structure, and Meaning of the Birth Story*

Exodus begins by continuing the strand of narrative from the end of Genesis. The Hebrews are still in Egypt—they are listed and numbered by the traditional names of the tribes (Exod. 1.1-5). Discontinuity and crisis emerge when Joseph and his generation die, and when the people continue to be fruitful and multiply (a covenantal blessing formula common in Genesis), a new pharaoh becomes fearful of the Hebrews' numbers. Edicts adding to their workload and authorizing the murder of infant boys follow. The whole focus of ch. 1 is thus on the horrible plight of the Hebrews as they increase in number.

The birth story of Moses takes up the first ten verses of ch. 2; his name appears only at the end of the pericope, and his parents are described only as Levites. In this short space, Moses' parents marry, his mother gives birth, he is placed in the ark (תבה, the term used in the story of Noah), and he is discovered, saved, and raised as a son by the daughter of Pharaoh. Immediately following the birth story comes the incident of Moses killing the overseer, which leads to his exile in Midian.

Many narrative gaps appear in the birth story, including: when and where it occurs in relation to ch. 1, why the mother had to give up the baby when she did, what the mother intended by placing the baby in the ark, whether and for how long the baby returned to its own mother to nurse, and what identity or status was assigned to the child in the Egyptian court. For later interpreters, the most pressing question was the balance of Hebrew and Egyptian identities, especially in the mind of Moses. But this question already reflects a bias toward biography as a description of Moses' subjectivity and personal identity. What is much more crucial from the standpoint of narrative continuity is the simple question of how the birth story fits into the narrative laid out in ch. 1.

The answer supplied by tradition, of course, is that Moses is the one who will deliver the Hebrews from their Egyptian servitude. But as Gressmann and other commentators have pointed out, there seem to be at least two independent narrative

---

3. There is no attempt to sketch the history of interpretation in either case, only to identify key issues in both texts and their subsequent traditions.

4. Derrida, *Of Grammatology*, pp. 18-22.

traditions at play. Jonathan Cohen identifies three parts in the story: the midwives, the ark, and the birth itself; he points out that the birth story makes no connection to the midwives.[5] As later sources have it (e.g. Josephus), the murder of the sons follows the announcement of the deliverer's birth. One would thus expect the midwives to save Moses, but instead, the ark tradition intervenes, and Moses is saved in the great tradition of Sargon, Cyrus, and other ancient heroes. Following Samuel Loewenstamm, Cohen avers that traditional legends announcing and describing Moses' birth have been reduced and spliced into their present context, the result of which is a 'complex narrative' filled with patterns of 'revealing and concealing' (e.g. the baby, the parents).[6]

The gaps in the story also compel the careful reader to be conscious that the text's meaning is not self-evident, and that the text is constructed out of distinct parts. Some of these parts are recognizable to the reader of Genesis. As James Ackerman has shown, Exodus 1–2 includes strong linguistic and thematic parallels to the stories of creation, the flood, and the tower of Babel.[7] To an audience 'literate' in ancient traditions, the hero birth/abandonment motif would be familiar as well, perhaps enough to allow a truncated version to imply missing elements (e.g. the annunciation). The first two verses naming the children of Israel who came to Egypt recall Genesis (especially Jacob's blessing in ch. 49) and anticipate the Blessing of Moses (Deut. 33), his last official act before he dies.

If the birth of Moses is an artful combination of distinct narrative elements designed to call attention to their own composition and structure—if, in other words, the medium is the message (or at least part of it)—then why did later interpreters such as Josephus elaborate and expand it? Why did they create a biography out of what Ackerman calls a 'quick collage of episodes'?[8] One explanation is that ancient traditions continued to shine through the lattices of biblical redaction, that such legends strive to reconstruct themselves. Cohen speaks of the 'recurrent desire of the pattern to return to its roots'.[9] Such an explanation is hard to disprove, because the evidence is unclear. On the one hand, nonbiblical parallels certainly suggest that Moses' birth belongs to a class of heroes' birth/abandonment stories, and that Moses is by analogy a hero like Sargon, Cyrus, or Oedipus. On the other hand, the primacy of the hero legend is not self-evident in Exodus, even if a longer version of the story is implied. When Philo and Josephus amplify the birth story, for instance, their purpose is polemical and their context is Hellenistic. These were Jewish leaders writing in defense of their tradition and against the derogation of their founder, Moses.

Josephus and others may have reconstructed missing parts of the birth story, but the choice to focus on a great individual meant the choice *not* to focus on the

5.   Cohen, *Moses Nativity Story*, p. 13.
6.   Cohen, *Moses Nativity Story*, pp. 20-24.
7.   James S. Ackerman, 'The Literary Context of the Moses Birth Story', in Gros Louis, Ackerman and Warshaw (eds.), *Literary Interpretations of Biblical Narratives*, pp. 74-119.
8.   Ackerman, 'Moses Birth Story', p. 96.
9.   Cohen, *Moses Nativity Story*, p. 65.

collective experience of a people or the complexities of the biblical text itself, which displays skillful patterns among its distinct elements. The legends in which he removes Pharaoh's crown, speaks at birth, and prophesies at age three, all strengthen the view of Moses as an extraordinary individual.[10] But as Ackerman shows, Exodus 1–2 forms a composite story of the people of Israel struggling between forces of life and death. Rather than linear narrative, the story coheres through motifs of water, wilderness, and survival at the hands of Egyptian oppression.[11] Allusions to Genesis further strengthen the text's thematic resonance.

Like the episodes of the veil, the heavy mouth, and the Torah and Song, Exodus 1–2 is a 'scriptural' text in that one must notice its composition in order to make sense of it. The plot is driven by formal, text-like utterances—the edicts of Pharaoh and the naming of Moses—but writing itself is absent. One could say that writing is evoked nonetheless, just as the absence of divine presence in the narrative evokes God. The literary quality of Exodus 1–2, its 'writtenness', is unavoidable, until it is concealed or eclipsed by the impulse to rewrite it as biography.

2. *Language, Structure, and Meaning of the Death Story*

The Moses death story invokes the incident of Massah-Meribah. The first version of the story (Exod. 17.1-7) shows Israel to be guilty of contentiousness, and the second (Num. 20.10-13) finds fault with Moses and Aaron for striking the rock twice and announces the punishment that they will not lead the people into the promised land. Some texts in Deuteronomy, such as Deut. 1.37, 3.26, and 4.21, attribute blame to the people, while others (Deut. 3.23-38; 4.21-22; 32.48-52) seem to accuse Moses. The death of Moses is announced and explained several times before Deuteronomy 34, and as Chapters 6 and 7 have shown, his last actions prepare for his death.

The scope of this review is limited to the narration of his death itself: Deut. 34.5-12. Like the birth story, the death story makes no explicit reference to writing, although it is so central to his work and last actions. The brevity of the death episode is perhaps more striking than that of the birth episode, though it compensates for brevity by its emphatically panegyric tone.

In fact, Deut. 34.5-12 is more concerned to extol the life of Moses than to describe his death. The event itself is told with a minimum of detail: 'And Moses the servant of YHWH died there in the land of Moab at the command of YHWH. And he [or they] buried him in a gave in the land of Moab opposite Beth Peor, and no one has known the place of his burial till this day.' The textual puzzle of whether the verb is singular or plural is striking: if it is plural, then presumably the people buried him, in which they *would* have known the grave site. But with the term עוד, the narrator implies a moment of storytelling much later than the story itself. The term also evokes the associations of duration and memorial that it has in Deuteronomy

---

10. Rella Kushelevsky, *Moses and the Angel of Death* (New York: Peter Lang, 1995), p. 243.
11. Ackerman, 'Moses Birth Story', pp. 109-14.

31–32 (see Chapter 6). If the verb is singular, then its antecedent is YHWH, which suggests a unique role for YHWH as gravedigger, suggesting at least that Moses' death is unlike any other.

At the age limit of 120 years (see Gen. 6), Moses' time has come, as the reader has been warned repeatedly by this point. But his death is also untimely, for, as the NRSV has it, 'his eye was not dim nor his natural force abated' (Deut. 34.7). In seeming contradiction to Moses' admission that he can 'no longer (עוֹד) go out and come back' (Deut. 31.2), get around, that is, here we have a denial of physical weakness. Moses' death may be necessary, but not for ordinary physical reasons.

The children of Israel observe a thirty-day mourning period, and we are then told that Joshua was filled with a spirit of wisdom, 'because Moses had put his hands upon him (see Deut. 31), and the children of Israel listened to him and did as YHWH had commanded Moses'. Moses' successor gains his power from YHWH, but only through the hands of Moses. With the narrative complete, the final three verses summarize Moses' achievements in a careful balance of hero veneration and respect for YHWH's activity: 'And no prophet has since (עוֹד) arisen in Israel like Moses, who know YHWH face to face' (34.10). From the standpoint of Deuteronomy 34, Moses is unique, but 18.15 and 18 do promise Israel a 'prophet like' Moses. From a literary perspective, the echo hardly seems accidental, so even this most unequivocal statement about Moses is more complex and ambiguous than might first appear.[12]

The term יָד returns in Deut. 34.12 as the strong arm of Moses, a phrase that often applies to YHWH himself (cf. 32.39-41). The focus remains on Moses, though piety requires a divine source for his power. A close, phrase-by-phrase translation of vv. 11-12 reveals this ambiguous balance:

> In all the signs and wonders
> Which YHWH sent him to do in the land of Egypt,
> To Pharaoh and to his servants, and to all his land;
> And in everything with strong arm and great terror
> That Moses did in the eyes of all of Israel.

Verses 11-12 seem to follow as an apodosis to v. 10, illustrating the uniqueness of Moses as the prophet who knows God face-to-face. The term 'all' (כֹל) appears six times in the passage, and the prefix –לְ ('to', 'in', or 'by') appears seven times, creating a chain of phrases that summarize Moses' career in the most complete, all-encompassing terms possible. In the first three lines (as translated above), Moses acts at the direction of YHWH; in the last two lines, YHWH's direction is only implicit, and the descriptive language ('strong arm and great terror') seem more suited to a deity than to a mortal servant.

Deuteronomy 34 offers more evaluation than narration. The basic circumstances of Moses' death—how he died, how and where he was buried, and even why he died—remain unclear, but his importance—as a unique prophet and worker of signs and wonders—is certain. Nevertheless, the absence of Torah (תּוֹרָה)—a term so

---

12. Jeffrey Tigay (*Deuteronomy*, p. 175) notes the tension and finesses it by distinguishing the role of prophet from the unique career of Moses.

central in chs. 31–32, even in the mythopoetic Song (32.4)—is striking. Nowhere in ch. 34 is Moses' work of writing and teaching mentioned, despite the evaluative purpose of the text. The closest the text comes to mentioning his writing is the communication implied by the epithets אבד יהוה and נביא. Why is writing excluded, and why are the circumstances of Moses' death obscured?

According to Loewenstamm, the biblical death of Moses is a compromise between a tradition of Moses' immortality and a pious account of his mortality:

> The Torah admits that Moses vanished on a high mountain and that no one knows where he is buried, but it adds that one may not interpret this as an assumption to God. Moses went up to the mountain only so that God might show him from there the land of Israel for which he yearned. He died there, yet he was not buried on the mountain close to god, but rather in the valley, as is the lot of a common man.[13]

Whether a tradition of Moses' ascent underlies Deuteronomy 34 is unknown, but Loewenstamm's cogent suggestion would explain the ambiguities and careful balance in Deuteronomy 34. Like Elijah, Moses is a figure whose mythological significance exceeds the bounds of piety, an issue that surfaces at the time of his death. This Moses is a legendary man of action, not the scribe and teacher found elsewhere in Deuteronomy. For this Moses, physical vigor and actions are eternally present, and any signs of frailty are unacceptable. The Moses of the mighty hand can only die under extraordinary circumstances.

The writing Moses, on the other hand, is already assured a permanent place in tradition. The tension between mortality and immortality in Deut. 34.10-12 does not concern the Moses who writes and teaches. As the analysis of Deuteronomy 31–32 demonstrates (Chapter 6), Moses and writing are endlessly intertwined in a legacy that appears to rank Torah above Joshua, text above personality, the Moses of writing above the Moses of leading, for posterity.

'Moses did not die like all other people, but like all other people, Moses died', writes Leon Wieseltier in *Kaddish*.[14] Even if the Deuteronomy 34 is not a toned-down story of Moses' ascent to God, it is certainly an extraordinary narrative. The unclear circumstances of the death and burial, along with the panegyric on Moses' great deeds, suggest a tension between Moses veneration and biblical piety. But the Moses venerated in ch. 34 is not the Moses of Torah but the Moses of האתות והמופתים ('signs and wonders'). The writing Moses is less tangible and vivid in a biographical sense, but more enduring and, I propose, more basic to the biblical portrayal.

13. Samuel Loewenstamm, 'The Death of Moses', in George Nickelsburg (ed.), *Studies on the Testament of Abraham* (Missoula, MT: Scholars Press, 1976), p. 198. The valley ('opposite Beth Peor') also recalls acts of faithlessness with Baal Peor (Num. 25.1-5).

14. Leon Wieseltier, *Kaddish* (New York: Alfred Knopf, 1998), p. 110. Elsewhere, Wieseltier notes: 'Rashi is struck by the fact that Moses died on the same date that he was born. This requires explanation. "So that the birth will atone for the death", he explains' (p. 582). See also pp. 96-99 and 583.

3. *The Death of Moses and the Writing of Moses*

While Moses is alive to the people in the story, he is long dead at the time of the text's inscription. For his contemporaries, Moses provides direct personal leadership; but the post-Mosaic people, although they have crossed the Jordan, rely on writings by and about Moses as an affirmation of their past. Deuteronomy emphasizes texts because of their importance to its audience; Moses' scribal activity legitimates texts and exalts him at the same time. Temporal ambiguities and the mixture of legal, parenetic, and poetic genres merge the ancient past of Deuteronomy with the scriptural present.

There is a dialectical relationship between Moses and written tradition: each magnifies and legitimates the other. The text (i.e. Torah) derives authority from its connection to Moses as a central figure of the narrative and an author of at least part of the text. Moses, in turn, derives authority simply through representation in the text as a unique prophet, servant of God, teacher, scribe, and worker of signs and wonders.[15] Neither Moses nor text can be understood without the other.

As the analysis of Deuteronomy 31–32 in Chapter 6 shows, the boundaries of texts become blurred in Deuteronomy 31–34, and they become referentially expanded in their parenetic context. The effect of this blurring and expansion is to reach beyond the narrative frame, in which Moses addresses the people before his death, to involve and even address the reader, through ambiguity (תורה), reference to the future (writing texts, seven-year cycle, עוד, and Blessing), and narrative frame-breaks such as in 34.10. The redactors of Deuteronomy 31–34 guide readers, by the text's reflexivity, discontinuity, and dual characterization of Moses (writing and written), to reflect on the conception of sacred text both as a stable authority and as a dynamic tradition that requires and encourages active interpretation. Such a model of the text, constituted through the interpretive process, complements a number of contemporary hermeneutical and literary theories.[16]

The three texts presented by Moses (תורה [Torah], Song, and Blessing) form a kind of typology of sacred texts. The Torah is the most important (since it equals life, according to 32.47) and yet the least clearly delineated, while the Song, which has a negative function as 'witness' (עד), has very clear literary boundaries. The Blessing, on the other hand, derives less importance from writing than the other texts; it represents a prophetic speech act and event rather than a text to be written, recited, and learned. At the same time, if Torah is given its widest possible reference in the text, then it may be understood to include the Song (thus 32.2) and the Blessing (cf. 33.4). The diversity of texts in Deuteronomy 31–34 reflects diverse notions of writing that nevertheless can be encompassed by the broad term תורה.

---

15. See Patrick D. Miller, Jr, '"Moses My Servant": The Deuteronomic Portrait of Moses', *Int* 41 (1987), pp. 245-55, and Aaron Wildavsky, *The Nursing Father: Moses as a Political Leader* (Tuscaloosa: University of Alabama Press, 1984), especially pp. 170-71.

16. See, e.g., Hans-Georg Gadamer, 'The Relevance of the Beautiful', in *idem, The Relevance of the Beautiful and Other Essays* (ed. Robert Bernasconi; trans. Nicholas Walker; Cambridge: Cambridge University Press, 1986), pp. 1-53, and Mikhail Bakhtin, 'Forms of Time and Chronotope in the Novel', in *idem, The Dialogic Imagination*, pp. 84-258 (252-53).

The ambiguity of תורה and the paradox that Moses is a writer and a character written about makes it difficult to extricate Moses' writings from the writing of Moses. Everything Moses does in Deuteronomy 31–34, including his writing, portrays him as an energetic and powerful servant of God. At the same time, the writing of Moses by the hidden narrator depicts a dying leader who claims to be physically weak. But it may be more appropriate to speak of Moses' writing and the writing of Moses in the middle voice (following Roland Barthes' notion of writing): Moses is writing/written,[17] or 'the writing being' and 'the being written'. Moses writes the תורה, a term whose reference can include the narrative that reports this inscription, thus encouraging the tradition of Mosaic authorship. But at the same time, Moses appears as a figure inscribed in the text, and in this sense Moses is written; the distinction of Moses as a writer and as a character written about ultimately dissolves.

Like the *Phaedo*, Deuteronomy presents a great man's last actions and the circumstances of his predetermined death, and, interestingly, both Moses and Socrates include writing among their final actions.[18] Complex narrative and poetic texts combine to address these questions and, also like the *Phaedo*, develop strategies of involving the reader in the sphere of the text's addressees.[19] In both cases, narrative discontinuity and parenetic discourse contribute to this effect without destroying the historiographic function of the texts. In order to make sense of Deuteronomy 31–34, the reader must recognize the reflexivity of the text: there is a story and a frame around the story; there is a speaker within the story (Moses) and a narrator outside the story; there is a text in which the inscription of texts is depicted. This reflexivity decontextualizes the immediate story and alerts the reader to the retrospective frame around it.[20]

Without diminishing the importance of Moses as a character in the story, the elements of the narrative frame and the three texts inscribed and recited in the story

17.   According to Roland Barthes, modern writing suggests a transformation of the verb *to write* from active to middle voice: 'It is my opinion that in the middle verb *to write* the distance between the writer and the language diminishes asymptotically… The field of the writer is nothing but writing itself, not as the pure "form" conceived by an aesthetic of art for art's sake, but, much more radically, as the only area [*espace*] for the one who writes' ('To Write: An Intransitive Verb?', in R.T. and F.M. De George (eds.), *The Structuralists: From Marx to Levi-Strauss* [Garden City, NY: Doubleday, 1972], pp. 155-67 [166]).

18.   Plato, *Phaedo*, in *The Collected Dialogues of Plato* (ed. Edith Hamilton and Huntington Cairns; Princeton, NJ: Princeton University Press, 1987), pp. 43-44.

19.   In the *Phaedo*, the story of Socrates' last conversation and death appears within a narrative frame in which an eyewitness, Phaedo, reports the events to an interlocutor who was not present (Echecrates); this frame establishes a connection between the interlocutor and the reader of the dialogue. The philosophical subject of the dialogue, the immortality of the soul, merges artfully with the narrative of Socrates' instruction and consolation of his students and his calm acceptance of death. See also Benjamin's account of the *Phaedo* as a 'parody of tragedy' in his *The Origin of German Tragic Drama*, pp. 113-15.

20.   See Jacques Derrida's meditations on Socrates, Plato and writing in his *The Post Card: From Socrates to Freud and Beyond* (trans. Alan Bass; Chicago: University of Chicago Press, 1987), pp. 9-19.

depict Moses as a writer of texts. These features activate an interpretive process that guides the reader to consider the subject of sacred texts. The תורה, Song, and Blessing represent three models of sacred texts as instruction, memorial witness, and prophetic utterance (see Chapters 6 and 7); תורה has the broadest reference (arguably including the Song and Blessing, the rest of Deuteronomy and, for later traditions, the whole Pentateuch) and the greatest significance: it educates and influences the people; it even constitutes their life. Still, the תורה does not replace or supersede Moses (as Weberian analysis may suggest); rather, it inscribes him as a writing and written figure.

Traditional attributions of biblical authorship to Moses may lack historical accuracy, but they reflect an interpretive sophistication often overlooked by modern scholars. Spinoza was not the first to observe the paradox of Moses writing his own death story. Rabbinic commentators had already developed a number of explanations: in one, Moses foresaw and wrote the account; another tradition suggests that Joshua wrote it for him; and a third suggests, incredibly, that Moses did not die at all.[21] A later, ingenious tradition suggested that death was a gradual process in which one part, the image (צלם) dies thirty days before the rest of the self. The departure of Moses' צלם thus alerted him to his impending demise.[22]

In several elaborate midrashim, God sends a succession of angels to take the soul of Moses. After Gabriel and Michael decline, God sends Sammael, the angel of death. But Moses, in the act of writing, is invincible:

Immediately Sammael went forth from God in great glee. He put on his sword and girded himself with ruthlessness, and in great rage went forth to meet Moses. When Sammael looked at Moses—who was writing down the Ineffable Name while darts of fire were shooting from his mouth, and the radiance of his countenance and speech shone like the sun so that he was like an angel of the Lord of hosts—fear and trembling seized Sammael. And when Moses, who had known of his coming, lifted his eyes and saw him, at once Sammael's eyes grew dim before he radiance of Moses' countenance and he fell upon his face.[23]

The scene is captured in a poem by Rilke:

No one, only the sombre, the fallen, angel
responded; took weapons, approached
the summoned with mortal intent. To hurtle
clattering, backwards, upwards,
crying into heaven: 'I can't!'

For calmly, without uplifting his bushy eyebrows,
Moses had simply noticed and gone on writing:
saving words and the name that endureth forever.
And his eye was pure to the very depth of his power.[24]

21. Thus one view in *Midrash ha-Gadol*; see Kugel, *The Bible as it Was*, p. 544.
22. Moshe Idel, *Golem* (Albany: State University of New York Press, 1990), p. 293 n. 24.
23. *Midrash Petirat Moshe*, in Kushelevsky, *Moses and the Angel of Death*, p. 243.
24. Rainer Maria Rilke, 'Der Tod Moses', Rilke-Archiv with Ruth Sieber-Rilke, *Sämtliche Werke* (6 vols.; Wiesbaden: Insel-Verlag, 1963), II, p. 102. The English translation appears in

Even to the fallen angel, Moses is a threatening figure whose power derives from the act of writing the name of God.

The categories of personal leadership, divine agency, and written communication run through the entire Hebrew Bible. Such an understanding need not be a naively univocal concept of authorship but, as the analysis of Deuteronomy 31–34 has tried to show, quite sophisticated in showing the interdependence of the figure of Moses and written texts in the Bible.[25] The contemporary reader of Deuteronomy has limited access to the original sources and historical background of Deuteronomy, but it does not follow that contemporary interpretation does violence to the text. My literary and philological analysis, a hermeneutical and therefore historically situated enterprise,[26] characterizes Deuteronomy as a heteroglot text that involves the reader actively in confronting the figure of Moses and the identity and function of sacred texts, including Deuteronomy itself. The openness and closure of Torah represent the inscription of Moses as a writing and written figure. In a short essay on Derrida, Maurice Blanchot relates Moses' writing and writtenness to his death:

> But the disappearance of the 'author' gives even greater necessity to teaching, writing (the trace prior to all text) and speech, to the speech within writing, the speech that does not vivify writing which otherwise would be dead, but on the contrary impels us to go towards others, caring for the distant and the near, without it yet being given to us to know that, before all else, this is the only path towards the Infinite.[27]

Blanchot's compact reading of the death of Moses doubles as a commentary on the literary and ethical work of Derrida and Levinas. Without saying so explicitly, Blanchot places Derrida's insights on writing, speech, and authorship in the biblical tradition of Moses' death.

4. *Writing and Memory*

To understand the role of writing in Deuteronomy 31–34, it is necessary to review other occasions of Moses' writing (Exod. 17.14; 24.4-7; 34.27; Num. 17.17; 33.2), as well as writing by other figures in the Hexateuch. Every instance of Moses' writing, from the words of the covenant to the wanderings of the people, follows a direct divine command (with the interesting exception of 31.9). The most important text written by Moses, the tablets of the covenant (Exod. 24.4; 34.27), is first or also written by YHWH (Exod. 24.12; 31.18), although, interestingly, Deuteronomy

---

Rainer Maria Rilke, *Poems 1906–1926* (trans. J. B. Leishman; London: Hogarth Press, 1968), pp. 214-15. See also George Eliot, 'The Death of Moses', in *Theophrastus Such, Jubal and Other Poems, and the Spanish Gypsy* (Chicago, IL; R.S. Peale, 1888), pp. 280-83.

25.   See Dennis T. Olson, *Deuteronomy and the Death of Moses* (Minneapolis: Fortress Press, 1994), especially pp. 136 and 172-82.

26.   See Hans-Georg Gadamer, *Truth and Method* (New York: Crossroad, 1988), pp. 235-74.

27.   Maurice Blanchot, 'Thanks (Be Given) to Jacques Derrida', in *idem, The Blanchot Reader* (ed. M. Holland; Oxford: Basil Blackwell, 1995), pp. 317-23 (323).

attributes both inscriptions to Y[HWH] (Deut. 4.13; 5.22; 9.10; 10.2-4).[28] Like the dual agency of Moses' prophetic speech (Exod. 4.10-17), Moses and Y[HWH] are also both responsible for the written covenant. Yet in Deuteronomy 31, when he can no longer come and go and he faces mortality, only Moses writes (and in v. 9 without explicit divine command). This difference sharpens the focus on Moses' writing in Deuteronomy 31–34. Though he clearly writes with divine sanction, the dramatic focus on Moses in his last moments inscribing at least two texts infuses them with special importance. If the texts gain legitimacy from their author, then their author and his life draw significance from the texts, especially through the two main functions of writing: witness and memory. To understand the nature of Moses' writing more completely, it is important to examine the term 'remember' (זכר), which like the term עוד (see Chapter 6), applies to the text in several ways.

According to Brevard Childs, where זכר refers to Israel, it stands not only for a mental state but also the act of 'actualizing the past':

> Actualization is the process by which a past event is contemporized for a generation removed in time and space from the original event. When later Israel responded to the continuing imperative of her tradition through her memory, that moment in historical time likewise became an Exodus experience. Not in the sense that later Israel again crossed the Red Sea. This was an irreversible, once-for-all event. Rather, Israel entered the same redemptive reality of the Exodus generation.[29]

Taking this point further, Childs claims, 'We do not have in the Old Testament "an original event". What we have are various witnesses to an event.'[30] Childs' semantic understanding of memory as actualization views the past event as neither absolute myth nor absolute history.[31] While the event happens 'once-for-all', memory actualizes it again for the people and thus makes it a witness to the same redemptive reality. The biblical text provides no access to the original event but only to the manner in which it is witnessed.

There are only two attestations of the term זכר in Deuteronomy 31–34, and both appear in the Song of Moses (32.7, 26).[32] The first (in 32.7) addresses Israel in the imperative: 'Remember the days of old, be aware of (בינו) the years from generation upon generation. Ask your father and he will relate it to you, our elders and they will tell you'. Here memory is associated, as Childs would argue, not only

---

28. Several references to the written contents of the ספר התורה (Deut. 28.58, 61; 29.20-27; 30.10; Josh. 1.8; 23.6) do not specify an author, although Exod. 24, 34, Deut. 31, and Josh. 8 imply Mosaic authorship. There are also a number of instances in which the people are commanded by Moses to write: Deut. 6.9; 27.2-8. Joshua writes a copy of Moses' ספר התורה in 8.32 and writes commandments in the ספר התורה in 24.26.

29. Brevard Childs, *Memory and Tradition in Israel* (Studies in Biblical Theology, 37; Naperville: Alec R. Allenson, 1962), pp. 80, 85.

30. Childs, *Memory and Tradition*.

31. Childs, *Memory and Tradition*, p. 83.

32. Childs (*Memory and Tradition* p. 46) recognizes a high occurrence of the verb as applied to Israel in Deuteronomy (thirteen times).

with mental states but also with the actualization of past events through spoken communication. Memory here evokes YHWH's past actions of redemption as a complaint against Israel in the רִיב tradition.[33] Israel must be admonished to remember how God established Israel among the nations.

The second use of the word appears in the noun זֵכֶר, which often appears parallel to שֵׁם ('name') and belongs to a whole series of passages that 'deal with the destruction of the enemy by means of cutting off all mention of the name'.[34] It will be recalled that Deut. 32.26 is the key turning point in the Song of Moses at which YHWH debates whether to destroy Israel and remove them from human memory but decides not to do so because of how the enemy might construe it (32.27; cf. Num. 14.10-19).

The most similar Pentateuchal use of the noun זֵכֶר, Exod. 17.14 (with a close parallel in Deut. 25.19), is also the first biblical reference to Moses' writing, in which YHWH tells Moses to record the defeat of Amalek in a book as a memorial (זִכָּרוֹן) that YHWH will *completely erase* (מָחֹה אֶמְחֶה) the memory (זֵכֶר) of Amalek (see Chapters 5 and 7). Memory and writing are also connected in the unforgotten (לֹא תִשָּׁכַח) status of the Song (31.21). This close connection between memory and writing, although negative, implies the centrality of writing to biblical thought: writing becomes a memory-preserving artifact.[35] Yet in contrast to the didactic purposes of תּוֹרָה, the purpose of writing in Exod. 17.14 appears only to be a recording of an event, and in this way it resembles the function of the Song. Memory does not require writing, but the two are closely linked. According to Yosef Yerushalmi, memory in the biblical period was served primarily by ritual and recital. He observes that 'meaning in history, memory of the past, and the writing of history are by no means to be equated. In the Bible, to be sure, the three elements are linked, they overlap at critical points, and, in general, they are held together in a web of delicate and reciprocal relationships.'[36] For Yerushalmi, memory constitutes a central and unique feature of Israelite identity: 'memory has become crucial to its faith and, ultimately, to its very existence'.[37] In this sense, the 'textual memorial' of the תּוֹרָה remains the focus of Deuteronomy 31–34, despite the legendary hagiography in Deuteronomy 34.

The categories of witness and memory apply to the תּוֹרָה, the Song, and the Blessing, but in different ways. As ritually recited instruction, the תּוֹרָה reactivates the covenant and the events of its reception. The Song has a negative function as witness against the people's future transgressions; it lives in their memory more as verbal artifact than as instruction. The Blessing, finally, reactivates the past by projecting predictions about the amphictyony onto Moses and the patriarchal blessing tradition of Genesis.

---

33. Childs, *Memory and Tradition* p. 49.
34. Especially Exod. 17.14 and Deut. 25.19. See Childs, *Memory and Tradition*, p. 71.
35. See Benjamin, 'The Storyteller', p. 98.
36. Yerushalmi, *Zakhor*, pp. 11, 14.
37. Yerushalmi, *Zakhor*, p. 9.

5. *Patterns in the Birth and Death Stories*

As different as they obviously are, the birth and death stories share a number of thematic and structural elements. The two episodes represent major transitions not only for Moses but also for the children of Israel. In fact, the tribes of Israel are named near the birth and death stories (Exod. 1, and the similarly ordered list in Gen. 49 and Deut. 33; see also Deut. 34.2); the people are accounted for during their Egyptian sojourn and just before they enter the promised land. There is also language of blessing near the birth and death stories: not only with Jacob's blessing in Genesis 49, but also with the formulaic statement that the people were fruitful and multiplied in Exod. 1.7 (cf. Gen. 1.22; 9.7; 16.10; 17.20; 35.11; 43.34). Jacob's blessing also forms a clear parallel to Exodus 33. These persistent literary patterns signal the reader that Moses' story is the people's story, that his identity depends on theirs. Though he disappears just before their triumph, he leaves them with a Torah, a memorial of the covenant and mirror of the people's life.

As the analysis of the Song and Blessing (Chapter 7) shows, the links between the blessings in Genesis 49 and Exodus 33 create symmetry and a canonical link between Jacob and Moses, the twelve sons and the twelve tribes, and the history of the people itself. Jacob blesses his children after they have come to Egypt from Canaan. Moses blesses the tribes of Israel when they have left Egypt to return to the land of Canaan. The journey of Joseph provides another frame: he travels in bondage to Egypt, enjoys remarkable success there before he dies, and his bones are carried with the people back to Canaan, according to his wishes. The instrumental, central figure in this story, of course, is Moses, though his actions and offices always exceed his personality.

Both episodes balance life against death: Moses is born against the background of horrible infanticide, but it is also a time of fertility. His death stands out against the background of increase and blessing outlined in Deuteronomy 33. Moses' death caps a long list of deaths (such as Aaron's, Deut. 32.50) of the first generation coming from Egypt, and it precedes the large-scale killing that follows in Joshua. Moses' birth among death and death among (promised) births make him distinctive, but his fate is always tied to the people as well: in birth he barely escapes death, and in death, which he accepts reluctantly (Deut. 3.24-25), he anticipates the birth of a sovereign people.

For Moses and many other heroes, water and rivers play crucial roles in the birth and death stories.[38] Moses' ark, of course, is placed on a branch of the Nile; water endangers, conceals, and finally delivers him to safety. Like the Red Sea, the river is a boundary or threshold he crosses to a new existence. The Jordan River, by contrast, is a boundary he may not cross (Deut. 3.25; 31.2); instead he may only go to its edge to look to the other side. Moses experiences unlikely survival on the Nile and an unlikely demise along the Jordan. Water is also the cause of Moses' death—specifically, the incident and Massah/Meribah/Kadesh. Perhaps to underscore that it

---

38. Dean A. Miller, *The Epic Hero* (Baltimore: The Johns Hopkins University Press, 2000), pp. 138-40.

is YHWH and not Moses who conquers the waters (see Exod. 15), the human agent of the Red Sea crossing undergoes judgment and death near a body of water.

The birth and death take place in hostile, foreign territory, making Moses a purely exilic figure for tradition. Like Joseph and Esther, he is the typical hero of the *Diasporanovelle*.[39] Even though the hero of the *Diasporanovelle* prevails over evil, the genre is always bittersweet, since the success of the hero does not guarantee the success of the people at large. In contrast to Joseph and Esther, however, Moses leads the people out of exile. Moses' death outside the promised land reverses the pattern of the *Diasporanovelle*, since the people attain a homeland denied to him.

6. *Body of Moses, Text of Moses*

Figure 1. *Fresco of Moses' Discovery in the Nile,*
Synagogue at Dura-Europos (third century)

In order to focus on Moses' body in the birth and death narratives, I turn to two very well-known (and different) images. The first is a fresco depicting the birth story of Moses from the third-century synagogue at Dura-Europos. The second, Matteo da Lecce's *Fight for the Body of Moses*, is a sixteenth-century fresco in the Sistine Chapel that replaced the original fifteenth-century fresco by Signorelli. In both images, Moses' body is the central image, and in both cases, it is endangered. With God in the background, Moses' body is the subject of a high-stakes drama of good against evil. In birth and death, Moses himself is quite powerless to affect the outcome; his body is handled like a puppet or talisman, lending power to the one holding it.

The Moses nativity fresco in the synagogue at Dura-Europos shows Moses' body changing hands. In a narrative that appears to move from right to left with the flow of the river, the panel begins with a figure on a throne near a fortified building (perhaps a palace) and flanked by two attendants, presumably Pharaoh issuing the decree to kill the infant males. Next to them are three women, one of whom is stooping down; the fresco is damaged at that point, but presumably she is placing

---

39. See Arndt Meinhold, 'Die Gattung der Josephsgeschichte und des Estherbuches: Diaspo-ranovelle I und II', *ZAW* 87 (1975), pp. 306-24, and *ZAW* 88 (1976), pp. 72-93.

the baby and ark into the river. Further to the left is a scene in which a nude woman stands in the water holding the infant Moses. His ark, a rectangular structure with a pitched roof, floats nearby in the water. The baby is shown again, above and to the left, in the arms of two women, presumably the attendants of Pharaoh's daughter.[40]

The three scenes are linked by hand gestures: Pharaoh and one of his attendants gesture toward the women in the next scene, two of whom (the midwives Shifrah and Puah?) gesture back to Pharaoh. Pharaoh's daughter holds Moses in her left arm and gestures up to the two attendants, also holding Moses, with her right arm. Separate draperies hang over each scene. A more subtle feature of the composition is the parallel between the palace on the far right and the ark on the far left: both are architectural structures with doors open, out of which powerful leaders have emerged. This symmetry suggests the episode in Josephus, for instance, where Moses seizes the crown of Pharaoh and hurls it to the ground. The fresco's narrative thus flows from one great leader to another.

But Moses is a very different sort of leader from Pharaoh; in the fresco he is a baby attended by women. Pharaoh is an adult attended by men. Pharaoh is surrounded by royal paraphernalia: throne, crown, palace, and well-dressed attendants, one of whom holds a book. Apart from the ark, Moses has no such props (though the damaged area may have included other elements), but only the ornate circular and cylindrical objects, perhaps a mirror and brush, held by one attendant. Nevertheless, he is the central figure of the narrative, appearing at least two and perhaps three times. The juxtaposition of Moses and Pharaoh is a study in contrasts—a palace and an ark, powerful man and weak infant, an official setting with male servants and a bathing scene with female servants. But, for the viewer, these visual contrasts only underscore the overwhelming reversals that lie in store for Moses and the Pharaoh—the weak figure will grow to be more powerful, and the power of the book (pictured with Pharaoh) will become synonymous with Moses.

The New Testament Letter of Jude refers to a struggle over Moses' dead body:

> Even as Sodom and Gomorrah, and the cities about them in like manner, giving themselves over to fornication, and going after strange flesh, are set forth for an example, suffering the vengeance of eternal fire. Likewise also these filthy dreamers defile the flesh, despise dominion, and speak evil of dignities. Yet when Michael the archangel contended with the devil and disputed about the body of Moses, he did not dare bring against him a railing accusation but said, 'The Lord rebuke you [Zech. 3.2]'. (Jude 7-9)

This text implies a narrative context that must be reconstructed. First, Michael is sent by YHWH to bury Moses; the substitution of an angel for such a task is a standard solution to anthropomorphic images of God. According to Loewenstamm, Satan challenges Michael, claiming the body 'because he is the lord of matter' and because of the sins of Adam and Moses.[41] Michael prevails, however, vindicating divine sovereignty.

---

40. Cohen, *Moses Nativity Story*, pp. 62-65.
41. Loewenstamm, 'The Death of Moses', p. 209.

Figure 2. *Matteo da Lecce's* Fight for the Body of Moses,
a fresco in the Sistine Chapel (sixteenth century)

It is difficult to reconstruct the conflict described in Jude, and scholars have debated its origins and influences. While Philo, Josephus, and the rabbinic sources do not mention a struggle over Moses' dead body, the contest between Moses and angels, especially Sammael, is attested. In the *Tanhuma*, an eighth–ninth century collection of midrash, Moses' plea not to die by the sword of Sammael leads to his death by God's mouth (Deut. 34.6). God places Moses' soul under the divine throne, and the angels then process before his bier.[42] In *Deuteronomy Rabbah*, there is also an account of a contest between Michael and Sammael that makes mention of Moses: '"Though I am fallen"—because of the demise of Moses; "I shall arise"—on account of the leadership displayed by Joshua…'[43] In the early medieval *Midrash Petirat Moshe*, God's mercy overrides the plan for Sammael to kill him, and the vivid death-scene anticipates the Lecce fresco:

> God was accompanied by three angels: Michael, Zagzagel, and Gabriel. Gabriel laid out Moses' bier, Michael spread out a purple sheet over it, and Zagzagel laid down a pillow at his bolster. Zagzagel stationed himself at Moses' feet; Michael,

---

42. Kushelevsky, *Moses and the Angel of Death*, p. 272.
43. Quoted in Kushelevsky, *Moses and the Angel of Death*, p. 92.

to his right; and Gabriel, to his left. Then God said to him: 'Fold both your hands and lay [them] on your breast. Close both of your eyes.' And Moses did so.[44]

But the contest over Moses' dead body appears to be a mainly Christian story, and the most complete retelling of the episode comes from the late (around ninth century) Greek text, the *Palaea Historica*. In this version, Sammael brings down Moses' body so that the people will worship it. At the command of God, Michael orders the release of the body, and the ensuing struggle, which like Jude quotes Zech. 3.2, leads to victory for the heavenly side.[45] The *Palaea Historica* version of the story, perhaps triggered by the mystery of the hidden burial place of Moses (Deut. 34.6), includes a clear moral lesson even though its narrative context is obscure: the body of Moses belongs to God and not the devil, and it should not be an object of worship. How much of this version corresponds to Jude 9 remains uncertain.

Why is Moses the object of such struggle for the author of Jude? One answer is that Moses' death is already established as a site for interpretive contention. But this only defers the question. Moses is the most ambiguous mortal in the Hebrew Bible, and as Deuteronomy 34 reveals, so is his mortality. Philo distinguishes Moses' body from his soul, and some rabbinic and patristic authors make similar distinctions between body and soul or even (in Clement and Origen) a double-Moses.[46] For a Christian writer with dualistic tendencies, Moses poses the additional problem of being a virtuous figure venerated in Jewish tradition, a foundational prophet who represents a superseded law. Yet for the author of Jude, if not for all Christians of the period, the body of Moses was a suitable and worthy battle site, and the victory for God and spirit over Satan and flesh comes to represent a victory for Christianity itself (and perhaps, by implication, a defeat for Judaism).

But the outcome is still unclear: has Michael won the body of Moses in order to raise it to God or only to bury it? Jewish and Christian traditions would agree that Moses' soul goes to God, but there is less clarity on the question of his body. If the outcome is physical assumption, then the biblical insistence on burial is thwarted, but if simple burial is indicated, then Michael's victory seems hollow. How, after all, are we to imagine a worse outcome for the body of Moses than burial and decomposition?

One explanation for the struggle over Moses' body is that the Bible leaves it up for grabs. The means and place of its burial unknown, the cause of death given more than one explanation, Moses' body is neither here nor there. The opposite is true for Joseph, whose bones are carried solemnly from Egypt to the promised land for burial in the tomb at Shechem bought by Abraham (Gen. 50; Exod. 13; Josh. 24).[47] Neither is Moses taken into heaven, as Elijah is (2 Kgs 3). Instead, Moses'

44. *Midrash Petirat Moshe*, in Kushelevsky, *Moses and the Angel of Death*, p. 221.
45. J. Daryl Charles, *Literary Strategy in the Epistle of Jude* (Scranton, PA: University of Scranton Press, 1993), p. 151.
46. Kugel, *The Bible as it Was*, p. 544.
47. Regina Schwartz, 'Joseph's Bones and the Resurrection of the Text: Remembering in the Bible', in *idem* (ed.), *The Book and the Text* (Oxford: Basil Blackwell, 1990), pp. 40-59.

body is buried in an *unmarked*, that is, *unwritten* grave, and hence the source of continuing speculation, continued writing.

This mystery may or may not illuminate the conflict depicted in Lecce's mural of the *Fight for the Body of Moses*. What is clear in the image is that the struggle over Moses' body opposes cosmic forces of good and evil, light and dark, with the implication that good will prevail. Moses' corpse is placed centrally in the painting. Like the scene of the bier in *Midrash Petirat Moshe*, Moses lies face up on a decorated bier while seven demons to his left and right contend with three angels above. Michael, the middle angel, wears armor and aims his spear at one of the demons. The other two angels, perhaps Gabriel and Zagzagel, challenge the other demons.

In the background to this scene, on the left, is a funeral procession in which Moses is carried down a steep and winding path, perhaps the Valley of Moab below Mt Nebo, where he dies (Deut. 34.1-6). Carol Lewine describes this as a burial by 'celestial beings'.[48] Taken together, these two scenes suggest that Moses has died as described in Deuteronomy 34, but that a cosmological conflict, the one alluded to in Jude, ensued thereafter. According to Lewine, the scene, which is paired in the Sistine Chapel with a scene of *Christ's Ascension into Heaven*, may have been included by Pope Sixtus IV to show the power of God and the popes over Satan. Another association of the fresco is the Lenten theme of liberating the Jews from the Babylonian captivity. In one sense, this liberation was the triumph of Christianity over Judaism, but it may also have alluded to the 'Babylonian captivity' of the papacy in Avignon one hundred years earlier (1377).[49] In any case, it is striking that Moses' death—a story barely attested in extant literature—spoke to the liturgical and historical context of Renaissance Christianity. The body of Moses—even in death—is a text that tradition has continued to write and rewrite.

7. *Conclusion*

Although writing is not an overt theme of the birth and death stories, the biblical narrative ambiguates, abbreviates, and marginalizes these episodes from the central concern with the people and written traditions of Israel. Post-biblical commentators have consistently amplified the birth and death stories, filling in narrative gaps and resolving ambiguities with a biographical emphasis on Moses. It is possible that Philo, Josephus, and other interpreters recovered layers of tradition muted by the biblical redactors, but they also neglected the biblical emphasis on the people and their traditions.

Writing mediates the stories, however, and even enters them: Moses' birth and death are each mandated by decree, a type of 'text' even when given orally. Against these decrees stands the principle of life—the saving of Hebrew infants, the removal of Moses' body from the water, and the crossing of the Jordan River. Life struggles against writing, *bios* against *graphé*, in the birth and death narratives. But

48.   Lewine, *The Sistine Walls and the Roman Liturgy*, p. 99.
49.   Lewine, *The Sistine Walls and the Roman Liturgy*, p. 99.

since the biblical text incorporates Moses' life, the birth and death episodes play endlessly within the boundaries of scriptural tradition.[50] In this way, life and text, birth and death, merge in biblical tradition, just as Moses insists that the Torah is the very life of Israel itself (Deut. 32.47).

My analysis of the birth and death scenes shows a Moses who is not only embodied but also written. Post-biblical tradition has focused on body at the expense of text, but since body and text are inextricable, there are traces of textuality even in the most embodied traditions. If the birth and death scenes are supplements to the main 'body' of narrative in Exodus, Numbers, and Deuteronomy, then the opposite is true for post-biblical traditions, which centralize Moses' biography, especially legends of his birth, heroic action, and death. This reversal from scriptural tradition to post-biblical biography arises through cultural change, misunderstanding, and anxiety before the text; but the repressed textuality of Moses returns when the body of Moses is textualized through narrative, art, and references to writing. The tradition of a struggle over Moses' body misses the point of biblical gaps and ambiguities: the body of Moses, so easily misplaced in the stories and traditions, resides safely in the pages of the Bible.

---

50. See Derrida, *Archive Fever*, pp. 94-95.

CONCLUSION

Moses undergoes multiple transformations in his post-biblical afterlife. Differences among these portraits come mostly from cultural and historical context: people constantly recreate Moses in their own image. Yet across centuries of rewriting run the dual patterns of Moses as a great individual in the breach of conflict and Moses as a conduit for revelation and writing.

How do these roles play out in the Bible? Biblical tradition typically limits Moses to the role of a mortal servant of God. The biblical account avoids lengthy glorification of his deeds and attributes, even inserting episodes that show his faults. As a prophet of God, however, Moses performs extensive duties—his speech and writing provide a rich account of how divine revelation was understood in ancient Israel. Despite their reluctance to glorify him, biblical authors and redactors used the legendary prestige of Moses to ascribe great words and actions to him, such as the 'words of the Torah' in Deuteronomy 31 and 32. In this ambivalent biblical portrait, the life of Moses—a balance of greatness and imperfection—is partly displaced by the writing of Moses.

But for post-biblical tradition the story is different. While the rabbis would privilege the Torah over the life of Moses, others, following the Hellenistic lead of Philo and Josephus, would typically magnify Moses at the expense of the text. His life came to overshadow his work. In psychoanalytic terms, the writing of Moses would be repressed, and as everyone knows, what is repressed must eventually return. How it returns, particularly in modern fiction, film, and scholarship, has been one question of this study. Exactly who returns, the biblical Moses who speaks and writes divine revelation, has been the other object of this study. This Moses of the 'heavy mouth' and 'veil' embodies subtle ideas of writing and revelation—his biblical portrait abounds in signs of a self-conscious and reflexive written tradition. Even in the birth and death episodes, the body of Moses becomes inseparable from, and finally secondary to, his text. My goal has been to explicate the role of Moses in the Bible and in post-biblical, especially contemporary, culture.

My path to the study of Moses began with the main question of my previous work: How do the Bible and biblical culture conceive of language, writing, and revelation? Moses was not a dominant figure of my childhood or socialization in a suburban American Catholic family, apart from the clichés of biblical stories and *The Ten Commandments*. It came as a surprise, therefore, to see how widely and obsessively Moses has preoccupied religious and popular culture down to the present. I expected post-biblical images of Moses simply to reveal a protean hero, typically more life than work, more great man than writing and revelation. Such was my initial impression of novels about Moses: Steffens' socialist *Moses in Red* and Mann's anti-Nazi *Tables of the Law*, for instance, portray Moses in harshly ideological, even propagandistic, ways.

I then realized that this tendency toward polemic, with all its various manifestations, was part of the tradition itself. In this sense, Moses illustrates Alasdair MacIntyre's notion of tradition as 'historically extended, socially embodied argument'.[1] A pivotal figure from the beginning, an eternal mediator and intercessor, Moses often appears in the midst of the most pressing controversies of the day: gender, race, and ideology in the twentieth century; the struggle of individual and group in the early modern period; Jews and Christians in the Middle Ages; Jews and pagans in late antiquity; and, in the Bible, Hebrews and Egyptians, as well as divisions over leadership and law among the Israelites.

I have concentrated on two related elements of the biblical and post-biblical Moses: polemic and writing. The struggles to escape slavery, establish covenant law, journey toward a homeland, and institute traditions of ritual and written instruction all emerge through fierce conflicts with Moses at their center. The biblical text itself appears to contain opposing views on the status and character of Moses. But Moses' heroic and legendary feats are often surpassed by his role as a writer and speaker of divine words—from his commission as a prophet and liberator in Exodus 4; through his struggles with dissent and recalcitrance among the Hebrews in the golden calf episode of Exodus 32–34 and Numbers 11–16; and especially in the closing words of his life and career in Deuteronomy 31–34, when specific texts—Torah, Song, and Blessing—are named, delivered, and recorded. Later portraits of Moses, in fiction or film, often radically change the contours and details of the biblical story, but the elements of polemic and writing persist.

In most of these polemical contexts, there are dominant, even stereotypical images of Moses as an individual—the great liberator, lawgiver, prophet, or leader. But beneath these stereotypes are dynamic tensions that Moses, like the myths of Levi-Strauss' structuralism, is meant to address if not resolve. Hurston's Moses is a solitary thinker as well as a great leader, a hoodoo man as well as the champion of liberty. Moses thrives in a climate of cultural conflict; new crises seem more manageable when they become retellings of the Moses story.

Underneath the dominant focus on Moses the individual, there lies a recessive Moses, a figure reflexively constituted by and about writing. The biblical portrait of Moses often resists the (dominant) urge to see Moses simply as a great man, even when you most expect it, as in the birth and death episodes (see Chapter 8). Instead, the Bible offers us an uncanny figure whose most significant actions are speech and writing. Constituted, as James Nohrnberg says, as a religious 'interruption', and responsible, as Jan Assmann says, for a crucial 'Mosaic distinction' in ancient culture, Moses must be conceived (as Martin Noth first showed) as a figure retrojected by tradition onto the past. Charged with the tremendous duty of creating a religious civilization under a transcendent deity, Moses becomes inseparable from the culture he is believed to have created.

---

1. MacIntyre, *After Virtue*, p. 222.

Revelation is inherently mysterious for the biblical Moses: the veil he wears after the golden calf episode in Exodus conceals and reveals at the same time, suggesting that biblical revelation itself is a dynamic process in which absence and silence combine with presence. Even in the most biographical episodes of Moses' life, his birth and death scenes, a tendency to abbreviate legendary material makes Moses' life inextricable from writing and revelation. In medieval Christian art, the veil of Moses is usually seen through the eyes of Paul, who typologically depicts Jesus as removing the veil of Moses. But revelation uncannily returns in many of these images, along with images of Synagogue and the personification of Nature.

The commission of Moses in Exodus 4 pays unusual attention to his speech difficulty in a text and context that suggest how Moses' writing—the occasion of the story itself—will come to matter more than his flawed speech (Chapter 5). Writing itself has the durative quality of a witness that will long outlive and surpass Moses (Chapter 6). Several types of writing—Torah, Song, Blessing—will warn against wrongdoing and teach righteousness. At the same time, these texts will remind readers of the multiple layers of the Bible—a text whose composition and redaction display the process of tradition-formation (Chapter 7). The models of writing as mystery, iteration, memorial, witness, and life itself provide powerful if unsystematic sources of biblical tradition, and their traces can be seen even in the most complete rewritings of biblical stories.

Traditions of authorship, signs and wonders, military success, and law accumulate around the biblical Moses, a process that only grows in the post-biblical period. Moses is thus an object of projection as well as repression, as Freud would have it. In *Moses and Monotheism*, Freud boldly claims that Moses was a great Egyptian leader killed by his Hebrew followers, and that this crisis and its repression link Jewish and Christian narratives (the parricides of Moses and Jesus) at the core of monotheistic religion. But while he indulged in historical speculations about the fate and identity of Moses, calling his study at one point a 'historical novel', Freud keenly recognized how the Moses question extends to the inner logic of Judaism and Christianity, as well as the anti-Semitism of the years 1937–39 when he was writing. Even for Freud, Moses would become an object of projection, a great individual whose story meshes with present-day polemics without completely losing the biblical emphasis on writing.[2]

My studies of fiction, film, scholarship, and art show how far the modern Moses has wandered from his biblical home. At the same time, in surprising ways perhaps beyond their authors' designs, these rewritings continue the tradition of Moses as a figure of polemic and writing. Moses consistently performs the cultural work of straddling opposites, addressing polemics, and embodying traditions of writing. The issues of gender, race, religious identity, and ideology in the novels and films are only contemporary versions of ancient questions that encircle Moses himself.

---

2.   One can see the emphasis on writing in Freud's Moses in the concept of memory itself, insofar as Moses stands for the key elements of monotheistic tradition. Freud's methods of analysis are also textual, especially here, where his subject is not an individual but a religious civilization. See Yerushalmi, *Freud's Moses*, and Bernstein, *Freud and the Legacy of Moses*.

And even in the most unbiblical novels, Hurston's and Mann's for example, the effort to resist long-standing stereotypes leads paradoxically to more 'biblical' versions of Moses. The work of modern biblical scholars recalls Paul de Man's notion of 'blindness and insight'; for all their historical and philological rigor, they have a surprising tendency to reproduce (by affirmation or, in Noth's case, denial) the commonly held modern view of Moses as a legendary hero.[3]

Rewritings of Moses show how robust biblical traditions can be, despite the post-biblical eclipse of biblical narrative. In the modern world, a Moses already established at the center of multiple polemics—between monotheists and pagans, Christians and Jews, hermeticists and religionists—assumes new responsibilities as the standard-bearer of Enlightenment values of liberty, equality, and rationality; group identity for African Americans, Protestants, and Jews; and the focus of debates on socialism and fascism. The issue of writing usually appears in these portraits as a literary motif, but it also runs on the deeper level at which writing is a form of authority, reason, and tradition. Artists, writers, and politicians as diverse as Zora Neale Hurston, Arnold Schoenberg, and Adolf Hitler would find Moses indispensable to their modern projects, even as they effaced his biblical portrait.

The modern Moses uniquely embodies the cultural tension between religion and reason. As Hent de Vries argues, 'all discourses concerning Western modernization…rest on the assumption that it is possible to make a clear-cut distinction between myth and *logos*, or reason, between the divine and the human, the sacred and the profane, the Christian and the secular'.[4] The institutions of modern culture—law, science, and government—all depend on this distinction between religion and the secular world. Yet critics from Walter Benjamin to Jean-Luc Marion have shown that denial of the religious foundations of modernity can lead to devastating results.[5] The eclipse of the biblical Moses is an eclipse of religion, along with the writing and revelation that constitute biblical tradition.

Moses' eternal return in the post-biblical world reveals the extent to which biblical tradition endures, even at the expense of the Bible. Yet the biblical texts themselves, with their complexity and ambivalence, enable this tradition to flourish, and they reward close analysis with patterns and insights that bear directly on the study of culture in its 'religious' and 'secular' forms. Writing and polemic are infinitely intertwined in the figure of Moses. In this way, this book has been a study of the dynamics of biblical tradition itself.

3.   Paul de Man, *Blindness and Insight: Essays in the Rhetoric of Contemporary Criticism* (Minneapolis: University of Minnesota Press, 1983), p. 141.

4.   Hent de Vries, *Philosophy and the Turn to Religion* (Baltimore: The Johns Hopkins University Press, 1999), p. 431.

5.   Walter Benjamin, 'Theses on the Philosophy of History', in *idem*, *Illuminations*, pp. 253-64; Jean-Luc Marion, *Sur la théologie blanche de Descartes* (Paris: Presses Universitaires de France, 1981), cited in de Vries, *Philosophy and the Turn to Religion*, p. 79 n. 53.

BIBLIOGRAPHY

Abrams, M.H., *Natural Supernaturalism* (New York: W.W. Norton, 1973).
Ackerman, James S., 'The Literary Context of the Moses Birth Story', in Gros Louis, Acker-
    man and Warshaw (eds.), *Literary Interpretations of Biblical Narratives*, pp. 74-119.
Agmon, Mordechai. 'The Idea of the Radiant Skin of Moses' Face and the Veil', *Beth Miqra*
    104 (1985), pp. 186-88 (Hebrew).
Albright, William, *Archaeology and the Religion of Israel* (Baltimore: The Johns Hopkins
    University Press, 1968).
—*The Biblical Period From Abraham to Ezra* (New York: Harper & Row, 1963).
—'Some Remarks on the Song of Moses in Deuteronomy XXXII', *VT* 9 (1959), pp. 339-46.
Allison, Dale, Jr, *The New Moses* (Minneapolis: Fortress Press, 1993).
Alter, Robert, 'Introduction', in Alter and Kermode (eds.), *The Literary Guide to the Bible*,
    pp. 11-35.
Alter, Robert, and Frank Kermode (eds.), *The Literary Guide to the Bible* (Cambridge, MA:
    Harvard University Press, 1987).
Ameriks, Karl, 'Introduction: Interpreting German Idealism', in *idem* (ed.), *The Cambridge
    Companion to German Idealism* (Cambridge: Cambridge University Press, 2000),
    pp. 1-17.
Anonymous, *Rescued from Egypt* (London: Thomas Nelson, 1873).
Aristotle, *The Poetics* (Cambridge, MA: Harvard University Press, 1982).
Asch, Sholem, *Moses* (trans. Maurice Samuel; New York: Putnam, 1951).
Assmann, Jan, *Moses the Egyptian: The Memory of Egypt in Western Monotheism* (Cam-
    bridge, MA: Harvard University Press, 1997).
Auerbach, Erich, *Mimesis* (trans. Willard R. Trask; Princeton, NJ: Princeton University Press,
    1974).
—*Moses* (trans. Robert A. Barclay and Israel O. Lehman; Detroit: Wayne State University
    Press, 1975).
Bakhtin, Mikhail, *The Dialogic Imagination* (ed. Michael Holquist; trans. Caryl Emerson and
    Michael Holquist; Austin: University of Texas Press, 1981).
—'Forms of Time and Chronotope in the Novel', in *idem*, *The Dialogic Imagination*,
    pp. 89-258.
Bal, Mieke, *Lethal Love: Feminist Literary Readings of Biblical Love Stories* (Bloomington:
    Indiana University Press, 1987).
—*Reading Rembrandt: Beyond the Word-Image Opposition* (New York: Cambridge
    University Press, 1991).
Banks, Lynne Reid, *Moses in Egypt: A Novel Inspired by 'The Prince of Egypt'* (New York:
    Dreamworks/Puffin, 1998).
Barthes, Roland, 'From Work to Text', in Josué Harari (ed.), *Textual Strategies* (Ithaca, NY:
    Cornell University Press, 1979), pp. 73-81.
—'To Write: An Intransitive Verb?', in R.T. and F.M. De George (eds.), *The Structuralists:
    From Marx to Levi-Strauss* (Garden City, NY: Doubleday, 1972), pp. 155-67.

Barton, John, 'Gerhard von Rad on the World-View of Early Israel', *Journal of Theological Studies* 35 (1984), pp. 301-23.

Barzel, Hillel, 'Moses: Tragedy and Sublimity', in Gros Louis, Ackerman and Warshaw (eds.), *Literary Interpretations of Biblical Narratives*, pp. 120-40.

Bellah, Robert N., 'Civil Religion in America', *Daedalus* 96 (1967), pp. 1-21.

Belleville, Linda, *Reflections of Glory: Paul's Polemical Use of the Moses-Doxa Tradition in 2 Corinthians 3.1-18* (JSOTSup, 52; Sheffield: JSOT Press, 1991).

Bellour, Raymond, *The Analysis of Film* (Bloomington: Indiana University Press, 2000).

Benjamin, Walter, 'The Art of the Storyteller', in *idem, Illuminations*, pp. 83-109.

—*Charles Baudelaire* (trans. Harry Zohn; London: Verso, 1989).

—*Gesammelte Schriften* (7 vols.; ed. Rolf Tiedemann and H. Schweppenhäuser; Frankfurt: Suhrkamp, 1991).

—*Illuminations* (trans. Harry Zohn; New York: Schocken Books, 1969).

'On Language as Such and on the Language of Man', in *idem, Reflections*, pp. 314-32.

—*The Origin of German Tragic Drama* (trans. John Osborne; London: New Left Books, 1977).

—*Reflections* (trans. Edmund Jephcott; New York: Schocken Books, 1986).

—'The Task of the Translator', in *idem, Illuminations*, pp. 69-82.

—'Theses on the Philosophy of History', in *idem, Illuminations*, pp. 253-64

—'Traumkitsch', in *idem, Gesammelte Schriften*, II, pp. 620-22.

—'The Work of Art in the Age of Mechanical Reproduction', in *idem, Illuminations*, pp. 217-51.

Berkove, Lawrence, '"The Minister's Black Veil": The Gloomy Moses of Milford', *The Nathaniel Hawthorne Journal* 8 (1978), pp. 147-57.

Berlin, Adele, *The Dynamics of Biblical Parallelism* (Bloomington: Indiana University Press, 1985).

—'Literary Exegesis of Biblical Narrative: Between Poetics and Hermeneutics', in Jason Rosenblatt and Joseph Sitterson, Jr (eds.), *'Not in Heaven': Coherence and Complexity in Biblical Narrative* (Bloomington: Indiana University Press, 1991), pp. 120-28.

—*Poetics and Interpretation of Biblical Narrative* (Bible and Literature Series, 9; Sheffield: Almond Press, 1983).

Bernstein, Richard J, *Freud and the Legacy of Moses* (Cambridge: Cambridge University Press, 1998).

Beyerle, Stefan, *Der Mosesegen im Deuteronomium* (Berlin: W. de Gruyter, 1997).

Blanchot, Maurice, 'Thanks (Be Given) to Jacques Derrida', in *idem, The Blanchot Reader* (ed. M. Holland; Oxford: Basil Blackwell, 1995), pp. 317-23.

Bleek, Fr., *Einleitung in das Alte Testament* (rev. J. Wellhausen; Berlin, 1878).

Blenkinsopp, Joseph, 'Jonathan's Sacrilege', *CBQ* 26 (1964), pp. 423-49.

Bloch, Ernst, *The Principle of Hope* (trans. N. Plaice, S. Plaice and P. Knight; 3 vols.; Cambridge: MIT Press, 1986).

Bloom, Harold, *The Book of J* (New York: Grove, 1990).

Bordwell, David, *On the History of Film Style* (Cambridge, MA: Harvard University Press, 1997).

Boston, James, 'The Wisdom Influence Upon the Song of Moses', *JBL* 87 (1968), pp. 198-202.

Breasted, J.H., *The Dawn of Conscience* (New York: Charles Scribner's Sons, 1933).

Brecht, Bertolt, *Brecht on Theater* (trans. John Willet; London: Methuen, 1974).

Britt, Brian, 'Apology for the Text', *Literature and Theology* 14 (2000), pp. 412-29.

—'The Book of Life: The Hebrew Bible as a Sacred Text in Deut. 31–34 and in the Philosophy of Walter Benjamin' (PhD dissertation, University of Chicago, 1992).

—'Contesting History and Identity in Modern Fiction About Moses', in Eric Ziolkowski (ed.),
     Literature, Religion, and East–West Comparison: Essays in Honor of Anthony C. Yu
     (Newark, DL: University of Delaware Press, forthcoming).
—'Deut. 31–32 as a Textual Memorial', *BibInt* 8 (2000), pp. 358-74
—'Prophetic Concealment in a Biblical Type Scene', *CBQ* 64 (2002), pp. 37-58.
—'Romantic Roots of the Debate on the Buber-Rosenzweig Bible', *Prooftexts* 20 (2000),
     pp. 262-89.
—'The Veil of Allegory in Hawthorne's *The Blithedale Romance*', *Literature and Theology*
     10 (1996), pp. 44-57.
—*Walter Benjamin and the Bible* (Lewiston, NY: Edwin Mellen Press, 2003 [first edn: New
     York: Continuum, 1996]).
Brock, Sebastian, 'Jacob of Serugh on the Veil of Moses', *Sobornost* 3 (1981), pp. 70-85.
Buber, Martin, *Moses* (Atlantic Heights, NJ: Humanities Press, 1989).
Buber, Martin, and Franz Rosenzweig, *Die Schrift und ihre Verdeutschung* (Berlin: Schocken
     Books, 1936).
Bucher, François (ed.), *The Pamplona Bibles; a Facsimile Compiled from Two Picture Bibles
     with Martyrologies Commissioned by King Sancho el Fuerte of Navarra (1194–1234)*
     (New Haven: Yale University Press, 1970).
Buck-Morss, Susan, *The Dialectics of Seeing* (Cambridge: MIT Press, 1989).
Burgess, Anthony, *Moses: A Narrative* (New York: Stonehill, 1976).
Calvin, John, *Calvin's Commentaries*, IV (trans. Charles Bingham; 22 vols.; Grand Rapids:
     Baker Book House,1989).
Charles, J. Daryl, *Literary Strategy in the Epistle of Jude* (Scranton: University of Scranton
     Press, 1993).
Chateaubriand, François René de, *Moïse, tragédie en cinq actes* (Paris: Acamédia, 1997).
Childs, Brevard, *The Book of Exodus: A Critical, Theological Commentary* (Philadelphia:
     Westminster Press, 1974).
—*Memory and Tradition in Israel* (Studies in Biblical Theology, 37; Naperville: Alec R.
     Allenson, 1962).
Cassuto, Umberto, *A Commentary on the Book of Exodus* (trans. Israel Abrams; Jerusalem:
     Magnes Press, 1967).
Chesnutt, Charles W., *The Conjure Woman* (repr., Ann Arbor: University of Michigan Press,
     1969).
Clair, Archer St., 'A New Moses: Typological Iconography in the Moutier-Grandval Bible
     Illustrations of Exodus', *Gesta* 26 (1987), pp. 19-28.
Coats, George W., *Moses: Heroic Man, Man of God* (JSOTSup, 57; Sheffield: JSOT Press,
     1988).
—'The Moses Narratives as Heroic Saga', in *idem* (ed.), *Saga Legend Tale Novella Fable*,
     pp. 33-44.
Coats, George W. (ed.), *Saga Legend Tale Novella Fable* (JSOTSup, 35; Sheffield: JSOT
     Press, 1985).
Cohen, Jonathan, *The Origins and Evolution of the Moses Nativity Story* (Leiden: E.J. Brill,
     1993).
Cohen, Morton, *Rider Haggard: His Life and Works* (London: Hutchinson, 1960).
Collingwood, R.G., *The Idea of History* (Oxford: Clarendon Press, 1946).
Copenhaver, Brian P. (ed.), *Hermetica* (Cambridge: Cambridge University Press, 1992).
Cox, Patricia, *Biography in Late Antiquity* (Berkeley: University of California, 1983).
Craigie, Peter C., *The Book of Deuteronomy* (Grand Rapids: Eerdmans, 1976).

Cross, Frank Moore, *Canaanite Myth and Hebrew Epic* (Cambridge, MA: Harvard University Press, 1973).

—*From Epic to Canon* (Baltimore: The Johns Hopkins University Press, 1998).

Cross, Frank Moore, and David Noel Freedman, 'The Blessing of Moses', *JBL* 67 (1978), p. 192.

Croutier, Alev Lytle, *Harem: The World Behind the Veil* (New York: Abbeville Press, 1989).

DeCerteau, Michel, *The Writing of History* (trans. Tom Conley; New York: Columbia, 1988).

DeMille, Cecil B., *The Autobiography of Cecil B. DeMille* (London: W.H. Allen, 1960).

Demsky, Aaron, 'Writing in Ancient Israel and Early Judaism: Part One, The Biblical Period', in Martin Jan Mulder and Harry Sysling (eds.), *Mikra* (Philadelphia: Fortress Press, 1988), pp. 1-20.

Derrida, Jacques, *Archive Fever* (trans. Eric Prenowitz; Chicago: University of Chicago Press, 1996).

—*Of Grammatology* (trans. Gayatri Spivak; Baltimore: The Johns Hopkins University Press, 1976).

—*The Post Card: From Socrates to Freud and Beyond* (trans. Alan Bass; Chicago: University of Chicago Press, 1987).

—'Sauf le nom (Post-Scriptum)', in *idem*, *On the Name* (ed. Thomas Dutoit; trans. John P. Leavey, Jr; Stanford: Stanford University Press, 1995), pp. 35-85.

—'Signature Event Context', in *idem*, *Margins of Philosophy* (trans. Alan Bass; Chicago: University of Chicago Press, 1982), pp.324-26.

De Vries, Hent, *Philosophy and the Turn to Religion* (Baltimore: The Johns Hopkins University Press, 1999).

Dion, Paul, 'The Horned Prophet (1 Kings 22.11)', *VT* 49 (1999), pp. 259-60.

Douglas, Ann, *The Feminization of American Culture* (New York: Knopf, 1977).

Dozeman, Thomas, *God on the Mountain* (Atlanta: Scholars Press, 1989).

—'Masking Moses and Mosaic Authority in Torah', *JBL* 119 (2000), pp. 21-45.

Driver, S.R., *A Critical and Exegetical Commentary on Deuteronomy* (ICC; New York: Charles Scribner's Sons, 1906).

Durkheim, Emile, *The Elementary Forms of Religious Life* (trans. Karen Fields; New York: Free Press, 1995).

Ebers, Georg, *Joshua: A Story of Biblical Times* (trans. Mary J. Safford; New York: D. Appleton, 1889).

Eckart, Dietrich, and Adolf Hitler, *Der Bolschewismus von Moses bis Lenin* (Munich: Hoheniechen Verlag, 1924).

Eilberg-Schwartz, Howard, *God's Phallus* (Boston: Beacon Press, 1994).

Eissfeldt, Otto, *Das Lied Moses Deuteronomium 32.1-34 und das Lehrgedicht Asaphs Psalm 78 Samt Einer Analyse der Umgebung des Mose-Liedes* (Berlin: Akademie-Verlag, 1958).

Eliot, George, 'The Death of Moses', in *Theophrastus Such, Jubal and Other Poems, and the Spanish Gypsy* (Chicago, IL; R.S. Peake, 1888), pp. 280-83.

Ellison, Ralph, 'Recent Negro Fiction', *New Masses* 40 (1941), p. 25.

Erikson, Erik, *Childhood and Society* (New York: Norton, 1950).

—*Identity: Youth and Crisis* (New York: Norton, 1968).

—*The Life Cycle Completed* (New York: Norton, 1982).

Etherington, Norman, *Rider Haggard* (Boston: Twayne, 1984).

Exum, J. Cheryl, *Plotted, Shot, and Painted: Cultural Representations of Biblical Women* (JSOTSup, 215; Sheffield: Sheffield Academic Press, 1996).

Fast, Howard, *Moses, Prince of Egypt* (New York: Crown, 1958).
Fewell, Dana Nolan, and David M. Gunn, 'Tipping the Balance: Sternberg's Reader and the Rape of Dinah', *JBL* 110 (1991), pp. 193-211.
Fishbane, Michael, *Biblical Interpretation in Ancient Israel* (Oxford: Clarendon Press, 1985).
—*Text and Texture* (New York: Schocken Books, 1979).
—'Varia Deuteronomica', *ZAW* 84 (1972), pp. 349-52.
Forshey, Gerald E., *American Religious and Biblical Spectaculars* (Westport, CT: Praeger, 1992).
Franko, Ivan, *Moses and Other Poems* (trans. Vera Rich and Percival Cundy; New York: Shevchenko Scientific Society, 1905).
Frei, Hans, *The Eclipse of Biblical Narrative* (New Haven: Yale University Press, 1974).
Fretheim, Terence E., *The Suffering of God* (Philadelphia: Fortress Press, 1984).
Freud, Sigmund, *Moses and Monotheism* (trans. Katherine Jones; New York: Vantage Books, 1967).
Friedman, Richard Elliott, *Who Wrote the Bible?* (New York: Harper & Row, 1989).
Gadamer, Hans-Georg, 'The Relevance of the Beautiful', in *idem*, *The Relevance of the Beautiful and Other Essays* (ed. Robert Bernasconi; trans. Nicholas Walker; Cambridge: Cambridge University Press, 1986), pp. 1-53
—*Truth and Method* (New York: Crossroad, 1988).
Gage, John, 'Gothic Glass: Two Aspects of a Dionysian Aesthetic', *Art History* 5 (1982), pp. 36-58.
Gager, John G., *Moses in Greco-Roman Paganism* (Nashville: Abingdon Press, 1972).
Gates, Henry Louis, Jr, *The Signifying Monkey* (Oxford: Oxford University Press, 1988).
Gates, Henry Louis, Jr, and K.A. Appiah (eds.), *Zora Neale Hurston: Critical Perspectives Past and Present* (New York: Amistad, 1993).
Geller, Stephen, 'The Dynamics of Parallel Verse: A Poetic Analysis of Deut. 32.6-12', *HTR* 75 (1982), pp. 35-56.
Gibson, David, 'We Revere the Bible... We Don't Read It', *Washington Post* (9 December 2000), B9.
Gilman, Sander, *Difference and Pathology: Stereotypes of Sexuality, Race, and Madness* (Ithaca, NY: Cornell University Press, 1985).
—'Salome, Syphilis, Sarah Bernhardt, and the Modern Jewess', in Linda Nochlin and Tamar Garb (eds.), *The Jew in the Text* (London: Thames & Hudson, 1995), pp. 97-120.
Girard, René, *Violence and the Sacred* (trans. Patrick Gregory; Baltimore: The Johns Hopkins University Press, 1977).
Goldstein, Bluma, *Reinscribing Moses* (Cambridge, MA: Harvard University Press, 1992).
Grant, Joan, *So Moses Was Born* (repr., New York: Arno Press, 1980 [1952]).
Graves, Robert, *My Head! My Head!* (New York: Haskell House, 1974).
Gregory of Nyssa, *The Life of Moses* (trans. Abraham Malherbe and Everett Ferguson; New York: Paulist Press, 1978).
Greig, Josef A., 'Some Formative Aspects in the Development of Gerhard von Rad's Idea of History', *Andrews University Seminary Studies* 16 (1978), pp. 313-31.
Greimas, Algirdas, *On Meaning: Selected Writings in Semiotic Theory* (trans. Paul J. Perron and Frank H. Collins; Minneapolis: University of Minnesota Press, 1987).
Gressmann, Hugo, *Albert Eichhorn und die Religionsgeschichtliche Schule* (Göttingen: Vandenhoeck & Ruprecht, 1914).
—'Die Aufgaben der alttestamentlichen Forschung', *ZAW* 42 (1924), pp. 1-33.
—*Mose und seine Zeit* (Göttingen: Vandenhoeck & Ruprecht, 1913).

—'Sage und Geschichte in den Patriarchersählungen', *ZAW* 28 (1910), pp. 1-34.

Groves, James, *Actualization and Interpretation in the Old Testament* (Atlanta: Scholars Press, 1987).

Habel, Norman, 'The Form and Significance of the Call Narratives', *ZAW* 77 (1965), pp. 297-323.

Hadot, Pierre, *Zur Idee der Naturgeheimnisse* (Wiesbaden: Franz Steiner Verlag, 1982).

Haggard, Rider H., *Moon of Israel* (New York: Longmans, Green & Co., 1919).

Hals, Ronald M., 'Legend', in Coats (ed.), *Saga Legend Tale Novella Fable*, pp. 45-55.

Hamburger, Käte, 'Thomas Manns Mose-Erzählung "Das Gesetz" auf dem Hintergrund der Überlieferung und der religionswissenschaftlichen Forschung', in Mann, *Das Gesetz*, pp. 58-112.

Handelman, Susan, *The Slayers of Moses* (Albany: SUNY Press, 1982).

Haran, Menahem, 'The Shining of Moses' Face: A Case Study in Biblical and Ancient Near Eastern Iconography', in W. Barrick and John Spencer (eds.), *In the Shelter of Elyon* (JSOTSup, 31; Sheffield: Sheffield Academic Press, 1984), pp. 159-73.

Hardy, W.G., *All the Trumpets Sounded* (New York: Popular Library, 1957).

Hareven, Alouph, *Panim el Panim* (Tel Aviv: Zmora-Bitan, 1991 [Hebrew]).

Harper, Frances Ellen Watkins, *Moses a Story of the Nile* (1869), in *Complete Poems of Frances E.W. Harper* (ed. Maryemma Graham; The Schomburg Library of Nineteenth-Century Black Women Writers; New York: Oxford University Press, 1988), pp. 34-66.

Hata, Gohei, 'The Story of Moses Interpreted Within the Context of Anti-Semitism', Louis H. Feldman and Gohei Hata (eds.), *Josephus, Judaism, and Christianity* (Detroit: Wayne State University Press, 1987), pp. 180-97.

Hawthorne, Julian, 'Nathaniel Hawthorne and his Wife: A Biography', in *The Works of Nathaniel Hawthorne*, XIV–XV.

Hawthorne, Nathaniel, *The American Notebooks*, in *The Centenary Edition of the Works of Nathaniel Hawthorne* (21 vols.; Columbus: Ohio State University Press, 1972).

—'Passages From the French and Italian Notebooks', in *The Works of Nathaniel Hawthorne*, X.

—*The Works of Nathaniel Hawthorne* (24 vols.; Boston: Houghton Mifflin & Co., 1891).

Hayes, John H., and J. Maxwell Miller (eds.), *Israelite and Judean History* (Philadelphia: Trinity Press International, 1977).

Hayward, Jane, 'Stained Glass at Saint-Denis', in Sumner Crosby *et al.* (eds.), *The Royal Abbey of St.-Denis in the Time of Abbot Suger* (New York: Metropolitan Museum of Art, 1981), pp. 61-71.

Hegel, Georg Wilhelm Friedrich, *Lectures on the Philosophy of Religion: One-Volume Edition, The Lectures of 1827* (ed. Peter C. Hodgson; trans. R.F. Brown, P.C. Hodgson and J.M. Stewart; Berkeley: University of California Press, 1988).

Hendel, Ronald, 'The Exodus in Biblical Memory', *JBL* 120 (2001), pp. 601-22.

Higashi, Sumiko, 'Antimodernism as Historical Representation in a Consumer Culture: Cecil B. DeMille's *The Ten Commandments*, 1923, 1956, 1993', in Vivian Sobchack (ed.), *The Persistence of History* (New York: Routledge, 1996), pp. 91-112.

Hill, Lynda Marion, *Social Rituals and the Verbal Art of Zora Neale Hurston* (Washington, DC: Howard University Press, 1996).

Hoffmann, Konrad, 'Sugers "Anagogisches Fenster" in St. Denis', *Wallraf-Richartz-Jahrbuch* 30 (1968), pp. 57-87.

Hurston, Zora Neale, *Moses, Man of the Mountain* (Urbana, IL: University of Illinois Press, 1984).

—*Their Eyes Were Watching God* (New York: HarperCollins, 1998).

—*Zora Neale Hurston: Folklore, Memoirs, and Other Writings* (New York: Library of America, 1995).

Idel, Moshe, *Golem* (Albany: State University of New York Press, 1990).

Ingraham, J.H., *The Pillar of Fire or Israel in Bondage* (Philadelphia: G.G. Evans, 1860).

Jakobson, Roman, 'Grammatical Parallelism and its Russian Facet', in Krystyna Pomorska and Stephen Rudy (eds.), *Language in Literature* (Cambridge, MA: Harvard University Press, 1987), pp. 145-79.

Jameson, Fredric, *The Political Unconscious* (Ithaca, NY: Cornell University Press, 1981).

Jansen, Werner, *Die Kinder Israel: Mose-Roman* (Braunschweig: Georg Westermann, 1927).

—*The Light of Egypt* (translation of *Die Kinder Israel*) (trans. William A. Drake; New York: Brentano's, 1928).

Josephus, *Josephus*. I. *Against Apion* (trans. H.St.J. Thackeray; LCL; Cambridge, MA: Harvard University Press, 1966).

   Josephus. IV. *Jewish Antiquities* (trans. H.St.J. Thackeray; LCL; Cambridge, MA: Harvard University Press, 1978).

Josipovici, Gabriel, *The Book of God* (New Haven: Yale University Press, 1988).

Kalisch, M., *A Historical and Critical Commentary on the Old Testament—Exodus* (London: Longman, Brown, Green & Longman, 1855).

Kant, Immanuel, 'On a Newly Arisen Superior Tone in Philosophy', in Peter Fenves (ed.), *Raising the Tone of Philosophy: Late Essays by Immanuel Kant, Transformative Critique by Jacques Derrida* (Baltimore: The Johns Hopkins University Press, 1993), pp. 51-81.

Keegan, Terence J., 'Biblical Criticism and the Challenge of Postmodernism', *BibInt* 3 (1995), pp. 1-14.

Kierkegaard, Søren, *The Concept of Anxiety* (trans. Reidar Thomte; Princeton, NJ: Princeton University Press, 1980).

Kirsch, Jonathan, *Moses: A Life* (New York: Ballantine, 1988).

Kleiner, Diana, *Roman Sculpture* (New Haven: Yale University Press, 1992).

Knight, Douglas A., *Rediscovering the Traditions of Israel* (Missoula, MT: Society of Biblical Literature, 1975).

Knowles, Michael, '"The Rock, His Work is Perfect": Unusual Imagery for God in Deuteronomy xxxii', *VT* 39 (1989), pp. 307-22.

Kodolanyi, Janos, *Und er fuhrte sie aus Agypten: Ein Moses-Roman* (Stuttgart: Steingruben-Verlag, 1965).

Kolb, Leon, *Moses the Near Easterner* (San Francisco: Genuart, 1956).

Kolve, V.A., *The Play Called Corpus Christi* (Stanford: Stanford University Press, 1966).

Kracauer, Sigfried, 'The Biography as an Art Form of the New Bourgeoisie', in *idem*, *The Mass Ornament* (trans. Thomas Y. Levin; Cambridge, MA: Harvard University Press, 1995), pp. 101-105.

—*The Mass Ornament* (trans. Thomas Y. Levin; Cambridge, MA: Harvard University Press, 1995).

—*Theory of Film: The Redemption of Physical Reality* (Princeton, NJ: Princeton University Press, 1997).

Kugel, James, *The Bible as it Was* (Cambridge, MA: Harvard University Press, 1997).

—*The Idea of Biblical Poetry* (New Haven: Yale University Press, 1981).

Kuhl, Curt, 'Die "Wiederaufnahme"—ein literarkritisches Prinzip?', *ZAW* 64 (1952), pp. 1-11.

Kushelevsky, Bella, *Moses and the Angel of Death* (New York: Peter Lang, 1995).

Labuschagne, Casper, 'The Setting of the Song of Moses in Deuteronomy', in M. Vervenne and J. Lust (eds.), *Deuteronomy and Deuteronomic Literature* (Leuven: Leuven University Press, 1997), pp. 111-29.

Leibert, Julius, *The Lawgiver* (New York: Exposition Press, 1953).

Lemche, Niels Peter, 'On the Problem of Studying Israelite History Apropos Abraham Malamat's View of Historical Research', *BN* 23 (1984), pp. 94-124.

—'Rachel and Lea. Or: On the Survival of Outdated Paradigmas in the Study of the Origin of Israel, II', *Scandinavian Journal of the Old Testament* 1 (1988), pp. 39-65.

Levenson, Jon, 'Who Inserted the Book of the Torah?', *HTR* 68 (1975), pp. 203-33.

Levinas, Emmanuel, excerpt from *Time and the Other*, in Seán Hand (ed.), *The Levinas Reader* (Cambridge, MA: Basil Blackwell, 1989), pp. 37-58.

Levinson, Bernard, *Deuteronomy and the Hermeneutics of Legal Innovation* (New York: Oxford University Press, 1997).

Levi-Strauss, Claude, *Structural Anthropology* (New York: Basic Books, 1963).

Lewine, Carol, *The Sistine Chapel Walls and the Roman Liturgy* (University Park, PA: Pennsylvania State University Press, 1993).

Lewis, Suzanne, *Reading Images: Narrative Discourse and Reception in the Thirteenth-Century Illuminated Apocalypse* (Cambridge: Cambridge University Press, 1995).

Lincoln, Bruce, *Theorizing Myth: Narrative, Ideology, and Scholarship* (Chicago: University of Chicago Press, 1999).

Lissauer, Ernst, *Der Weg des Gewaltigen* (Chemnitz: Gesellschaft der Bücherfreunde, 1931).

Liverani, Mario, 'Storiografia politica hittita—II: Telipinu, ovvero: della solidarietà', *OA* 16 (1977), pp. 105-108.

Loewenstamm, Samuel, 'The Death of Moses', in George Nickelsburg (ed.), *Studies on the Testament of Abraham* (Missoula, MT: Scholars Press, 1976), p. 198.

Lohfink, Norbert, 'Der Bundesschluss im Land Moab-Redaktionsgeschichtliches zu Deut. 28,68-32,47', *BZ* 6 (1962), pp. 32-55.

—'Zur Fabel des Deuteronomiums', in G. Braulik (ed.), *Bundesdokument und Gesetz: Studien zum Deuteronomium* (Herders Biblische Studien, 4; Freiburg: Herder, 1995), pp. 65-78.

—'Zur Fabel in Dtn 31–32', in R. Bartelmus, T. Krueger and H. Utzschneider (eds.) *Konsequente Traditionsgeschichte* (Göttingen: Universitätsverlag, 1993), pp. 255-80.

Long, Burke O., *1 Kings, With an Introduction to Historical Literature* (Grand Rapids: Eerdmans, 1984).

—'Framing Repetitions in Biblical Historiography', *JBL* 106 (1987), pp. 385-99.

Low, Gail Ching-Liang, *White Skins/Black Masks* (London: Routledge, 1996).

Lowe, John, *Jump at the Sun* (Urbana, IL: University of Illinois Press, 1994).

Louis, K. Gros, J. Ackerman and T.S. Warshaw (eds.), *Literary Interpretations of Biblical Narratives* (Nashville: Abingdon Press, 1974).

Lubich, Frederick A., ' "Fascinating Fascism": Thomas Manns "Das Gesetz" und seine Selbstde-Montage als Moses-Hitler', *German Studies Review* 14 (1991), pp. 553-73.

Lukacs, Georg, *The Theory of the Novel* (trans. Anna Bostock; Cambridge: MIT Press, 1971).

Lundbom, Jack R., 'God's Use of the *Idem Per Idem* to Terminate Debate', *HTR* 71 (1978), pp. 193-201.

Lux, Rudiger, 'Der Tod Moses als "besprochene und erzählete Welt" ', *Zeitschrift für Theologie und Kirche* 84 (1987), pp. 395-425.

Luyten, Jos, 'Primeval and Eschatological Overtones in the Song of Moses (DT 32, 1-43)', in Norbert Lohfink (ed.), *Das Deuteronomium: Entstehung, Gestalt und Botschaft* (Leuven: Leuven University Press, 1985), pp.46-47.

MacIntyre, Alasdair, *After Virtue: A Study in Moral Theory* (Notre Dame, IN: University of Notre Dame Press, 1984).

Makoschey, Klaus, *Quellenkritische Untersuchungen zum Spätwerk Thomas Manns* (Thomas-Mann-Studien, 17; Frankfurt: Vittorio Klostermann, 1998).

Malinowski, Bronislaw, *Magic, Science and Religion* (Garden City, NY: Doubleday, 1954).

Man, Paul de, *Blindness and Insight: Essays in the Rhetoric of Contemporary Criticism* (Minneapolis: University of Minnesota Press, 1983).

Mann, Thomas, *Das Gesetz* (ed. Kate Hamburger; Frankfurt: Ullstein, 1964).

—*Letters of Thomas Mann* (trans. Richard and Clara Winston; New York: Knopf, 1971).

—*The Tables of the Law* (trans. H.T. Lowe-Porter; New York: Knopf, 1943).

Marion, Jean-Luc, *Sur la théologie blanche de Descartes* (Paris: Presses Universitaires de France, 1981).

Marks, Herbert, 'On Prophetic Stammering', in Schwartz (ed.), *The Book and The Text*, pp. 60-80.

Mayes, A.D.H., *Deuteronomy* (Grand Rapids. Eerdmans, 1981).

McCarthy, Judy, '"The Minister's Black Veil": Concealing Moses and the Holy of Holies'. *Studies in Short Fiction* 24 (1987), pp. 131-38.

McDannell, Colleen, *Material Christianity* (New Haven: Yale University Press, 1995).

Meinhold, Arndt, 'Die Gattung der Josephsgeschichte und des Estherbuches: Diasporanovelle I und II', *ZAW* 87 (1975), pp. 306-24, and *ZAW* 88 (1976), pp. 72-93.

Mellinkoff, Ruth, *The Horned Moses in Medieval Art and Thought* (Berkeley: University of California Press, 1970).

Meyer, Eduard, *Die Israeliten und ihre Nachbarstämme* (Halle: Max Niemeyer, 1906).

Miles, Margaret, *Image as Insight* (Boston: Beacon Press, 1985).

Miller, Dean A., *The Epic Hero* (Baltimore: The Johns Hopkins University Press, 2000).

Miller, Patrick D., Jr, '"Moses My Servant": The Deuteronomic Portrait of Moses', *Interpretation* 41 (1987), pp. 245-55.

Mitchell, W.J.T., *Iconology* (Chicago: University of Chicago Press, 1986).

—*Picture Theory* (Chicago: University of Chicago Press, 1994).

Mankekar, Purnima, *Screening Culture, Viewing Politics* (Durham: Duke University Press, 1999).

Momigliano, Arnaldo, *The Development of Greek Biography* (Cambridge, MA: Harvard University Press, 1971).

Morand, Kathleen, *Claus Sluter: Artist at the Court of Burgundy* (Austin: University of Texas Press, 1991).

Morgan, David, *Visual Piety* (Berkeley: University of California Press, 1998).

Mulvey, Laura, *Fetishism and Curiosity* (Bloomington: Indiana University Press, 1996).

Nadel, Alan, 'God's Law and the Wide Screen: *The Ten Commandments* as Cold War "Epic"', *PMLA* 108 (1993), pp. 415-30.

Nicholson, Ernest, *The Pentateuch in the Twentieth Century* (Oxford: Clarendon Press, 1998).

Niehoff, Maren R., *Philo and Jewish Identity and Culture* (Tübingen: J.C.B. Mohr [Paul Siebeck], 2001).

Nietzsche, Friedrich, *On the Genealogy of Morals* (trans. Walter Kaufmann; New York: Vintage Books, 1967).

Noerdlinger, Henry S., *Moses and Egypt; The Documentation to the Motion Picture The Ten Commandments* (Los Angeles: University of Southern California Press, 1956).

Norhnberg, James, *Like Unto Moses: The Constituting of an Interruption* (Bloomington: University of Indiana Press, 1995).

Noth, Martin, *Exodus* (Philadelphia: Westminster Press, 1962).

—*A History of Pentateuchal Traditions* (trans. Bernhard W. Anderson; Chico, CA: Scholars Press, 1981) (German original, *Überlieferungsgeschichte des Pentateuch* [Stuttgart: W. Kohlhammer, 1948]).

Oden, Robert, *The Bible Without Theology* (Urbana, IL: University of Illinois Press, 1987).

Olson, Dennis T, *Deuteronomy and the Death of Moses* (Minneapolis: Fortress Press, 1994).

Origen, *Homilies on Genesis and Exodus* (trans. R. Heine; Washington: Catholic University Press, 1981).

Osswald, Eva, *Das Bild des Mose in der kritischen alttestamentlichen Wissenschaft seit Julius Wellhausen* (Berlin: Evangelische Verlaganstalt, 1962).

Panofsky, Erwin, *Abbot Suger on the Abbey Church of St.-Denis and its Art Treasures* (Princeton, NJ: Princeton University Press, 1979).

Pardee, Dennis, 'Ugaritic and Hebrew Metrics', in Gordon D. Young (ed.), *Ugarit in Retrospect: Fifty Years of Ugarit and Ugaritic* (Winona Lake, IN: Eisenbrauns, 1981), pp. 113-30.

—*Ugaritic and Hebrew Poetic Parallelism: A Trial Cut* (VTSup, 39 ; Leiden: E.J. Brill, 1988).

Pardes, Ilana, *The Biography of Ancient Israel* (Berkeley: University of California Press, 2000).

—'Moses Goes Down to Hollywood: Miracles and Special Effects', *Semeia* 74 (1996), pp. 15-32.

Paul, Robert A., *Moses and Civilization* (New Haven: Yale University Press, 1996).

Perlitt, Lother, *Vatke und Wellhausen* (Berlin: Alfred Töpelmann, 1965).

Philo, *Philo*. VI. *On the Life of Moses* (ed. G.P. Goold; trans F.H. Colson; Cambridge, MA: Harvard University Press, 1994).

Piaget, Jean, *Structuralism* (New York: Basic Books, 1970).

Plato, *Phaedo*, in *The Collected Dialogues of Plato* (ed. Edith Hamilton and Huntington Cairns; Princeton, NJ: Princeton University Press, 1987).

Polzin, Robert, 'Deuteronomy', in Alter and Kermode (eds.), *The Literary Guide to the Bible*, pp. 92-101.

—*Moses and the Deuteronomist* (New York: Seabury, 1980).

—*Samuel and the Deuteronomist* (Bloomington: Indiana University Press, 1989).

Posnock, Ross, *Color and Culture* (Cambridge, MA: Harvard University Press, 1998).

Promey, Salley, *Painting Religion in Public: John Singer Sargent's Triumph of Religion at the Boston Public Library* (Princeton, NJ: Princeton University Press, 2000).

Propp, William H., 'Exodus 1–18' (AB, 2; Garden City, NY: Doubleday, 1999).

—'The Skin of Moses' Face—Transfigured or Disfigured?', *CBQ* 49 (1987), pp. 375-86.

Pseudo-Dionysius, *Pseudo-Dionysius: The Complete Works* (trans. Colm Luibheid; New York: Paulist Press, 1987).

Pseudo-Philo, *Biblical Antiquities* (trans. J.R. James; New York: Ktav, 1971).

Purdue, Leo, *The Collapse of History: Reconstructing Old Testament Theology* (Overtures to Biblical Theology; Minneapolis: Fortress Press, 1994).

Rad, Gerhard von, *Deuteronomy: A Commentary* (trans. Dorothea Barton; Philadelphia: Westminster Press, 1966).

—*Old Testament Theology* (trans. D. Stalker; 2 vols.; New York: Harper & Row, 1962).

—*Theologie des Alten Testaments* (2 vols.; Munich: Chr. Kaiser Verlag, 1987), I, p. 64.

Ramban, *Commentary on the Torah: Deuteronomy* (trans. Rabbi Charles B. Chavel; New York: Shilo, 1976).

Rashi, *The Pentateuch and Rashi's Commentary: Deuteronomy* (eds. Rabbi Abraham Ben Isaiah and Rabbi Benjamin Sharfman; Brooklyn: S.S. & R., 1950).

Rauschning, Hermann, 'A Conversation With Hitler', in *The Ten Commandments*, pp. ix-xiii.

Reis, Pamela Tamarkin, 'The Bridegroom of Blood: A New Reading', *Judaism* 40 (1991), pp. 324-31.

Resnick, Irven M., 'Medieval Roots of the Myth of Jewish Male Menses', *HTR* 93 (2000), pp. 241-63.

Ri, Su-Min (Andreas), 'Mosesmotive in den Fresken der Katakombe der Via Latina im Lichte der Rabbinischen Tradition', *Kairos* 17 (1975), pp. 57-92.

Ricoeur, Paul, *Interpretation Theory* (Fort Worth: Texas Christian University Press, 1976).

—'Toward a Hermeneutic of the Idea of Revelation', in *idem*, *Essays on Biblical Interpretation* (Philadelphia: Fortress Press, 1985), pp. 73-118.

Rilke, Rainer Maria, *Poems 1906–1926* (trans. J.B. Leishman; London: Hogarth Press, 1968).

—'Der Tod Moses', in Rilke-Archiv with Ruth Sieber-Rilke, *Sämtliche Werke* (6 vols.; Wiesbaden: Insel-Verlag, 1963), II, p. 102.

Ripa, Cesara, *Baroque and Rococo Pictorial Imagery* (ed. Edward Maser; New York: Dover, 1971).

Robinson, Armin, 'Editor's Foreword', in *The Ten Commandments* (New York: Simon & Schuster, 1944).

Rofé, Alexander, 'The Question of the Composition of Deuteronomy 31 in Light of a Conjecture about a Confusion in the Columns of the Biblical Text', *Shnaton* 3 (1978–79), pp. 49-76 (Hebrew).

Rohrer-Walsh, Jennifer, 'Coming-of-Age in *The Prince of Egypt*', in Walsh and Aichele (eds.), *Screening Scripture*, pp. 77-99.

Rosenberg, Isaac, *Moses: A Play* (London: Imperial War Museum, 1990).

Said, Edward, *Orientalism* (New York: Vintage Books, 1978).

Sandmel, Samuel, *Alone Atop the Mountain* (Garden City, NY: Doubleday, 1973).

Sarna, Nahum, *Exodus: The Traditional Hebrew Text with the New JPS Translation* (Philadelphia: Jewish Publication Society of America, 1991).

Schelling, Freiedrich, *Philosophie der Mythologie (1837/1842)* (ed. Klaus Vieweg and Christian Danz; Munich: Wilhelm Fink, 1996).

Schiller, Friedrich, *Die Sendung Moses* (ed. Karl-Heinz Hahn, Schillers Werke: Nationalausgabe, 17; Weimar: Hermann Böhlaus, 1970), pp. 377-413.

Schmid, Herbert, *Mose: Überlieferung und Geschichte* (Berlin: Alfred Töpelmann, 1968).

Schreckenberg, Heinz, *The Jews in Christian Art* (trans. John Bowden; New York: Continuum, 1996).

Schwartz, Regina, 'Joseph's Bones and the Resurrection of the Text: Remembering in the Bible', in *idem* (ed.), *The Book and the Text*, pp. 40-59.

Schwartz, Regina (ed.), *The Book and the Text* (Cambridge, MA: Basil Blackwell, 1990), pp. 40-59.

Scolnic, Benjamin E., 'Moses and the Horns of Power', *Judaism* 40 (1991), pp. 569-79.

Scullion, John J., 'Translator's Introduction to Hermann Gunkel', in Gunkel, *The Stories of Genesis* (Berkeley: BIBAL Press, 1994), pp. xv-xviii.

Seiferth, Wolfgang, *Synagogue and Church in the Middle Ages* (trans. Lee Chadeayne and Paul Gottwald; New York: Frederick Ungar, 1970).

Sellin, Ernst, *Mose und seine Bedeutung für die israelitisch-jüdische Religionsgeschichte* (Leipzig: A. Deichertsche Verlagsbuchhandlung, 1922).

Seow, C.L., *Ecclesiastes: A New Translation with Introduction and Commentary* (AB, 18C; Garden City, NY: Doubleday, 1997).

Sheen, Erica, '*The Ten Commandments* and *The Prince of Egypt*: Biblical Adaptation and Global Politics in the 1990s', *Polygraph* 12 (2000), pp. 85-99.

Sherwood, Yvonne, *A Biblical Text and its Afterlives* (Cambridge: Cambridge University Press, 2000).

Sifre: A Tannaitic Commentary on the Book of Deuteronomy (trans. Reuven Hammer; New Haven: Yale University Press, 1986).

Silberman, Lou H., 'Wellhausen and Judaism', *Semeia* 25 (1983), pp. 75-82.

Silver, Daniel Jeremy, *Images of Moses* (New York: Basic Books, 1982).

Smend, Rudolf, *Das Mosebild von Heinrich Ewald bis Martin Noth* (Beiträge zur Geschichte der Bbilischen Exegese, 3; Tübingen: J.C.B. Mohr, 1959).

—'Wellhausen und das Judentum', *ZTK* 79 (1982), pp. 249-82.

Sobel, Ileene Smith, (introduction by Elie Wiesel), illustrations by Mark Podwal, *Moses and the Angels* (New York: Delacorte Press, 1999).

Sonnet, Jean-Pierre, *The Book Within the Book: Writing in Deuteronomy* (Leiden: E.J. Brill, 1997).

Southon, Arthur E., *On Eagles' Wings* (New York: McGraw–Hill, 1939).

Spriggs, D.G., *Two Old Testament Theologies* (London: SCM Press, 1974).

Steffens, Lincoln, *Moses in Red* (Philadelphia: Dorrance & Co., 1926).

Sternberg, Meir, *The Poetics of Biblical Narrative* (Bloomington: Indiana University Press, 1985).

Sterngold, James, 'Just Like Real Life? Well, Maybe a Little More Exciting—Scholars Get Cameo Roles as Film Consultants', *The New York Times* (26 December 1998), A23.

Strong, Donald, *Roman Art* (New York: Penguin Books, 1988).

Swarzenski, Georg, *Die Illuminierter Handschriften und Einzelminiaturen des Mittelalters und der Renaissance in Frankfurter Besitz* (Frankfurt: Joseph Baer, 1929).

Talmon, Shemaryahu, 'The Presentation of Synchroneity and Simultaneity in Biblical Narrative', in *idem, Literary Studies in the Hebrew Bible* (Jerusalem: Magnes Press, 1993), pp. 112-33.

Tarr, Judith, *Pillar of Fire* (New York: Forge, 1995).

Thomson, Thomas L., 'Martin Noth and the History of Israel', in Steven McKenzie and M. Patrick Graham (eds.), *The History of Israel's Traditions* (JSOTSup, 182; Sheffield: Sheffield Academic Press, 1994), pp. 81-90.

Tigay, Jeffrey H., '"Heavy of Mouth" and "Heavy of Tongue": On Moses' Speech Difficulty'. *BASOR* 231 (1978), pp. 57-67.

—*The JPS Torah Commentary: Deuteronomy* (Philadelphia: Jewish Publication Society of America, 1996).

Uffenheimer, Benyamin, 'Buber and Modern Biblical Scholarship', in Haim Gordon and Jochanon Bloch (eds.), *Martin Buber: A Centenary Volume* (New York: Ktav, 1984), pp. 163-211.

Untermeyer, Louis, *Moses* (New York: Harcourt, Brace & Company, 1928).

Uricchio, William and Roberta E. Pearson, *Reframing Culture: The Case of the Vitagraph Quality Films* (Princeton, NJ: Princeton University Press, 1993).

Van Loggem, Manuel, *Mozes: Roman* (Amsterdam: Meulenhoff, 1968).

Van Seters, John, *The Life of Moses* (Louisville, KY: Westminster/John Knox Press, 1994).

Von Arndt, Meinhold, 'Die Gattung der Josephsgeschichte und des Estherbuches: Diasporanovelle II', *ZAW* 88 (1976), pp. 72-93.

Walsh, Richard and George Aichele (eds.), *Screening Scripture: Intertextual Connections Between Scripture and Film* (Harrisburg, PA: Trinity Press, 2002).

Wan, Sze-Kar, 'Charismatic Exegesis: Philo and Paul Compared', *The Studia Philonica Annual* 6 (1994), pp. 54-82.

Warner, G., *Queen Mary's Psalter: Miniatures and Drawings by an English Artist of the 14th Century; Reproduced from Royal Ms. 2 B. VII in the British Museum* (London: British Museum, 1912).

Watson, Wilfred G.E., *Classical Hebrew Poetry* (JSOTSup, 26; Sheffield: JSOT Press, 1984).

Watt, Ian, *The Rise of the Novel* (London: Penguin Books, 1966).

Watts, James W., 'The Legal Characterization of Moses in the Rhetoric of the Pentateuch'. *JBL* 117 (1998), pp. 415-26.

Weber, Max, *The Sociology of Religion* (trans. Ephraim Fischoff; Boston: Beacon Press, 1963).

Weinfeld, Moshe, *Deuteronomy and the Deuteronomic School* (Oxford: Oxford University Press, 1972).

Weitzman, Steven, 'Lessons from the Dying: The Role of Deuteronomy 32 in its Narrative Setting', *HTR* 87.4 (1994), pp. 377-93.

—*Song and Story in Biblical Narrative* (Bloomington: Indiana University Press, 1997).

Wellhausen, Julius, *Prolegomena to the History of Israel* (Atlanta: Scholars Press, 1994).

—*Prolegomena zur Geschichte Israels* (Berlin: Georg Reimer, 1899).

Wieseltier, Leon, *Kaddish* (New York: Alfred Knopf, 1998).

Wilch, J.R., *Time and Event* (Leiden: E.J.Brill, 1969).

Wildavsky, Aaron, *The Nursing Father: Moses as a Political Leader* (Tiscaloosa: University of Alabama Press, 1984).

Williams, James G., *The Bible, Violence and the Sacred* (San Francisco: HarperCollins, 1991).

Wilson, Dorothy Clarke, *Prince of Egypt* (repr., New York: Pocket Books, 1951 [1949]).

Wörner, Karl H., *Schoenberg's 'Moses and Aaron'* (trans. Paul Hamburger; New York: St Martin's Press, 1963).

Wright, G.E., 'The Lawsuit of God: A Form-Critical Study of Deuteronomy 32', in B.W. Anderson and W. Harrelson (eds.), *Israel's Prophetic Heritage* (New York: Harper, 1962), pp. 26-67.

Wright, Melanie J., *Moses in America: The Cultural Uses of Biblical Narrative* (Oxford: Oxford University Press, 2003).

Yates, Frances, *Giordano Bruno and the Hermetic Tradition* (Chicago: University of Chicago Press, 1964).

Yerushalmi, Yosef, *Freud's Moses: Judaism Terminable and Interminable* (New Haven: Yale University Press, 1991).

—*Zakhor: Jewish History and Jewish Memory* (Seattle: University of Washington Press, 1982).

Young, James E., *The Texture of Memory* (New Haven: Yale University Press, 1993).

—*Writing and Rewriting the Holocaust* (Bloomington: Indiana University Press, 1988).

Yu, Anthony C., *Rereading the Stone: Desire and the Making of Fiction in Dream of the Red Chamber* (Princeton, NJ: Princeton University Press, 1997).

Zevit, Ziony, 'Roman Jakobson, Psycholinguistics, and Biblical Poetry', *JBL* 109 (1990), pp. 385-401.

Ziolkowski, Theodore, *Fictional Transfigurations of Jesus* (Princeton, NJ: Princeton University Press, 1972).

Žižek, Slavoj, *Enjoy Your Symptom!* (New York: Routledge, 2001).

INDEX OF AUTHORS